The Fruits of Empirical Linguistics
Volume 2: Product

Studies in Generative Grammar 102

Editors

Henk van Riemsdijk
Jan Koster
Harry van der Hulst

Mouton de Gruyter
Berlin · New York

The Fruits of Empirical Linguistics

Volume 2: Product

Edited by

Susanne Winkler
Sam Featherston

Mouton de Gruyter
Berlin · New York

Mouton de Gruyter (formerly Mouton, The Hague)
is a Division of Walter de Gruyter GmbH & Co. KG, Berlin.

The series Studies in Generative Grammar was formerly published by
Foris Publications Holland.

♾ Printed on acid-free paper which falls within the guidelines
of the ANSI to ensure permanence and durability.

Library of Congress Cataloging-in-Publication Data

The fruits of empirical linguistics / edited by Sam Featherston, Susanne Winkler.
2 v. cm.
Includes bibliographical references and index.
Contents: v. 1. Process – v. 2. Product.
ISBN 978-3-11-021338-6 (vol. 1 : hardcover : alk. paper)
ISBN 978-3-11-021347-8 (vol. 2 : hardcover)
1. Computational linguistics – Methodology. 2. Discourse analysis – Data processing. I. Featherston, Sam II. Winkler, Susanne, 1960–
P98.F78 2009
410.285–dc22
2009016914

Bibliographic information published by the Deutsche Nationalbibliothek

The Deutsche Nationalbibliothek lists this publication in the Deutsche Nationalbibliografie; detailed bibliographic data are available in the Internet at http://dnb.d-nb.de.

ISBN 978-3-11-021347-8
ISSN 0167-4331

Cover design: Christopher Schneider, Laufen.
Printed in Germany.

Table of contents

Volume 1: Table of contents

German verb-first conditionals as unintegrated clauses: A case study in converging synchronic and diachronic evidence[*]

Katrin Axel and Angelika Wöllstein

Introduction

According to standard assumptions, German verb-first (= V1) conditionals are embedded clauses that occupy the prefield of their apodosis clause. We will argue against this analysis, showing that the V1-conditional is syntactically "unintegrated" in its apodosis. It follows that the apodosis cannot be a bona fide declarative verb-second (= V2) clause. We will support this claim with synchronic data from Present-Day German and data from historical text corpora. While the synchronic and diachronic data provide new insights by themselves, it is their combination that crucially corroborates our analysis of V1-conditionals as unintegrated clauses.

1. V1-conditionals – the phenomenon

The conditional construction is bipartite: the conditional clause of the construction is referred to as protasis, the consequent clause answering to the protasis is referred to as apodosis. A typical example of a German V1-conditional construction is given in (1). In the clause marked by square brackets, the finite verb *glaubt* 'believes' has moved to C°. There is no introductory conjunction. The resulting V1-clause has a strictly conditional interpretation.

(1) [*Glaubt man den Plakaten* t_i] *jagt ein Großereignis das*
believes one the placards chases one mega-event the
nächste.
next
'If one may trust the placards, one mega-event is chasing the other'
(TüBa-D/Z,n° 3802)

A comparative perspective shows that practically all Germanic languages, past or present, allow V1-conditionals, cf. Iatridou and Embick (1993: 191). Examples from Present-Day English and Dutch are given in (2a) and (2b), respectively.

(2) a. *Had John eaten the calamari, he might be better now.* (Iatridou and Embick 1993: 197)

b. *Heeft een schepsel een mond dan heeft het een neus.*
has e creature a mouth then has it a nose
'Has a creature a mouth, then it has a nose' (Dutch)

The traditional assumption is that V1-conditionals have the same structure as conditionals introduced by a conditional conjunction (cf. König and van der Auwera 1988, Iatridou and Embick 1993, Zifonun et al. 1997, Bhatt and Pancheva 2006). Since the German *wenn*-conditional is assumed to be embedded in the prefield (= SpecC) of its apodosis clause, the V1-conditional is assigned the same embedded analysis; cf. (3a)–(3b).

(3) a. [$_{SpecC}$ [$_{CP}$ *Glaubt man den Plakaten*] [$_{C'}$ [$_{C°}$ *jagt*$_j$] [$_{IP}$ *ein*
believes one the placards chases one
Großereignis das nächste t_j]]]
mega-event the next
'If one may trust the placards, one mega-event is chasing the other'

b. [$_{SpecC}$ [$_{CP}$ *Wenn man den Plakaten glaubt*] [$_{C'}$ [$_{C°}$ *jagt*$_j$] [$_{IP}$
if one the placards believes chases
ein Großereignis das nächste t_j]]]
one mega-event the next

Given this analysis, the expectation is that German conditional V1-clauses should meet the diagnostic criteria for syntactic embedding. In section 2 we will present data showing that this expectation is not fulfilled: the V1-clauses do not meet the criteria for syntactic embedding, but in fact exhibit 'unintegrated' or even paratactic properties. Furthermore, there is no complete overlap in the semantic function of *wenn*- and V1-clauses and, as our corpus investigation shows, their topological distribution differs as well. Therefore we propose that the structure of German V1-conditionals is unintegrated, as shown in (4a, b), where the V1-protasis (= CP2) is adjoined to its apodosis (= CP1). Note that the linear word order in (4) does not differ from (3a).

(4) a. [$_{CP1}$ [$_{CP2}$ *Glaubt man den Plakaten*] [$_{CP1}$ [$_{C°}$ *jagt*$_j$] [*ein Großereignis das nächste* t_j]]]

b.

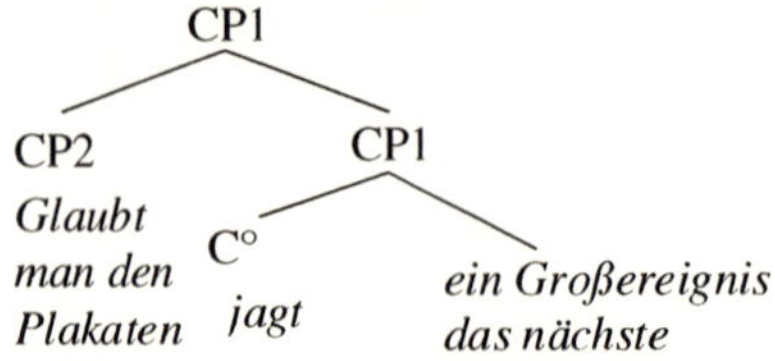

In the next section we will present synchronic evidence based upon joint work with Marga Reis, (cf. Reis and Wöllstein 2008) supporting this analysis.

2. Synchronic Data: Present-Day German

2.1. Syntactic structure – diagnostics for syntactic embedding of V1- vs. *wenn*-conditionals

To show that V1- and *wenn*-conditionals do not have the same syntactic structure, we examine their behavior with respect to four well-established diagnostic criteria: (i) Binding, (ii) Scope of left-peripheral focus particles, (iii) Focus-background structure and (iv) Question-answer pairs in elliptical constructions.

2.1.1. Binding

In general, coreference between pronoun and quantifier is possible if the left-peripheral clause is embedded in the matrix clause (cf. Frey 2004: 205) as can be seen in (5a). If we replace the *wenn*-clause by a V1-conditional, binding is no longer possible, see (5b). This is analogous to (5c), which shows that binding and clause integration interact (Frey 2004: 228). Following König and van der Auwera (1988: 16) the adverbial clause (= protasis) is structurally unintegrated if the apodosis has a V2-pattern.

(5) a. *Wenn sein*$_i$ *Sohn was erreicht hat, ist jeder*$_i$ *Vater*
if his son what achieved has is every father
glücklich.
happy
'Every father is happy if his son has achieved something'

b. **Hat sein*$_i$ *Sohn was erreicht, ist jeder*$_i$ *Vater glücklich.*
has his son what achieved is every father happy
'Every father is happy if his son has achieved something'

c. **Hat sein*$_i$ *Sohn was erreicht, so ist jeder*$_i$ *Vater*
has his son what achieved so is every father
glücklich.
happy
'Every father is happy if his son has achieved something'

2.1.2. Scope of left-peripheral focus particles

Focus particles such as *sogar* 'even' and *nur* 'only' are elements which require a phrasal constituent in their scope. In (6a) the verb *kommst* 'come' in the adverbial clause fulfills this requirement because the *wenn*-clause is integrated and serves as a constituent of the matrix clause which is in the scope of the particle *nur* 'only'. The ungrammaticality of (6b) shows that the V1-clause may not occur within the scope of focus particles (see also Iatridou and Embick 1993: 198).The natural explanation is that *wenn*-clauses structurally belong to the apodosis but V1-clauses do not, that is, they are unintegrated.

(6) a. *Nur wenn du KOMMST, backe ich einen Kuchen.*
only if you come bake I a cake
'Only if you come, I will bake a cake'

b. (**Nur*) *KOMMST du, backe ich einenKuchen.*

2.1.3. Focus-background structure

In a focus-background structure, *wenn*-clauses are able to carry the main stress of the entire construction, cf. (7a). As illustrated by (7b)–(7d), V1-conditionals seem unable to do the same, rather, both clauses form focus-background structures of their own (Reis 2000: 217).

(7) a. *Wenn ich MillioNÄR wäre, würde ich es tun.*
if I millionaire were would I it do
'If I were a millionaire, I would do this.'

b. ??*Wäre ich MillioNÄR, würde ich es tun.*

c. ??*Wäre ich Millionär, würde ich es TUN.*

d. *Wäre ich MillioNÄR, würde ich es TUN.*

Iatridou and Embick claim (1993: 198) that the reason why V1-conditionals may not be focussed at all is because the proposition expressed by the V1-clause is always presupposed to be discourse-old. This implies that the difference in information structure between V1- and *wenn*-clauses does not reflect a syntactic difference: V1-clauses are held to be embedded just like *wenn*- 'if'-clauses. While it is correct that cases like (7b) are deviant, Iatridou and Embick fail to take into account data such as (7c) and (7d), which show that it is the lack of an explicit indication of two separate focus-background structures in V1-constructions that is at fault. This is again evidence for the unintegrated status of V1-conditionals.

2.1.4. Question-answer pairs in elliptical constructions

As observed by Altmann (1987: 27) and, independently, by Iatridou and Embick (1993: 199), *wenn*-conditionals may figure as elliptical answers but V1-conditionals may not, cf. (8a) vs. (8b). Since bona fide clause constituents may always function as elliptical answers, this is further evidence that V1-conditionals are unintegrated, unlike *wenn*-conditionals. Additional confirmation can be seen in the fact that German V2-argument clauses, which have been shown to be (relatively) unintegrated as well, contrast with canonical *dass* 'that' complement clauses in the same way (see Reis 1997).

(8) [*Unter welchen Umständen würden Sie einen Bentley*
under which circumstances would you a Bentley
kaufen?]
buy
'In what circumstances would you buy a Bentley?'

a. *Wenn ich Millionäre wäre.*
if I millionaire were.
'If I were a millionaire.'

b. **Wäre ich Millionär.*

So far, we have provided four syntactic arguments for the claim that *wenn*-conditionals and V1-conditionals have different structures. The former is integrated, the latter is not. In the following two subsections we will present evidence from semantic and topological distribution to further support our claim.

2.2. Semantics: overlap in meaning and function between V1- and *wenn*-conditionals?

As is well-known, *wenn*-clauses occur in different adverbial functions and may serve as complements as well (Fabricius-Hansen 1980: 161). Beside the true conditional contexts they can also be attested in unconditional contexts. Since *wenn*-clauses are compatible with these various functions and meanings, they can be regarded as unspecific. In this section we provide evidence that there are differences in the semantic distribution of V1- vs. *wenn*-conditionals, in that V1-conditionals are much more restricted and therefore more specific.

Bhatt and Pancheva (2006: 639) paraphrase the interpretation of the most common kind of conditional structures discussed in the literature, viz. the hypothetical conditionals, in the following way: "[...] the proposition expressed by the antecedent clause specifies the (modal) circumstances in which the proposition expressed by the 'main' clause (=apodosis) is true. Thus, (9a) states that the possible worlds/situations in which [*Karl reads*] (the denotation of the conditional clause) are possible worlds/situations in which [*he falls asleep*] (the denotation of the 'main' clause)."

(9) a. *Wenn Karl liest, schläft er ein.*
if Karl reads sleeps he
'If Karl reads, he falls asleep'

b. *Liest Karl, schläft er ein.*
reads Karl sleeps he

As (9b) shows, V1-clauses occur in this central interpretation as well.[1] But *wenn*-clauses in German have a much wider distribution than that; they may even occur in contexts where a truly conditional interpretation is excluded, cf. (10) and (11). If V1-conditionals were just a variant of *wenn*-conditionals as generally assumed, they should also be licenced in these contexts. But they are not: V1-clauses neither allow 'unconditional' or 'speech act conditional' interpretations as in (10a-b), no matter whether the apodosis is V1 (the exception) or V2 (the rule),[2] nor are they acceptable in complement function, nor are they really licit in factive/echoic (12a) and *ex falso quodlibet*[3] constructions (12b).[4]

(10) a. ??*Bin ich ehrlich /Wenn ich ehrlich bin, habe ich /ich habe*
am I honest /if I honest am have I /I have
darüber noch nicht nachgedacht.
about-it yet not considered
'To be honest, so far I haven't thought about it'

b. **Darf ich es offen sagen /Wenn ich es offen sagen*
may I it frankly say /if I it frankly say
darf, halte ich /ich halte das Ganze für einen Schwindel.
may take I /I take the whole for a fake
'To put it bluntly, I think the whole thing is a fake'
((10b) with *wenn*-clause from Pittner 2003: example (13b))

The fact that V1-clauses, unlike *wenn*-clauses, only occur with a truly conditional interpretation holds in contexts where the V1-clauses do not function as adverbial clauses at all: Whereas *wenn*-clauses may substitute for *dass* 'that'-clauses appearing in the complement function of matrix predicates, V1-clauses may not. The same is shown in Reis (1997) for V2-clauses. More precisely, as Reis and Wöllstein (2008) have noted, 'V1-substitute' requires a salient conditional relationship – preferably a hypothetical one – between antecedent and consequent.[5]

(11) a. *Mir ist lieber, wenn du nicht kommst.*
me is preferably if you not come
'I would prefer if/that you would not come.'

b. **Mir ist lieber, kommst du nicht.*

A further effect of the hypothetical conditional relationship on grammaticality can be observed in factive conditionals.[6] In factive and echoic conditionals the protasis has a factive reading. As example (12a) shows, V1-clauses are barely allowed in factive conditionals. For the *ex falso quodlibet* interpretation in (12b) the truth-value of the protasis is derivable from the truth-value of the 'apodosis'. Dancygier (1993: 421) characterizes them as containing "a blantantly false [or] irrelevant conclusion as necessarily derivable from p and thus presenting p as false."

(12) a. ??*Bleibt ihr schon so lange /Wenn ihr schon so lange*
remain you already so long /if you already so long
bleibt, könnt ihr auch mithelfen.
remain can you MOD$_{\text{PCTL}}$ assist
'If you are going to stay that long, you can help'

b. ??*War das die Zarentochter /Wenn das die Zarentochter*
was this the czar's-daughter /if this the czar's-daughter
war, bin ich die Wiedergeburt von Queen Victoria.
was am I the rebirth of Queen Victoria
'If this was the Czar's daughter, I am a reincarnation of Queen Victoria' (The examples in (12) are taken from Reis and Wöllstein 2008).

Both factive conditionals and the *ex falso quodlibet* constructions contain a predetermined truth-value, given from either the protasis or the apodosis. In both cases V1-clauses are very marked. This suggests that V1-conditional constructions do not tolerate fixed truth-values. Reis (2008) concludes that conditional constructions with V1 typically show a hypothetical conditional interpretation and seem to be restricted to material implication.

To sum up: the differences between *wenn* and V1 discussed in this subsection can be considered to be semantically driven. Given that V1 has a unique function and meaning, there is only a partial overlap with *wenn*, namely in hypothetical conditional and temporal constructions. No overlap in meaning or function can be observed with the 'unconditional' (e.g. the 'speech act') interpretation and generally if the consequent or the antecedent has a fixed truth-value as with factive/echoic and *ex falso quodlibet* constructions. Thus, V1- vs. *wenn*-clauses do not have the same semantic properties.

2.3. Topological distribution of *wenn*- vs. V1-clauses – corpus investigation

Given the substantial differences between V1- and *wenn*-conditionals both in syntactic behaviour and in semantic function and meaning, one might expect differences in their topological distribution as well.

Comrie (1986: 83) among others generally confirms Greenberg's (1963) generalization that "in conditional statements, the conditional clause (= protasis) precedes the conclusion (=apodosis) in all languages". However, it is also undisputed that both orders are possible (see e.g. Comrie 1986, Bhatt and Pancheva 2006). Does this hold for the conditional constructions under investigation as well?

2.3.1. *Postposed placement*

We carried out a corpus investigation in the treebanks TIGER and TüBaD/Z. As it turned out, V1-conditionals are hardly ever postposed (8%), whereas *wenn*-conditionals are abundantly attested in this position (81%).[7,8]

Besides this quantitative contrast there is also a qualitative one: All V1-conditionals that are postposed in the treebanks are in conjunctive mood (= subjunctive). The data in (13) show pre- and postposed V1-conditionals (marked by brackets): The introspective data in (13a)' and (13b) illustrate this contrast.

(13) a. [*Will nur einer die Trennung*], *entscheidet das*
wants$_{IND}$ only one the divorce decides the
Gericht.
court
'If only one wants the divorce, the court decides'

a.′ **Das Gericht entscheidet,*[*will nur einer die Trennung*].

b. *Zudem verlangt es von ihm, die parlamentarische*
moreover demands it from him, the parliamentary
Zustimmung einzuholen, [*sollte er Bodentruppen in*
consent to obtain should$_{CONJI}$ he ground troops in
den Krieg schicken wollen].
the war send want
'Moreover, it demands that he obtain parliamentary consent should he want to send ground troops into the war'

With *wenn*-conditionals there is no such restriction concerning verbal mood. What may be decisive here is that verbal mood plays a crucial role in strengthening semantic dependency: While conjunctive mood indicates interpretative dependency, hence integration, indicative does not.

2.3.2. *Medial placement*

To a limited extent both *wenn*-conditional clauses (14a) and V1-conditional clauses (14b) occur in the middle field. However, there is evidence that in this position V1-clauses are unintegrated parentheticals: In spoken language, they must be set off by parenthetical intonation. The same observation has been made for English *if*-conditionals in medial position (see Bhatt and Pancheva 2006: 645).

(14) a. *Die Berliner Schauspielerin Alice Treff, wenn man*
the berliner actress Alice Treff if one
Eingeweihten glauben will, wird heute 85 Jahre.
insider believe will becomes today 85 years
(COSMAS: MMM/106.15201)
'If you believe those in the know, the actress Alice Treff will be 85 today'

b. *Was außer einer guten Examensnote für den*
what beside a good grade-in-the-exam for the
Berufsweg, [soll er denn in Topetagen, hinaufführen,] alles
career shall it PCL in top-floor lead-up all
nötig ist, darüber informiert das Handbuch
necessary is about-it informs the handbook
„Berufsplanung für den Management-Nachwuchs“.
“Berufsplanung für den Management-Nachwuchs”.
(TIGER s5411)
'What you need, apart from good exam results, for your career, if it is to lead up onto the top floor, is the subject of the handbook B f d M N.'

2.3.3. *Word order options in the apodosis after preposed conditionals*

After preposed V1-conditionals we do not only find instances of V1-apodosis, but also of V1+*so*-apodosis, cf. (15a) (similar examples with V1+*dann*-apodosis are also attested) and of V1+'V2'-apodosis, in which the prefinite position in the apodosis is not occupied by resumptive *so*, but by all sorts of fronted XPs, cf. (15b) (cf. König and van der Auwera 1988: 116).[9] Both of these patterns are unintegrated (cf. also the binding data for V1+*so* apodosis in (5c)).

(15) a. *Glaubt man dem Festivalleiter Werner Rucicka, so*
believes one the festival-manager Werner Rucicka then
stand es um den Dokumentarfilm nie besser.
stood it about the documentary film never better
(TIGER, s22082)
'If we can believe the festival manager W R, the documentary film has never been in better shape.'

b. *Gäbe es ihn nicht, man müsste ihn*
existed$_{CONJ}$ it he$_{ACC}$ not one must$_{CONJ}$ he$_{ACC}$
im Interesse einer wachsamen, lebendigen Demokratie
on-behalf-of a alert lively democracy
erfinden. (TIGER, s46743)
invent
'If it/he did not exist, one would have to invent it/him in the interests of a lively and alert democracy.'

According to König and van der Auwera (1988: 16), examples such as (15b) show certain characteristics that also are present in the case of unintegrated hypothetical *wenn*-clauses with V2-apodosis: The construction is in subjunctive mood and the apodosis often contains an anaphoric element (= *ihn* in (15b)). Without these characteristics, such non-epistemic and non-indicative patterns normally occur with V1-apodosis and not with V2-apodosis, as Reis (p.c.) states.

2.4. Interim conclusion

In contrast to *wenn*-conditionals, V1-conditionals do not meet the diagnostic criteria for syntactic embedding. Furthermore, the semantics of *wenn*- and V1-conditionals show only a partial overlap. Finally, the topological distribution of V1-conditionals is more restricted than that of *wenn*-conditionals: V1-conditionals can hardly ever be postposed. Thus there is good evidence that V1-conditionals are different from *wenn*-conditionals, and that – in contrast to what is traditionally assumed – they are not embedded in the apodosis clause but unintegrated, i.e. linked to the apodosis clause by adjunction. This analysis, however, has the undisputable consequence that the apodosis in V1-conditional constructions is a V1-clause as well, cf. again (4), here repeated as (16).

(16) [$_{CP1}$ [$_{CP2}$ *Glaubt man den Plakaten*] [$_{CP1}$ [$_{C°}$ *jagt*$_j$] [$_{IP}$ *ein Großereignis das nächste* t$_j$]]]

This looks like an undesirable consequence for the traditional structural hypothesis. It is at variance with what is usually assumed about the distribution of V2-

vs. V1-declaratives in present day German. Thus, rounding off our synchronic analysis requires showing that this is necessary after all.

2.5. Independent evidence for a V1-apodosis in Present-Day German

In German, as in fact in many other Germanic languages, a marked V1-order is possible in declaratives (e.g. Platzack 1987, Lindström 2001; for German, e.g. Auer 1993, Diessel 1997, Önnerfors 1997, Reis 2000). The most common type is the so-called narrative type, cf. (17), which is sometimes also referred to as 'narrative inversion'. However, in German V1 is possible in non-narrative declaratives as well, cf. Önnerfors (1997: section 6) and Reis (2000). One example is the so-called 'causal type' (Önnerfors 1997: 155). This type of clause always follows an antecedent in the discourse, contains the modal particle *doch* and is interpreted roughly as a causal adverbial clause, cf. (18).

(17) *Hab ich ihr da ganz frech einen Kuss gegeben.*
have I her there totally bold a kiss given
Then, I just went ahead and kissed her.
(Example taken from Reis 2000: 90)

(18) *(Der Bau des Polders ist ungewiss,) steht ihm*
the construction of-the-polder is uncertain stands it
doch der Widerstand der Anwohner gegenüber.
PCL_{MOD} the Opposition of-the resident opposite
(Pasch et al. 2003: 515)
'The building of the polder is uncertain since it faces the resistance of the residents.'

There are even cases in which a V1-declarative is preceded by what is structurally a main clause but interpreted as subordinate: In (19a) the first clause shows main clause verb order (V2) and contains the particle *kaum* 'hardly'. It is followed by a declarative V1-clause. The *kaum*-clause is clearly syntactically unintegrated, because it has a V2-pattern and analogously to V1-conditionals binding into the apodosis is not possible, cf. (19b).

(19) a. *Kaum war er am Bahnhof angelangt, fuhr schon der*
hardly was he at station arrived pulled already the
Zug ein.
train in
'Hardly had he arrived at the station, the train pulled in.'

b.?/**Kaum war (fast) jeder*$_i$ *endlich in Urlaub gefahren,*
hardly was nearly everyone finally in holiday gone
bekam er$_i$ *Heimweh.*
became he home.sickness
'Hardly had almost everyone$_i$ gone on holiday at last, before he$_i$ got homesick.'

The *kaum*-construction – just like the V1-conditional construction – exhibits paratactic properties (see Reis 2007).Thus, V1-order even occurs after clauses that are clearly not integrated, but are interpreted as being subordinate to the V1-clause.

Finally, let us take a look at possible cases of adverbial clauses preceding non-declarative V1-clauses such as imperatives, (20a), and *yes/no*-interrogatives, (20b).

(20) a. *Wenn du noch Zeit hast, spül doch die Teller*
if you still time have clear barely the plates
noch ab!
yet
'If you still have time, wash the plates'

b. *Während ich noch weg bin, kannst du schon mal*
during I still away am, can you yet already
anfangen zu kochen?
begin to cook
'While I am still away, can you get on and start cooking'

Since imperatives and *yes/no*-interrogatives are V1-sentence types that are generally assumed to have no prefield position, they provide further evidence for the existence of an adjunction structure. The same is true for conditional clauses with a V2-apodosis as in (15b) (repeated as (21)):

(21) *Gäbe es ihn nicht, man müsste ihn im Interesse einer wachsamen, lebendigen Demokratie erfinden.*

We conclude that there is evidence for productive declarative V1-order also in non-narrative contexts in Present-Day German. Furthermore, there is independent confirmation for an adjunction analysis in the case of interrogative and imperative apodosis clauses. Thus, it is by no means implausible to assume that the apodosis is an instance of a declarative V1-clause in V1-conditional constructions as well, as is predicted by our adjunction analysis.

3. Diachronic Data

Our diachronic data provide further evidence for the claim that V1-conditionals have always been unintegrated clauses. While canonical adverbial clauses underwent a syntactic change from matrix-external adjunction to syntactic embedding in late Middle High German (= MHG) and Early New High German (= ENHG) times, V1-conditionals retained their unintegrated status. The construction with a V1-apodosis after the left-peripheral V1-conditionals was a very late innovation that did not take place until the 17th century. We shall argue that the apodosis is a variant of (non-narrative) declarative V1-order that began to be attested in independent contexts in ENHG times.

3.1. V1-conditionals and canonical adverbial clauses in Old and Middle High German

V1-conditionals are of old origin: They can be traced back to the earliest attested period of the German language, i.e. to Old High German (= OHG) times, (20a). As Behaghel (1928: 636) points out the phenomenon is probably Pan-Germanic even though it is not attested in Gothic.

(20) a. [$_{\text{CP}}$ [$_{\text{CP}}$ [$_{\text{C}}$ *Ni*[10]- *duas*$_{\text{i}}$] *thu* *só* t_i] … [$_{\text{CP}}$ *lon*$_{\text{j}}$ [$_{\text{C}}$ *ni-*
NEG do you so benefit NEG
hábes$_{\text{k}}$] *thu* *es* *nihéin* t_j t_k]]
have you it any
'If you don't do it, you won't have any benefit from it' (Otfrid II 20,7 (c. 870))

b. [$_{\text{CP}}$ [$_{\text{CP}}$ [$_{\text{C}}$ *Uuírt*$_{\text{i}}$] *er* *ferlâzen* t_i] … [$_{\text{CP}}$ *ér*$_{\text{k}}$ [$_{\text{C}}$ *ríhtet*$_{\text{j}}$]
becomes he released he erects
síh *áber* t_k *ûf* *ze_hímele* t_j]]
REFL however up to sky
'But if it (the bough) is released, it will erect itself towards the sky'
Si hanc curuans dextra remisit . recto uertice spectat cęlum.
(Notker *Boethius* III 118,16–17 (first half of 11th century))

Interestingly, the word order in the apodosis clause differs from that in Present-Day German. Instead of showing V1-order, the finite verb occurs in second position (or in third position if one also counts the V1-conditional). The finite verb in the apodosis is not directly preceded by the V1-conditional, but by a further XP in SpecC, i.e. the fronted direct object *lôn* in (20a) and the fronted subject pronoun *ér* in (20b). In Present-Day German this word order is no longer possible in the normal case as can be easily seen if the translation shows the same V2-order in the apodosis: **verhältst du dich nicht so, keinen Lohn bekommst du dafür*; **wird er verlassen, er richtet sich aber auf zum Himmel.*[11]

This strange word order pattern violates the V2-constraint, which was already quite well established in OHG times (Axel 2007). It is not only characteristic of V1-conditionals, but also of canonical adverbial clauses, both conditional adverbial omes as in (21a)[12] and other types of adverbial clauses (e.g. temporal ones). We use the term 'canonical' adverbial clauses to refer to subordinate clauses that are introduced by adverbial subordinators (e.g. *oba* 'if' in (21a), *dhuo* "when, as", cf. (22b)) and exhibit (structural) verb-final order.

(21) a. … [$_{CP}$[$_{CP}$ *oba* *thu* *uuili.*] [$_{CP}$ *thú*$_j$ [*maht*$_i$] t_i *mih*
if you will you can me
gisubiren. t_j]]
cleanse
'If you are willing, you can make me clean'
… si úis potes mé mundare.,
(Tatian 179,23–24 (c. 830))

(22) b. [$_{CP}$ [$_{CP}$*Dhuo* *ir* *himilo* *garauui* *frumida*], [$_{CP}$*dhar*$_i$
when he heavens' equipment created there
[$_C$ *uuas*$_j$] *ih* t_i t_j]]
was I
'When he fashioned the heavens, I was there'
Quando praeparabat cęlos, aderam;
(Isidor 91–92 (c. 790))

As is argued in Axel (2002, 2004), in OHG and MHG times canonical adverbial clauses were syntactically unembedded (= unintegrated clauses). This is why they could not occur in the prefield (i.e. SpecC according to traditional theory), a matrix-internal position.

Further evidence for their unintegrated status comes from their positioning with respect to matrix clauses introduced by sentence-particles. In OHG, *yes/no*-interrogatives still sometimes displayed the sentence-typing particle *eno/inu*. As demonstrated in Axel (2007: 210), such sentence-typing particles occupy a very peripheral position. Interestingly, adverbial clauses are placed even further to the left as is witnessed by several examples in Tatian (Axel 2004: 31f.). V1-conditionals are not attested in front of *eno* but this is probably an accidental gap in the data.[13] However, they do occur in front of the particle *iâ* 'yes' in Notker's texts:

(23) [CP *Kuúnnin óuh tie úbelen . . . dáz kûot tés sie*
attain however the evil-ones the good that$_{GEN}$ they
gérônt]. ***iâ*** *neuuârîn sie dánne úbele?*
seek PCL NEG.were they then evil
'But if evil men attain the good they seek, they cannot be evil?'
Mali uero si adipiscerentur bonum. quod appetunt. mali esse non possent?
(Notker Boethius IV 188,1–2 (c. 1000–1050))

That adverbial clauses were not syntactically embedded in their superordinate clause can furthermore be seen in complex sentences in which the matrix/apodosis clause is a subordinate clause itself. In this case a (preposed) adverbial clause is placed to the left of the subordinator (e.g. the complementizer *thaz* 'that') in OHG (and MHG) (Erdmann 1874, I: § 104, Kracke 1911, Axel 2002, 2004). We were not able to find any OHG examples with V1-conditionals occurring to the left of subordinate apodosis clauses. Again, this is probably an accidental gap in the data, the OHG corpus being relatively small. Many texts from the Middle period do witness this type of construction, however, as the following example from the Prose Lancelot illustrates. Here a V1-conditional occurs to the left of an object clause introduced by the complementizer *das*.

(24) *(sie) hett angst, [begriff er sie],* ***das*** *er ir laster mocht*
she had fear caught he her that he her disgrace might
thun,
do
'She was afraid that he might put her to disgrace if he got hold of her.'
(Prose Lancelot 52,19 (c. 13th century))

This word order pattern is ruled out in Present-Day-German where the adverbial clause has to be placed either in the middle or in final field of the subordinate matrix/apodosis clause it modifies. It should be noted that the left-peripheral placement of the adverbial clauses violates Chomsky's principle that adjunction to maximal projections is only possible if these are non-arguments (Chomsky 1986: 6).

All this evidence strongly suggests that neither canonical adverbial clauses nor V1-conditionals were syntactically embedded in their matrix/apodosis clauses in OHG (and MHG) times. Then the two structures should be identical in OHG. Axel (2002, 2004) proposes that canonical adverbial clauses were base-generated in their left-peripheral position and adjoined to the matrix-CP. We may assume the same structure for V1-conditionals:

(25) [$_{\mathrm{CP1}}$ [$_{\mathrm{CP2}}$ V1-conditional] [$_{\mathrm{CP1}}$ apodosis]]

The only difference from the Present-Day German structure in (25) is that in those cases where the apodosis was a root declarative, in OHG (and MHG) times it generally exhibited a V2-pattern[14] in which the prefield could be filled by any kind of XP that has been topicalized from its apodosis-internal position. As was shown above, a V2-apodosis is no longer possible today.

The historical root of the adjunction construction is the so-called correlative diptych (Haudry 1973). This type of clause combining was common with both relative and adverbial (relative) clauses and can be traced back to Indo-European times. It is attested in Latin, Hittite and Sanskrit, for example. As Bianchi (1999) demonstrates, at a descriptive level the archaic construction is composed of two clauses, the main clause and a dependent, i.e. relative, clause, the latter appearing at the left or right margin. The relative element (marked by bold face in the examples below) is usually fronted. The main clause contains the correlative element (marked by underlining). This element either also occurs at the left periphery of the main clause or remains in its clause-internal base position. The relative element and the correlative are interpreted as roughly co-referential. A Latin example of the correlative diptych expressing temporal subordination is given in (26).

(26) [[*tum*$_i$ *denique* … *nostra* *intellegimus* *bona*], [***quom***$_i$ …
then really our (we)understand happiness when
ea amisimus]]
it (we) loose
'We realize our happiness when we lose it' (Haudry 1973, 159, glosses and translation adapted from Bianchi 1999: 98)

In OHG adverbial clauses, the dependent clause is introduced by the fronted 'relative head' in the form of a demonstrative adverb.[15]. The main clause contains a correlative element, which is often, though not always, homonymous with the demonstrative adverb functioning as the 'relative head'. The same construction is abundantly attested in Old English (Mitchell 1982, Bianchi 1994).

(27) *Inti* [$_{\mathrm{CP}}$ [$_{\mathrm{CP}}$ ***thanne*** *her cumit,*] [$_{\mathrm{CP}}$ *thanne thuingit her uueralt*
and when he comes then convicts he world
fon sunton …]]
from sins
'And when he comes, then he will convict the word of sins'
& cum unerit ille argu& mundum de peccato
(Tatian, 585,3–4 (c. 830))

In OHG, the correlative element is not always fronted in the main clause. Sometimes it stays in its base position in the middle field as the following example from Isidor illustrates:

(28) [$_{CP}$ ***dhanne*** *ir … abgrundiu uuazssar umbihringida*] … *mit*
then he abysses water encircled with
imu uuas ih <u>*dhanne*</u> *al dhiz frummendi*
him was I then all this making
quando certa uallabat abyssos, … cum eo eram cuncta componens
'When he encircled the abysses …, I was then carrying all of this out with him'
(Isidor 92–94 (c. 790))

A further variant of this correlative structure are cases where there is no overt correlative element at present, cf. e.g. (22b) above. As Kiparsky (1995) argues for the old Indo-European languages (notably for Latin, Sanskrit, Hittite), the correlative is a silent *pro* in those cases, cf. (29). The silent correlative seems to have been restricted to those cases where it was an adjunct and not an argument (Kiparsky 1995).

(29) [$_{CP}$ [$_{CP}$ *Dhuo ir himilo garauui frumida*], [$_{CP}$*dhar*$_i$ [$_C$ *uuas*$_j$] *ih* <u>pro</u> t_i t_j]]

It is unclear whether the analysis with a(n optionally) silent correlative adverb in the main clause can also applied to other types of adverbial clauses, notably to the conditional ones introduced by *oba* as in (21a); or to the conditional ones with V1-order as in (20). However, nothing really hinges on this question. The important point is that in the area of adverbial subordination (as, in fact, with 'normal' non-adverbial relative clauses) there are residues of an archaic type of clause combination, viz. the correlative diptych. The dependent clauses in the correlative diptych are base-generated adjuncts to CP. In other words, there was an adjunction position for clausal material to the left of SpecC, which was of very old origin (cf. also Kiparsky 1995). V1-conditionals (as in fact their V-end counterparts) were placed in this peripheral position and not in SpecC.

In MHG times, V1-conditionals retained their unintegrated status. When preposed, they were placed to the left of the prefield of the main/apodosis clause (Behaghel 1929, Paul [1928] 1969: §495, Knaus 1995, Axel 2002, 2004). Often, though not always, there was a correlative adverb in the apodosis clause.

(29) [$_{CP}$ [$_{CP}$ *wil er icht darwiedder sprechen*], [$_{CP}$ ***ich*** *wil es*
wants he not there-against speak I want it
ware machen . . .]]
true make
'If he does not want to speak against it, I will make it true . . . '
(Prose Lancelot 36,2 (13th century))

The same is true for canonical adverbial clauses. However, in late MHG the development of canonical adverbial clauses and V1 diverged. This process must have started in the late 13th century and, as will be shown in the following section, kept on until well into the ENHG period.

3.2. Canonical adverbial clauses: The rise of syntactic embedding

The decisive period for the question raised in this study is the ENHG period (c. 1350–1650) and the beginning of the New High German period. In order to be able to show the time course of the major developments in the syntax of adverbial subordination we carried out a corpus study. We investigated the Bonn online ENHG corpus, which is a collection of 40[16] digitalized texts of different dialect regions from four time periods.

In the ENHG corpus the left periphery of declarative main clauses after preposed canonical adverbial clauses[17] exhibits the following three surface word order patterns: (i) the adverbial clause is followed by a full V2 main clause whose prefield may be occupied by any kind of XP (AdvC–XP–V_{fin}), (30a); (ii) the adverbial clause is followed by a full V2 main clause whose prefield is occupied by a correlative adverb (AdvC–corr.adv.–V_{fin}) (this is a subtype of type (i)), (30b); (iii) the adverbial clause is directly followed by the finite verb, (30c). In the following examples, the adverbial clause is given in square brackets, the finite verb in the apodosis is underlined and the prefinite XP or correlative adverb is highlighted by bold face.

(30) a. [*swenne er gelernet die gotes wisheit*], ***er*** <u>*heldet*</u> *sie*
when/ he learns the God's wisdom he holds it
lange in sinem herzem
long in his heart
"If he experiences God's wisdom, he will keep it in his heart for a long time"
(Altdeutsche Predigten 3,10–11 (Upper Saxon, 1sthalf 14th century))

b. [*wann mir ein solche junckfraw in Portugal zů einer*
when me a such maiden in Portugal to a
Ehegemaheln zůston moͤch]/ <u>*wolt*</u> *ich all mein*
spouse be-entitled might wanted I all my
hab und gůt in Hispanien zů barem gelt
possessions and belongings in Spain to cash money
machen
make
'If I were entitled to take such a maid as my wife in Portugal, I would cash in all my possessions in Spain'
(Jörg Wickram: Nachbarn 35,18–20 (Straßburg 1556))

c. *Ob aber der schmertz ... zů lang blib*] ***so*** <u>*ist*</u>
if however the pain too long stayed$_{CONJ}$ so is
gůt ... das man nem Oleum rosarum
good that one takes oil of.roses
"If, however, the pain remains for too long, it would be good to take rose oil"
(Hieronymus Brunschwig: Chirurgie 22(B),7–9 (Straßburg 1497))

The following table illustrates how frequent these three different patterns were in the four different time subperiods:

Table 1. Frequency of the three surface word order patterns after preposed canonical adverbial clauses in the Bonn online ENHG corpus

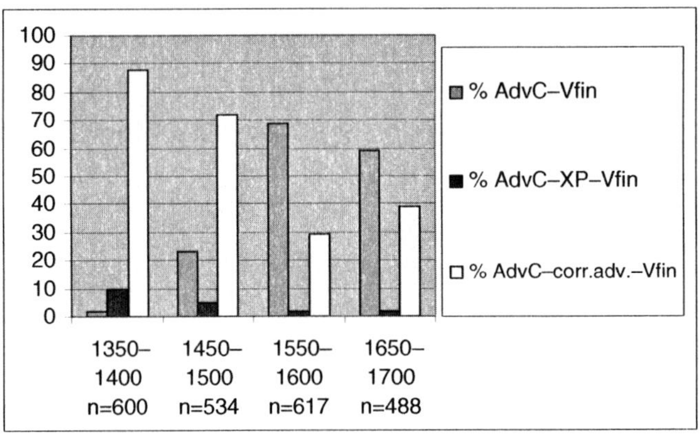

As can be seen, between 1350 and 1400, the by far most frequent pattern is the one in which the adverbial clause is followed by a correlative adverb occurring in the prefield of the main clause. However, the pattern AdvC–XP–

V_{fin}, which is ungrammatical in Present-Day German with the core types of canonical adverbial clauses, is also realized in 10% of the cases, which is a considerable amount. The pattern AdvC–V_{fin} which is the most frequent one in Present-Day German, is realized in only 2 % of the cases. Early instances of this type of example are already attested in late MHG times, for example in the late MHG part of the Prose Lancelot (Axel 2002). However, in the second subperiod (1450–1500) its frequency is significantly higher ($\chi^2(1) = 111{,}30$; $p < .01$). Furthermore, there is a significant difference between the second and third (1550–1600) subperiod ($\chi^2(1) = 252{,}04$; $p < .01$). While from a diachronic viewpoint, the AdvC–V_{fin} pattern is gaining ground in the ENHG period, the AdvC–XP–V_{fin} pattern is on the decline: There are significant drops in frequency between the first and second ($\chi^2(1) = 5{,}8$; $p < .05$) and between the second and third subperiods ($\chi^2(1) = 10{,}472$, $p < .01$). If one also looks at the data qualitatively, it emerges that the 'residual' examples from the second half of the ENHG period (i.e. between 1550 and 1700) largely exhibit the same characteristics that have been found to apply to the corresponding Present-Day German cases (König and van der Auwera 1988; cf. also fn. 7 above): The vast majority of them are counterfactual conditionals, concessive clauses or special types of conditional clauses such as speech act or irrelevance conditionals.

How can these developments be analyzed? Axel (2002, 2004) argues that the rise of the AdvC–V_{fin} pattern and the accompanying decline of the AdvC–XP–V_{fin} are the surface reflexes of an underlying change in the syntactic status of adverbial clauses from left-peripheral adjunction (AdvC–XP–V_{fin}) to syntactic embedding. In other words, adverbial clauses have developed into clauses that can occupy a matrix-internal adjunct position. One such position is the prefield (= SpecC). So in the AdvC–V_{fin} pattern, the adverbial clause occurs in the SpecC-position of the main clause:[18]

(31) [$_{CP}$ [$_{CP}$ *wann mir ein solche junckfraw … zů einer Ehegemaheln zůston möcht*] [$_{C'}$ *wolt ich all mein hab und gůt in Hispanien zů barem gelt machen*]]

There are further grammatical changes that are direct reflexes of or related to the underlying change from adjunction to embedding.

In those cases where the matrix clause was a subordinate clause itself, the old pattern where the adverbial clause was placed to the left of the complementizer was pushed back. Instead, in the second half of the ENHG period, adverbial clauses begin be attested to the right of the complementizer, i.e. in the middle field of the subordinate clause (cf. also Behaghel 1932: 296, Reichmann and Wegera 1993: § S 318).

(32) ... [CP *daß* [*wenn sie auff Erden gewest*] */man sie mit*
that if they on earth been one they with
Prűglen hätte todschmeissen sollen.]
clubs had dead.bash should
'... that one should have bashed them to death with clubs if they had been on earth'
(Gotthard Heidegger: Mythoscopia 41, 9–11 (Zurich 1698))

A further change is the development of the stacking of adverbial clauses. In OHG and MHG texts there are virtually no cases where pre-posed or post-posed adverbial clauses are themselves the superordinate clause of a further adverbial clause. There are cases, notably in MHG prose texts, in which more than one adverbial clause occur in either pre- or post-posed position. However, in almost all these cases the adverbial clauses are of the same degree, that is they are not in a hypotactic relation to each other, but are both directly dependent on the root clause. By contrast, in ENHG times, complex sentences become to be attested in which a (pre- or post-posed) adverbial clause is itself the matrix clause of another adverbial clause that it embeds:

(33) *behielt im nichts anderst vor/ dann ein sunder*
kept him nothing else PCL$_{\text{VERBAL}}$ then a special
gemach/ [*damit er ein rhů haben möcht/* [*wann es im*
chamber so.that he his quietness have may when it him
gelegen was]]
suited was
'he kept nothing else for him than a special chamber so that he could have his peace and quiet whenever it suited him"
(Jörg Wickram: Nachbarn 28,15–17 (Straßburg 1556))

A further change pertains to the inventory of adverbial subordinate conjunctions, which was subject to an intense re-organization during the late MHG and ENHG period (Axel 2004).

3.3. V1-conditionals: The rise of the V1-apodosis

As was outlined in the last section, the ENHG period is characterized by massive changes in the grammar of subordination, notably with adverbial subordination. One surface reflex that can be easily quantitatively studied in corpora is that adverbial clauses increasingly become attested in the position directly in front of the matrix finite verb (= AdvC–V_{fin} surface pattern). Interestingly,

V1-conditionals did not participate in this development. This can be seen in the following table:

Table 2. Frequency of the three surface word order patterns after preposed V1-conditionals in the Bonn online ENHG corpus

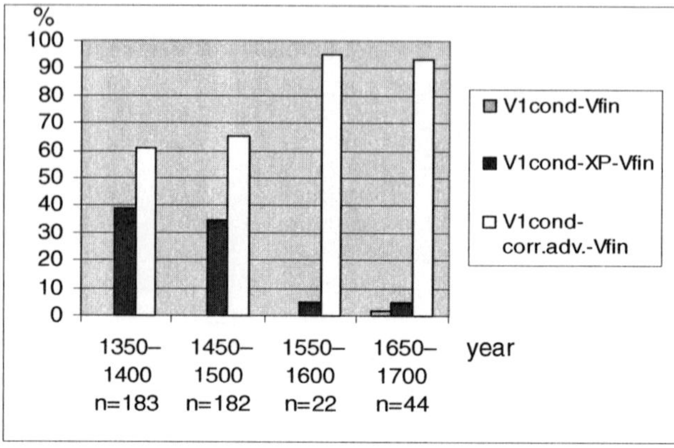

Let's first look at the first subperiod (1350–1400). It can be seen that the frequency of the V1cond–XP–V_{fin} surface pattern, (34), was quite high (39 %), much higher than in the case of canonical adverbial clauses (s. Table 1).

(34) [*slet man die frucht ab*], ***der boum*** *brenget des ander jares*
slays one the fruit off the tree brings the other year
noch groͤzzer frucht.
even bigger fruit
'If one cuts off the fruit, the tree will bear an even bigger fruit in the following year later'
(Altdeutsche Predigten 20,20–21 (mid 14th century))

There is, however, a parallel in the diachronic development: As in the case of canonical adverbial clauses, this pattern is also on the decline with V1-conditionals even though this decline is somewhat delayed compared to the canonical adverbial clauses. As can be seen in the second half of the ENHG period (1550–1600, 1650–1700), the frequency is signifcantly lower than in the first half (1350–1400, 1450–1500) ($\chi^2(1) = 27{,}02$; $p < .01$). Interestingly, in the case of V1-conditionals the V1cond–XP–V_{fin} pattern it is not pushed back by the V1cond–V_{fin} pattern, but by the correlative pattern. In the second half of the ENHG period, the correlative pattern is realized in over 90 % of the cases. In the vast majority of examples, the correlative is the adverb *so*:

(35) [*hastu rechte gelouben . . .*], ***so*** *bistu sin wirdich*
have-you right faith so are.you his$_{GEN}$ worthy
'If you have the right faith, you will be worthy of him'
(Altdeutsche Predigten 5, 28–29 (Upper Saxon, 1^{st}half 14th century))

With V1-conditionals, the V1cond–V_{fin} pattern, cf. (36), is not attested in the corpus until the second half of the 17th century. Since there are gaps of 50 years in the corpus, we do not have any data from the subperiod 1600–1650. So we do not know for sure when V1-conditionals started to appear. Nevertheless, we can conclude that in the corpus the pattern V1cond–V_{fin} arises at least 250 years later than the pattern AdvC–V_{fin}.

(36) [*Wuͤrde es aber mein Gluͤck vnd Beruff seyn/*
would it however my fortune and profession be
dasselbige zu foͤrdern]/ *wolte ich mein Leben von Hertzen*
that.same to promote wanted I my life from heart
gern darmit zubringen.
with.pleasure there.with spend
'If, however, it were my fortune and profession to promote that, I would be happy from the bottom of my heart to spend my life with it'
(Walter Ralegh: Amerika 5, 24–25 (Frankfurt/M. 1599))

There is thus a considerable delay compared to the rise of the AdvC–V_{fin}-construction with canonical adverbial clauses. This strongly suggests that these two developments are not reflexes of the same underlying phenomenon: If the hypothesis is correct that the spread of the AdvC–V_{fin} pattern with canonical adverbial clauses in the ENHG period is one major surface reflex of the rise of structural embedding, it looks as if V1-conditionals have not participated in this syntactic change.[19]

So in the case of V1-conditionals the major surface developments in the ENHG period are: an increase of the correlative pattern (= *so*-apodosis) at the expense of the V1cond–XP–V_{fin} pattern, the very late rise of the V1cond–V_{fin} pattern. The first two developments do not reflect a change in the underlying syntax: as was demonstrated above for Present-Day German, (5c), V1-conditionals followed by a *so*-apodosis are unintegrated/unembedded clauses. The same is true for those followed by a V2-apodosis that is not introduced by a correlative adverb. So V1-conditionals have retained their unintegrated status. What has changed is the surface manifestation in the apodosis where the filling of the prefield has become more restricted: instead of placing an XP of any type in this position, there was a strong diachronic tendency to favour the correlative adverb *so*. But why was the pattern without a correlative adverb in the V2-apodosis driven back between the middle of the 15th and 2nd half of the 16th century? Even in languages with very strict V2-grammars such as Present-Day German, extensions of the left periphery by clauses or non-sentential XPs are tolerated when a resumptive pronoun or adverb occurs clause-internally, as is the case in the Left-Dislocation or Hanging-Topic construction. In OHG and MHG, clause combining with adverbial clauses constituted a systematic exception to this 'rule'. However, during the first half of the ENHG period canonical adverbial clauses have increasingly gained access to the matrix Spec-position, as a result of which pre-SpecC-placement without a following resumptive or correlative adverb (AdvC–XP–V_{fin}) was pushed back and marginalized to special types of adverbial clauses. This marginalization may explain why the grammar could no longer tolerate the V1cond–XP–V_{fin} pattern in the case of V1-conditionals. Since V1-conditionals have not developed into embedded clauses and could not occupy the SpecC-position in the apodosis, the predominance of the V1cond–XP–V_{fin} pattern could only the circumvented by the spread of the correlative pattern with *so*.

In the 17th century, a further innovation took place: the rise of the V1-apodosis. Once this innovation had entered into the grammar, a competition must have taken place between the V1- and the *so*-apodosis in the course of which the V1-apodosis gained ground. This must have taken place in the last 300 years, between 1700 and the present. We do not have any systematic corpus data from the New High German period, but we know that in Present-Day German the V1-apodosis is much more frequent than the *so*-apodosis.

What we still need to explain, however, is how the V1-apodosis might have developed in the first place. This will be done in the following section.

3.4. The rise of new types of V1-declaratives

We have argued that V1-conditionals did not participate in the change from peripheral adjunction to clause-internal embedding. Their unintegrated status has been diachronically stable. If this is correct, the rise of the V1cond–V_{fin} pattern must be analyzed as a newly arising syntactic structure of the apodosis and not of the V1-conditional. The new structure would be a declarative clause with V1-order, that is with no SpecC-position. In section 2.5 we argued that this is indeed a feasible analysis for the Present-Day German data since there is evidence for the existence of non-narrative declarative V1-order in independent contexts. How plausible is this analysis from a diachronic perspective?

It is a well-known fact that in the late ENHG (16th century onwards) period new types of so-called V1-declaratives began to spread (= so-called späte Spitzenstellung im Aussagesatz 'late V1-order in declaratives', Behaghel 1932: 27–29). It should be noted that the phenomenon of V1-declaratives as such is characterized by a discontinuous diachronic development:[20] In MHG texts, V1-declaratives are hardly attested (Maurer 1926, Paul [1919] 1968: 71), they only begin to rise after the middle of the 15th century – first with verbs of saying in *inquit* formulae, later also with dynamic verbs in narrative contexts. Interestingly, besides the well-known 'narrative type' new types of V1-declaratives developed in the 16th century and became more frequent in the 17th century.

One such type is V1-declaratives containing the modal particle *doch* that occur in argumentative contexts and usually receive a causal interpretation (see (18b) for a Present-Day German example). This type begins to be attested from the 16th century onwards, cf. (39) for an example from the Bonn corpus. Some early examples occur in Luther's works (cf. Behaghel 1932: 39 for an example). Again, this type of V1-declarative still occurs in Present-Day German, cf. (37).

(37) Virt[iganes]. … *Und ob gleich der Koͤnig beschlossen hat/ … den meisten Theil voran#zu schicken/ werden doch so viel Schiffe zuruͤckbleiben/ dabey man allen Difficultaͤten wird begegnen koͤnnen.* (Even though the king has decided to send forth the major part, enough ships will stay so that all difficulties [= a potential rape of the princess, K.A.] can be encountered)

Sel[enissa]. *Sind* ***doch*** *alle Fabeln voll Goͤtter/ welche*
are DOCH all fairytales full gods who
Jungfern geraubet haben.
maiden robbed have
'since indeed all fairytale are full of gods who have raped maidens"
(Weise: Jugendlust 143, 20–25 (Leipzig 1648))

Furthermore, there is the phenomenon of V1-declaratives after main clauses containing the particle *kaum* (see (19a) for a Present-Day German example). Clauses with this particle have never been able to stand on their own, they have always been followed by a second clause and this second clause is either a V1-clause, or a V2-clause introduced by the resumptive adverb *so* or *da*.[21] Some of the 16th and 17th century texts in the Bonn corpus contain *kaum*-clauses, but in all of them the second clause follows the resumptive pattern. However, the pattern with a V1-apodosis is attested in texts from outside the corpus (cf. also Grimm and Grimm 1873 (volume 5), p. 357 for further examples):

(38) *das volk het kaum ihr wunsch verricht,* <u>*verlor*</u> *das schiff*
the folk had hardly her request out.carried lost the ship
sich aus dem gsicht
REFL out the sight
'Hardly had the people carried out her request, when the ship disappeared'
(Fischart, *gl. schiff* (1577, 527) (cited from Grimm and Grimm 1873, vol. 5: 357))

Moreover, Maurer (1926: 204) discusses a type of declarative V1-order that is quite characteristic of the language of the Chronicles (so-called *Urkundensprache*) and serves to establish a strong connection between two main clauses following each other in discourse. This connective effect is so strong that the first clause is interpreted as being subordinate to the second one with V1-order even though it is structurally a main clause:

(39) *Am dinstagk bin ich ken Aldem Lessen kuemmen vnd*
on.the Tuesday am I toward Aldem Lessen come and
mich dem erzbischoff lassen ansagen. <u>*Hatt*</u> *er mich lassen*
me the archbishop let announce has he me let
entphan …
receive
'When, on Tuesday, I approached A.L. and let myself announce to the archbishop, he let me be received …' (Brandenburgian Document (1521a) (cited from Maurer 1926: 204, translation according to Maurer's commentary))

To sum up, the rise and spread of V1-declaratives in the ENHG period did not only pertain to the well-known narrative type, but also to various other types. It is thus not inconceivable that this innovation also spread over to the apodosis clauses of the syntactically unintegrated V1-conditionals.

4. Conclusion

Our aim was to present evidence from synchrony and diachrony to defend the claim that V1-conditionals are not syntactically embedded, but adjoined.

Diachronically, V1-conditionals did not participate in the rise of embedding and this finds its synchronic reflex in the fact that in Present-Day German they do not satisfy the diagnostic criteria for syntactic embedding. Furthermore, there are differences in syntactic distribution and semantics between V1-conditionals and conditional *wenn*-clauses, an observation which strongly suggests two diverging analyses: In contrast to *wenn*-clauses and to what is traditionally assumed, V1-conditionals are not embedded into the apodosis clause but unintegrated, i.e. linked to the apodosis clause by adjunction.

The implication of the adjunction analysis is that synchronically the apodosis is a declarative V1-clause. At first sight this appears to be an unorthodox proposal. However, it is supported by the observation that not only are V1-declaratives more wide-spread than commonly assumed, but they also occur after structurally unintegrated *kaum*-clauses that are interpreted as being subordinate. Further plausibility for our proposal comes from the fact that diachronically there is a rough temporal correlation between the innovation of the V1-apodosis and the rise of certain types of (non-narrative) V1-declaratives in independent contexts.

What we have not addressed so far is the question why a V2-grammar should tolerate the adoption of a declarative V1-structure. Even though V1-declaratives do occur in many Germanic languages, this is still a marked sentence type after all. It is conceivable that surface equivalence may be responsible for this.[22] In fact, V1-conditionals 'look' like embedded canonical adverbial clauses: [[V1] [V1]] and [[V-end] V2] have the same surface word order.

In our case study we have drawn on data from synchrony as well as diachrony – still seemingly distant fields under a generative perspective – showing that they provide converging evidence for the unintegrated status of V1-conditionals. In this vein, our paper can be read as a plea for systematically using diachronic developments as evidence for synchronic analyses alongside (properly) synchronic data in a modular theory of grammar.

Notes

* This work was supported by the Deutsche Forschungsgemeinschaft within the SFB 441 'Linguistische Datenstrukturen'. The synchronic part of our paper is based upon joint work with Marga Reis, cf. Reis and Wöllstein (2008). The treebank searches (Present-Day German) were carried out in collaboration with our colleague Stephan Kepser, whom we thank. Thanks also to Oliver Bott for his assistance with the statistics and Janina Rado for proof reading. For helpful comments we thank the editors Susanne Winkler and Sam Featerston. We are also much obliged to our project leaders Marga Reis and Hubert Truckenbrodt as well as to many others members of the SFB. All remaining errors are our own.

1. Just like *wenn*-clauses, V1-clauses occur in temporal adverbial function (see e.g. König and van der Auwera 1988, Köpcke and Panther 1989).

2. Bhatt and Pancheva (2006: 639) describe a speech act conditional as "an implicit performative clause embedding the surface main clause, and this performative is the true consequent in a (hypothetical) conditional structure". In German, some types of speech act conditionals may occur with V1- as well as V2-apodosis, cf. (10a) and (10b), but the pattern with V2-apodosis is more common (cf. Pittner 2003 for an overview). V2-apodosis also occurs after so-called relevance conditionals: *Wenn du durstig bist, Bier ist im Kühlschrank* 'If you are thirsty, there is beer in the fridge', which also disallows V1-conditionals. As for the general distribution of V2 apodosis, see Section 2.3.3.
3. *ex falso quodlibet/ex falso sequitur quodlibet* = "Anything follows from falsehood". These sentences are also referred to as non-predictive conditionals in Dancygier (1993).
4. Examples of V1-clauses in concessive function are very rare. The following example is taken from Zifonun et al. (1997: 2313):

   War der Versuch auch missglückt, gab er die Hoffnung doch
   was the attempt also failed gave he the hope however
   nicht auf.
   not up
   'Although the attempt had failed, he still didn't give up hope'
5. It should be mentioned that V1-clauses also occur in adversative adverbial function, where *wenn*-clauses are exceedingly rare (Zifonun et al. 1997: 2325). How this fact fits into a consistent picture of the semantics of *wenn*- vs. V1-clauses is a question for further research.
6. In factive and echoic conditionals the protasis has a factive reading. V1-clauses are very marked in echoic conditionals, which suggest that the truth-value of the V1-clause may not be presupposed. Thus, echoic conditionals can be argued to be bad for the same reason as the example in (12b). (Note that in this example, the V1-clause is followed by a V2-clause.)

   ??*Wisst ihr ohnehin schon Bescheid, warum fragt ihr noch?*
   know you anyway yet notice why ask you still
   'If you already know, why are you still asking'
7. Since it is generally assumed that German *wenn*-clauses frequently occur in preposed position as well (Pittner 1999), we carried out a further study based on COSMAS subcorpora (*St. Galler Tagblatt* (23.–26.04.1997) and the *Vorarlberger Nachrichten* (02.–07.1997)). It showed that there was no preference for pre- or postposing of conditional *wenn*-clauses: Of the 301 conditional *wenn*-clauses we found, 122 were preposed and 117 postposed. (62 concessive or elliptical *wenn*-clauses in parenthetical position were not included). We want to thank Melanie Stahr for her help with this study.
8. See Wöllstein (2008) for an explanation why unintroduced adverbial clauses do not show an inversion of the prototypical semantic sequence: 'condition' precedes 'consequence'.

9. When a *wenn*-clause occurs that precedes a V2-apodosis (cf. fn. 6), the *wenn*-clause is an unintegrated clause. Like V1-conditionals, those *wenn*-clauses are prosodically separated from the apodosis clause, cf. Günthner (1999: 215f.) and form their own focus-background structure. Note that continuous intonation in V1-clauses does not necessarily imply that the apodosis is syntactically embedded, cf. Truckenbrodt (2005: 279) and Günthner (1999: 215) for counterevidence. Günthner shows that continuous intonation even occurs with independent intonation contours in the cases of unintegrated *wenn*-clauses.
10. The negation particle *ni* is an X°-clitic that has procliticized to the finite verb.
11. Note however, that this word order pattern is still marginally possible with counterfactual conditionals (both *wenn* and V1), certain types of speech act conditionals and concessives (König and van der Auwera 1988). Cf. also fn. 6.
12. Note that in (21a) the subject pronoun *thú* has been inserted contrary to the Latin in the apodosis and thus the German word order in the apodosis differs from that in the Latin (given in the fourth line), which suggests that this is a native pattern.
13. The particle *eno* or *inu* is mainly attested in Tatian and Isidor, respectively. Neither of these texts displays any V1-conditionals, however. This is probably due to the fact that they are relatively close renderings of the Latin originals. Since in the corresponding Latin examples conditional clauses are always introduced by adverbial subordinators, the translators always chose to maintain this in their translations. By contrast, a substantial number of V1-conditionals occur in Otfrid's Gospel Book, which is a poetical synopsis of the Gospels in chronological order and not a translation, and in Notker's works, which are paraphrases and commentaries of the ancient texts rather than mere translations.
14. If one also counts in the V1-conditional, the surface word order pattern in the apodosis is in fact V3. For simplicity's sake, we always refer to the surface word order in the (part of the) apodosis or matrix clause that follows the preposed V1-conditional or adverbial clause clause.
15. In Lower German the demonstrative adverb that introduces the adverbial clause is sometimes followed by the overtly realized relative particle *the*, which suggests that it has not yet be re-analysed as an adverbial conjunction in C°, but is still an adverb phrase occupying SpecC.
16. In the present version, the online corpus comprises 40 texts, but when we carried out our corpus study, text 117 (*Deo Gratias*) was not included. So the corpus of the present study contained only 39 texts.
17. Recall that we use the term 'canonical' only to refer to those adverbial clauses that are introduced by an adverbial subordinator and have (structural) verb-final order.
18. The question of how the pattern with the correlative adverb in the prefield of the matrix clause should be analyzed is more difficult to answer. As long as we do not find any evidence that adverbial clauses could occupy the SpecC-position, it seems to be indisputable that in the AdvC-corr.adv.–V_{fin} pattern, they are base-generated in their peripheral position and that only the correlative adverb is base-generated in the main-clause internal position in the middle field and moved to SpecC. Once

adverbial clauses themselves can be embedded in the main-clause and there arises a competition between the innovative embedding structure and the archaic adjunction structure, two analyses can be envisaged. In Present-Day German left-peripheral *wenn*-clauses, Frey (2004) distinguishes two constructions: Hanging Topic Left Dislocation (correlative adverb = *so*) and German Left Dislocation (correlative adverb = *dann*). It has been argued that in Hanging Topic Left Dislocation the dislocated XP (= the *wenn*-clause in this case) is base-generated in its peripheral position, whereas in the German Left Dislocation construction it is moved there from within the main clause. So, theoretically both these analyses could apply to the Adv-corr.adv.–V_{fin} pattern as soon as the competition between adjoined and embedded clauses has arisen. It may in fact have been this ambiguity that led to the innovation of embedded adverbial clauses in the first place: the old adjunction construction may have been re-analyzed as an instance of German Left Dislocation of an embedded clause. It would be beyond the scope of this article to pursue this any further. In the case of non-sentential dislocated XPs, it can be demonstrated that the two constructions differ for instance with respect to the requirement of case agreement between the XP and the resumptive pronoun: with Hanging Topic Left Dislocation case agreement is optional, while with German Topic Left Dislocation it is obligatory. This diagnostic cannot be applied to adverbial constituents as they do not bear case. Frey points out that in the case of the *wenn*-causes there are differences in the binding properties. Such intricacies can, of course, not be tested in historical corpora.

19. Note that according to Kroch (1989), the surface contexts of a given underlying change differ with the extent that they favour the innovative construction or not: contexts that favour the innovating option show a higher rate of overall use than others. What is the same is the rate of change for each context (Constant Rate Effect). Also the onset of the change occurs at the same time in all contexts. It could thus be argued that V1-conditionals are a less favourable surface context for the rise of embedding than canonical adverbial clauses so that it shows lower overall use of the innovative V1cond–V_{fin} pattern. However, we would still expect attestations of the innovative pattern in the first three subperiods. It could be objected that the lack of these early attestations is an accidental gap in the data since V1-conditionals are, of course, less frequent than the various semantic types of canonical adverbial clauses taken together so that their total number may be too low for the relevant pattern to be realized in the data. Note, however, that the relevant examples do show up in the last subperiod in which the total number of V1-conditionals is only 44, while they are not attested in the first two subperiods in which the total numbers are more than 4 times as high (182/183).

20. In OHG V1-order often occurred in the context of certain types of verbs (unaccusative verbs, impersonal predicates) and in sentences with existential/presentational constructions. These types of V1-declaratives were lost in the MHG period as a result of independent developments such as the innovation of the prefield expletive *es* and a spread of the quasi-argument *es* (Axel 2007). Furthermore, there existed the well-

known type of the narrative V1-declarative that also occurs in other (old and modern) West and North Germanic languages.

21. There is furthermore a third pattern in which the *kaum*-clause is followed by a subordinate clause with verb-end order introduced by the conjunction *als*. In a further variant the second clause is introduced by the co-ordinating conjunction *und* 'and', which is followed by the finite verb. Since it is unlikely that *und* is an XP occupying SpecC, this can be regarded as a variant of V1-order in the clause following the *kaum*-clause. (See Reis 2007 for a fuller treatment of Present-Day German *kaum*-clauses.)
22. Further phenomena where surface equivalence has been argued to play a role are backformation in word formation, pseudo-affixes (Wegener 2003), haplology, agreement mismatches (Ehrich 2007).

References

Corpora

Das Bonner Frühneuhochdeutschkorpus
Online access to the digitalized texts: http://pcdas.ikp.uni-bonn.de:3000/Leitseite/index.html

TüBaD/Z corpus
(Tübinger Baumbank Corpus. Treebank including c. 30.000 clauses from German newspaper *TAZ*) (tuebadz_release3_060713.cdat)

TIGER corpus
(Linguistic Interpretation of German corpus. Treebank including 50.000 clauses from German newspaper *Frankfurter Rundschau*) (tiger_release_dec05.cdat)

COSMAS II
(St. Galler Tagblatt (23.–26.04.1997) and Vorarlberger Nachrichten (02.–07.1997))

Primary Sources

[Isidor]
Der althochdeutsche Isidor. Nach der Pariser Handschrift und den Monseer Fragmenten. Hans Eggers (ed.). Tübingen: Niemeyer. 1964.

[Notker *Boethius*]
Notker der Deutsche: Boethius "De consolatione Philosophiae". Buch I/II. Buch III. Buch IV/V. Petrus W. Tax (ed.). Tübingen: Niemeyer 1986. 1988. 1990.

[Otfrid]
Otfrids Evangelienbuch. Oskar Erdmann (ed.), 6th edition by Ludwig Wolff. Tübingen: Niemeyer. 1973. (cited)

[Prose Lancelot]]
Lancelot und Ginover. Hans-Hugo Steinhoff (ed.). Volume 1. 1st edition. Frankfurt/M.: Deutscher Klassiker Verlag. 1995.

[Tatian]
Die lateinisch-althochdeutsche Tatianbilingue Stiftsbibliothek St. Gallen Cod. 56. Achim Masser (ed.) (in cooperation with Elisabeth De Felip-Jaud). Vandenhoeck & Ruprecht. 1994.

Secondary References

Altmann, Hans
1987 Problematik der Konstitution von Satzmodi als Formtypen. In: Jörg Meibauer (ed.), *Satzmodus zwischen Grammatik und Pragmatik. Referate anlässlich der 8. Jahrestagung der Deutschen Gesellschaft für Sprachwissenschaft. Heidelberg 1986*, 22–56. Tübingen: Niemeyer.

Auer, Peter
1993 Zur Verbspitzenstellung im gesprochenen Deutsch. *Deutsche Sprache* 21: 193–222.

Axel, Katrin
2002 Zur diachronen Entwicklung der syntaktischen Integration linksperipherer Adverbialsätze im Deutschen. *Beiträge zur Geschichte der deutschen Sprache und Literatur* 124: 11–43.
2004 The syntactic integration of preposed adverbial clauses on the German left periphery: a diachronic perspective. In: Horst Lohnstein and Susanne Trissler (eds), *The Syntax and Semanctic of the Left Periphery*, 23–58. Berlin/New York: Mouton de Gruyter.
2007 *Studies on Old High German. Left Sentence Periphery, Verb Placement and Verb-Second.* Amsterdam/Philadelphia, Benjamins.

Bhatt, Rajesh and Roumyana Pancheva
2006 Conditionals. In: Martin Everaert and Henk van Riemsdijk (eds), *The Blackwell Companion to Syntax*, volume 1, 638–687. Oxford: Oxford University Press.

Behaghel, Otto
1928 *Deutsche Syntax. Eine geschichtliche Darstellung.* Vol. III. Heidelberg: Winter.
1929 Der Nachsatz. *Beiträge zur Geschichte der deutschen Sprache und Literatur* 53: 401–419.
1932 *Deutsche Syntax. Eine geschichtliche Darstellung.* Vol. IV. Heidelberg: Winter.

Bianchi, Valentina
Consequences of Antisymmetry. Mouton de Gruyter: Berlin.

Chomsky, Noam
1986 *Barriers*. Cambridge, MA: The MIT-Press.

Comrie, Bernard
1986 Conditionals: A typology. In: Elizabeth Traugott, Alice ter Meulen, Judy S. Reilly and Charles A. Ferguson (eds.), *On Conditionals*, 77–99. Cambridge: Cambridge University Press.

Dancygier, Barbara
1993 Interpreting conditionals: time, knowledge and causation. *Journal of Pragmatics* 19: 403–434.

Diessel, Holger
1997 Verb-first constructions in German. In Marjolijn Verspoor, Kee D. Lee and Eve Sweetser (eds.), *Lexical and syntactical constructions and the construction of meaning*, 51–68. Amsterdam: John Benjamins.

Ehrich, Veronika
2007 Der Bloße Singular in koordinativen Verknüpfungen. *Neue Beiträge zur Germanistik*. 6.3: 9–30.

Erdmann, Oskar
1874. *Untersuchungen über die Syntax der Sprache Otfrids*. Teil 1: Die Formationen des Verbums in einfachen und in zusammengesetzten Sätzen. Halle/S.: Verlag der Buchhandlung des Waisenhauses.

Frey, Werner
2004 Notes on the syntax and pragmatics of German Left Dislocation. In: Horst Lohnstein and Susanne Trissler (eds.), *The Syntax and Semantics of the Left Periphery*, 203–234. Berlin/New York: Mouton de Gruyter.

Günthner, Susanne
1999 Wenn-Sätze im Vor-Vorfeld. *Deutsche Sprache* 27: 209–235.

Greenberg, Joseph H.
1963 Some universals of grammar with particular reference to the order of meaningful elements. In: Joseph H. Greenberg (ed.), *Universals of Language*, 73–113. London: MIT Press.

Grimm; Jacob and Wilhem Grimm.
1873 *Deutsches Wörterbuch*. Volume 5. Leipzig: S. Hirzel.

Haudry, Jean
1973 Parataxe, hypotaxe et corrélation dans la phrase latine. *Bulletin de la Société de Linguistique de Paris* LXVIII: 147–186.

Horacek, Blanka
1957 Zur Verbindung von Vorder- und Nachsatz im Deutschen. *Beiträge zur Geschichte der deutschen Sprache und Literatur (Halle)* 79. Sonderband, 415–439.

Iatridou, Sabine and David Embick
1993 Conditional Inversion. *Proceedings of NELS* 24: 189–203.

Kiparsky, Paul
1995 Indo-European origins of Germanic syntax. In Adrian Battye and Ian Roberts (eds), *Clause Structure and Language Change*, 140–170. Oxford: Oxford University Press.

Knaus, Harald
1995 Deutsche Syntax – diachron. Verb-dritt-Sätze im Mittelhochdeutschen und Frühneuhochdeutschen. MA thesis, University of Stuttgart.
König, Ekkehard and Johan van der Auwera
1988 Clause integration in German and Dutch conditionals, concessive conditionals and concessives. In: John Haiman and Sandra A. Thompson. (eds.), *Clause Combining in Grammar and Discourse*, 101–134. Amsterdam: Benjamins.
Köpcke, Klaus-Michael and Klaus-Uwe Panther
1989 On correlations between word order and pragmatic function of conditional sentences in German. *Journal of Pragmatics* 13: 685–711.
Kroch, Anthony
1989 Reflexes of grammar in patterns of language change. *Language Variation and Change* 1: 199–244.
Lindström, Liina
2001 Verb-initial clauses in narrative. In Mati Erelt (ed.), *Estonian: Typological Studies*, 138–168. V. Tartu: University of Tartu
Maurer, Friedrich
1926 *Untersuchungen über die deutsche Verbstellung in ihrer geschichtlichen Entwicklung*. Heidelberg: Winter.
Mitchell, Bruce
1985 *Old English Syntax*. 2 vols. Oxford: Clarendon Press.
Önnerfors, Olaf
1997 *Verb-Erst-Deklarativsätze. Grammatik und Pragmatik*. Stockholm: Almqvist & Wiksell.
Platzack, Christer
1987 The Scandinavian languages and the Null-Subject Parameter. *Natural Language and Linguistic Theory* 5: 377–401.
Paul, Hermann
1968 *Deutsche Grammatik*. Vol. III. Tübingen: Niemeyer [reprint of the edition from 1919]
Pittner, Karin
1998 *Adverbiale im Deutschen. Untersuchungen zu ihrer Stellung und Interpretation*. Tübingen: Stauffenburg.
2003 Sprechaktbedingungen und bedingte Sprechakte: Pragmatische Konditionalsätze im Deutschen. *Linguistik online* 5, 1/00.
Polikarpow, Alexander
1996 Zum Problem der asyndetischen Subordination in der Syntax der gesprochenen deutschen Sprache. *Deutsche Sprache* 24: 154–168.
Reichmann, Oskar and Klaus-Peter Wegera (eds.)
1993 *Frühneuhochdeutsche Grammatik*. Tübingen: Niemeyer.

Reis, Marga
1997 Zum syntaktischen Status unselbständiger Verbzweit-Sätze. In: Christa Dürscheid. Karl-Heinz Ramers, and Monika Schwarz (eds.), *Sprache im Fokus. Festschrift für Heinz Vater zum 65. Geburtstag*, 121–144. Tübingen: Niemeyer.
2000 Anmerkungen zu Verb-erst-Satz-Typen im Deutschen. In: Rolf Thieroff et al. (eds.), *Deutsche Grammatik in Theorie und Praxis*, 215–227. Tübingen: Niemeyer.
2007 Anmerkungen zur *kaum-als*-Konstruktion im Deutschen. [Ms. Universität Tübingen].
2008 When and why V1-conditionals? A Late Reply to Iatridou & Embick 1993. [Ms. Univ. Tübingen]

Reis, Marga and Angelika Wöllstein
2008 Zur Struktur von V1-Gefügen. [Ms. Universität Tübingen].

Truckenbrodt, Hubert
2005 A short report on intonation phrase boundaries in German. *Linguistische Berichte* 203: 273–296.

Wegener, Heide
2003 Normprobleme bei der Pluralbildung fremder und nativer Substantive. *Linguistik Online* 16: 4/03. 119–157.

Wöllstein, Angelika
2008 *Konzepte der Satzkonnexion*. Tübingen: Stauffenburg.

Zifonun, Gisela, Ludger Hoffmann, Bruno Strecker et al.
1997 *Grammatik der deutschen Sprache*. Berlin/New York: Mouton de Gruyter.

Optionality in verb cluster formation[*]

Markus Bader, Tanja Schmid and Jana Häussler

1. Introduction

In this paper we discuss a curious kind of optionality that is found with West-Germanic verb cluster formation. This kind of optionality differs from widely known cases of optionality like heavy NP shift in English or scrambling in German by the lack of any motivation, be it in terms of information structure or in terms of weight; all structural options can be used interchangeably without any difference in meaning. A well-known English example of this kind of optionality is quantifier-floating in English (e.g., Radford 1997). Another example is particle climbing in Dutch which is shown in (1) (see among others Bennis 1992; Evers 2003; Seuren 2003).

(1) Particle climbing in Dutch, taken from Seuren (2003)

a.	..., *dat*	*ze*	*het*	*boek*	*[zou*	*willen*	*mogen*	***op** bergen]*
	that	she	the	book	would	like	be-allowed	put-away

b. ..., *dat ze het boek [zou willen* ***op*** *mogen bergen]*

c. ..., *dat ze het boek [zou* ***op*** *willen mogen bergen]*

d. ..., *dat ze het boek [* ***op*** *zou willen mogen bergen]*

While the linear structure of the verbs in the cluster is rigid, a verbal particle like *op* may freely occur in any cluster-internal position preceding the lexical verb or, as Seuren (2003, page 274) puts it, verbal particles "(...) may climb through the V-cluster without limits (...)."

A less well-known but very similar kind of optionality is found in Colloquial German verb cluster formation. As with particle climbing in Dutch, an element, which in the German case is the finite auxiliary, is free to appear in several positions inside the verb cluster. We will concentrate on this case in the main part of our paper but come back to Dutch particle climbing in the final discussion where we will argue that we are dealing with a single kind of optionality here which is instantiated in different ways in Dutch and German.

In section 2 we give a short introduction to verb cluster formation in German. We will summarize experimental evidence on 3- and 4-verb clusters in section 3, sum up an analysis given in Bader and Schmid (to appear b) that accounts for this evidence in section 4, present new experimental findings on 5-verb clusters confirming and extending our data obtained so far in section 5 and finally summarize and point out some general implications of our work in section 6.

2. Verb cluster formation in German

As would be expected from an SOV language, verbs in German normally select their dependent elements to the left. This order is obligatory for DP objects as shown in (2) but it also occurs when a verb selects a verbal complement as shown in (3).

(2) …, *dass Peter [ein Buch ← schreibt]*
that P. a book writes
'that Peter writes a book'

(3) a. …, *dass Peter [ein Buch ← geschrieben ← hat]*
that P. a Book written has

b. …, *dass Peter [ein Buch ← geschrieben ← haben ← könnte]*
that P. a book written have could

c. …, *dass [ein Buch ← geschrieben ← worden ← sein ← könnte]*
that a book written been be could

The standard order of verbs and their verbal complements thus adheres to the schema in (4).

(4) $V_{selected} \leftarrow V_{selecting}$

There are, however, some well-known exceptions to this general picture in Standard German. When $V_{selecting}$ is represented by the perfect tense auxiliary *haben* and $V_{selected}$ by a modal verb, then the perfect tense auxiliary has to be inverted to the front of the cluster, resulting in the order *Aux-(V…)-Mod* as shown in (5) for 3- and 4-verb clusters.

(5) a. …, *dass Peter ein Buch* HAT → *schreiben* ← ***wollen***
that P. a book has write want

b. …, *dass das Auto* HAT → *repariert* ← *werden* ← ***müssen***.
that the car has repaired be must

We will abstract away from a further peculiarity of this construction, namely that the modal verb has to appear in the bare infinitive instead of the selected past participle, the so-called 'Infinitivus Pro Participio (IPP)'-effect, (see Schmid 2005 for an overview), and concentrate on verb order here. Furthermore, we will only discuss perfect tense clusters as in (5) (for future tense clusters, which are more liberal with respect to verb order even in Standard German, see Bader and Schmid (to appear b)).

According to the authoritative prescriptive grammar of German, no other verb orders apart from order *Aux-(V...)-Mod* are allowed in cases like (5) (Duden-Grammatik [Fabricius-Hansen et al. (2005)], §684). However, we find a lot of variation across German dialects and varieties as shown in (6).

(6) a. Variants of Austrian and Bavarian (Martina Wiltschko p.c.):
...., *dass er es schreiben* ***wollen*** *HAT*
that he it write want has

b. Pattern typical for Austrian and Bavarian (see Abraham 1995; Weiß 1998)
..., *dass er es* schreiben HAT ***wollen***

c. Swiss German (see Lötscher 1978)
..., *dass er es HAT wollen* schreiben

Furthermore, there is often more than one possible order in dialects as shown in (7).

(7) Sankt Gallen German (Schmid 2005)

a. ..., *das I das immer HA mache* **wöle**
that I that always have make want

b. ..., *das I das immer* mache *HA* ***wöle***

c. ..., *das I das immer* ***wöle*** mache *HA*

The large amount of variation found for verb clusters including modal verbs as well as a small set of other semi-functional verbs like *lassen* ('to let') raises the question of whether native speakers of German indeed adhere to the strict Standard German pattern. In a series of experiments, Bader and Schmid (to appear b) have found that this is not the case.

Native speakers of German are more liberal than prescriptive grammars ("Standard German") in a precisely defined way: In addition to full inversion of the auxiliary as in the Standard German order *Aux-(V...)-Mod* they also allow for partial inversion as in *(V...)-Aux-Mod.* We call the grammar that comprises these orders "Colloquial German". This result raises further questions about the correct generalization of German verb clusters as well as the correct syntactic account of the observed grammaticality distribution. We will look at these questions in more detail in the remainder of this paper.

3. Verb order variation in 3- and 4-verb clusters

Bader and Schmid (to appear b) conducted a number of experiments investigating German verb clusters. For reasons of space we only summarize the basic experiment on 3-verb clusters and a follow-up experiment on 4-verb clusters.

Both experiments looked at verb clusters with modal verbs in the perfect tense by means of speeded grammaticality judgments (SGJ). In an SGJ experiment, participants judge sentences as either grammatical or ungrammatical under controlled and timed conditions. In the experiments reported here, sentences were presented word-by-word with a presentation rate of about 350 ms per word. To ensure fast responses, participants had to give their grammaticality judgments within a deadline of 2000 ms after the last word of the sentence was presented. Although there are alternative methods in order to obtain experimentally controlled grammaticality judgments, like rating sentences on a 5- or 6-point scale or magnitude estimation (cf. Cowart 1997; Featherston 2007), speeded grammaticality judgments have the advantage that they offer a spontaneous assessment of the grammatical status of the constructions in question. In addition, in all experiments reported here, experimental sentences were embedded in a large list of filler sentences with a ratio of experimental to filler sentences of about 1 : 5, which prevents participants from focusing on any particular kind of syntactic construction. Finally, Bader and Häussler (submitted) conducted a direct comparison of speeded grammaticality judgments and magnitude estimation by letting participants judge the same sentences (including sentences containing 3-verb clusters of the sort considered here) with the help of both methods, and received very similar results.

In the 3-verb cluster experiment of Bader and Schmid (to appear b), all six permutations that arise by manipulating the order of *Aux*, *V* and *Mod* were tested. The goal of this experiment was to determine the degree to which native speakers of German accept these six orders. The sentences differed in two dimensions: Order of the auxiliary (either in first, second, or third position), and order between lexical verb and modal verb (either V < Mod or Mod < V). Both dimensions are shown schematically in Table 1.

Table 1. Dimensions of verb order variation

	Aux = 1	Aux = 2	Aux = 3
V < Mod	Aux-V-Mod	V-Aux-Mod	V-Mod-Aux
Mod < V	Aux-Mod-V	Mod-Aux-V	Mod-V-Aux

Five modal verbs were used in the experimental material: *können* ('can'), *müssen* ('must'), *wollen* ('want'), *dürfen* ('may'), *sollen* ('should'). Each modal verb appeared in six sentences and was always used in the bare infinitive.[1] A sample sentence is given in (8).

(8) a. ..., *dass Peter ein Buch (HAT) lesen (HAT)* ***müssen*** *(HAT).*
that P. a book has read has must has

b. ..., *dass Peter ein Buch (HAT)* ***müssen*** *(HAT) lesen (HAT).*
that P. a book has must has read has

If the experimental participants were adhering closely to Standard German, high percentages of judgments 'grammatical' should be received for order *Aux-V-Mod* and low percentages for the remaining five orders. This expectation based on prescriptive grammar did not turn out to be correct.

The results of Experiment 1 from Bader and Schmid (to appear b) are shown in Figure 1.

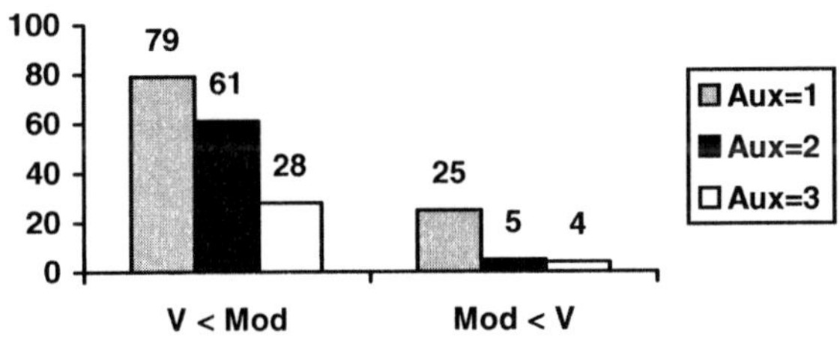

Figure 1. Percentages of judgments 'grammatical' in Experiment 1 of Bader and Schmid (to appear b).

The Standard German order *Aux-V-Mod* received the best judgments (79% grammatical), but the partially inverted order *V-Aux-Mod* was also judged surprisingly good: with 61% grammatical much better than Standard Grammar would predict. The remaining orders, in contrast, obtained low grammaticality scores, as expected (ranging from 4–28%).

These results were confirmed by a series of follow-up experiments. On average, the Standard German order *Aux-V-Mod* was accepted 85% of the time and the non-standard order *V-Aux-Mod* 70% of the time. Importantly, this finding was independent of the geographical background of the participants. This is the reason why Bader and Schmid (to appear b) called the grammar allowing exactly these two orders *Colloquial German.*

In contrast to other claims in the literature (e.g., Sapp 2006; Schmid and Vogel 2004), they found no effect of extra-syntactic factors like focus on the acceptability of verb orders. They therefore assume "real" optionality of the orders *Aux-V-Mod* and *V-Aux-Mod* in the perfect tense of modal verbs.

To summarize so far, Colloquial German has been found to be more liberal than Standard German in allowing two verb orders in 3-verb clusters in which a modal verb occurs in the perfect tense. At the same time, Colloquial German is quite restrictive in that only these two orders (out of a set of six possible orders) are grammatical. On the basis of these data, one may arrive at the following generalization for Colloquial German verb clusters: First, the lexical verb has to precede the modal verb, and second, the auxiliary must obligatorily be inverted – either fully (i.e., to the first position) or partly.[2] To test the validity of this generalization concerning auxiliary inversion in Colloquial German, Bader and Schmid (to appear b) conducted a follow-up experiment on 4-verb clusters. The major results of this experiment will be briefly summarized next.

Bader and Schmid (to appear b) looked at 4-verb clusters which were obtained from 3-verb clusters of the sort discussed above by passivizing the inner main verb. Thus, instead of a single main verb in the infinitive, the verbal complex contained the passive auxiliary *werden* ('to be') and a past participle main verb in addition to the modal verb and the perfect auxiliary. A sample sentence is shown in (9).

(9) 4-verb clusters: … *dass das Auto* … ('that the car …')

a. repariert *werden* ***müssen*** *HAT*
   repaired be must has
   '(…) had to be repaired'

b. repariert *werden HAT* ***[müssen]***

c. repariert *HAT [werden* ***müssen]***

d. *HAT [*repariert *werden* ***müssen]***

In the data presented here only the factor "placement of the auxiliary" (either first, second, third, or last position) varies whereas the position of the modal verb with respect to its complex complement is kept the same (modal after $V\text{-}Aux_{\text{passive}}$).[3]

In Standard German, the auxiliary must always be in first position, i.e., only order (9d) would be grammatical according to prescriptive grammar (Duden-Grammatik [Fabricius-Hansen et al (2005)], §684). The expectation for Colloquial German on the basis of Experiment 1 is quite different: All three orders in which the auxiliary is inverted, i.e., in which it appears either in first, second, or third position, should be accepted. As shown in Figure 2, this expectation was borne out.

The Standard German order with the auxiliary in first position was judged best but the other two orders with inverted auxiliary (Aux = 2 and Aux = 3) reached a high level of judgments 'grammatical' as well (80–88%). Only the

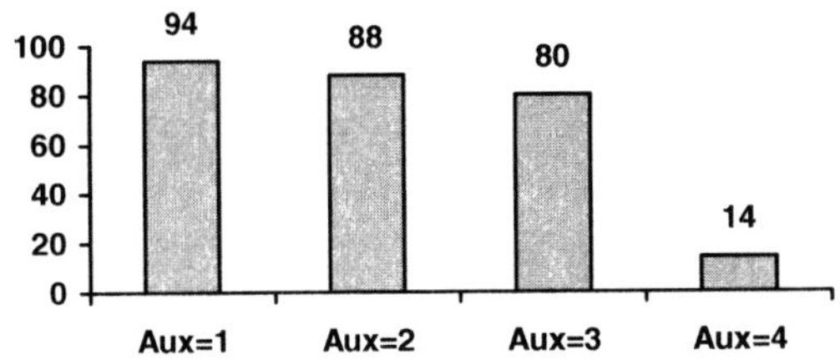

Figure 2. Percentages of judgments 'grammatical' in Experiment 4 of Bader and Schmid (to appear b).

last verb order, in which the auxiliary was not inverted (Aux = 4), was judged ungrammatical.

The experimental evidence summarized so far has shown that Colloquial German verb clusters differ from verb clusters in Standard German. In Colloquial German, the perfective auxiliary may occur in any position to the left of the modal verb. This leads to two grammatical verb orders in 3-verb clusters and three grammatical orders in 4-verb clusters in contrast to only one licit order in Standard German. In other words, Colloquial German shows optionality of auxiliary placement here whereas Standard German does not.

Yet another difference between Standard and Colloquial German is found with 2-verb clusters consisting of modal verb and auxiliary. In contrast to English, German modal verbs may appear without an (overt) verbal complement as shown in (10).

(10) a. ..., *dass er nach Paris* ***gewollt*** *HAT.*
that he to Paris wanted has
'..., that he wanted to go to Paris.'

b. ..., *dass er nach Paris HAT* ***wollen.*** (Colloquial German)
that he to Paris has want
'... that he wanted to go to Paris.'

Semantically, sentences like (10) are understood as containing a motion verb. An analysis in which the syntactic structure of such sentences actually contains an empty verb 'GO' has been proposed by van Riemsdijk (2002); Bader and Schmid (to appear a) discuss how van Riemdsijk's proposal can be integrated into the analysis presented in the next section.

With respect to order, Standard German allows auxiliary inversion only in clusters of at least three verbs. Thus, (10b) with the auxiliary in front of the modal verb is excluded in Standard German. In Colloquial German, however, the order in (10b) is a grammatical option, too (see Bader and Schmid (to appear a)). In summary, auxiliary inversion applies to verb clusters of any length in Colloquial German but is restricted to complex clusters (clusters with three or more verbs) in Standard German.

We summarize the observations on Colloquial German by the generalization in (11).[4]

(11) *Auxiliary inversion in Colloquial German*
An auxiliary selecting a modal verb inverts to any position in front of the modal verb, obligatorily in the perfect tense and optionally in the future tense.

We next present the analysis given in Bader and Schmid (to appear b) for the data introduced so far before we test whether the generalization in (11) is valid for 5-verb clusters as well.

4. Optionality in Auxiliary Placement: A Syntactic Proposal

Bader and Schmid (to appear b) present a syntactic analysis which modifies and extends the verb cluster analysis proposed in Williams (2003).[5] The four most important properties of this analysis may be summarized as follows: First, verb clusters are base generated and not derived by movement. Second, the analysis belongs to the family of analyses making use of *functional composition* (taken from Categorial Grammar, see Geach 1970 and subsequent work). Third, it places most of the information relevant for ordering into the lexicon, and last, optionality comes free in this approach.

Williams (2003) defines the formal language CAT which is a restricted variant of Categorial Grammar. Central to CAT is the Rule of Combination which is shown in (12) (in a slightly different notation than in Williams 2003).

(12) *Rule of Combination* (Williams, 2003: 205)
$X_{\_Y} + Y_{\_Z} \quad \rightarrow [X{+}Y]_{X\_Z}$

This rule is to be read as follows: "$X_{\_Y}$" is a syntactic unit of category X which subcategorizes for a syntactic unit of category Y. "$Y_{\_Z}$" is accordingly a syntactic unit of category Y which subcategorizes for a syntactic unit of category Z. Since "$X_{\_Y}$" selects "$Y_{\_Z}$", application of the Rule of Combination results in a unit which is of category X and subcategorizes for Z.

The application of the Rule of Combination is schematically illustrated in (13). The tree in (13a) shows the structure that results if the subcategorization feature of Y is empty (functional application), and the structure shown in (13b) if the subcategorization feature is not empty but a category Z (functional composition).

(13) a. b.

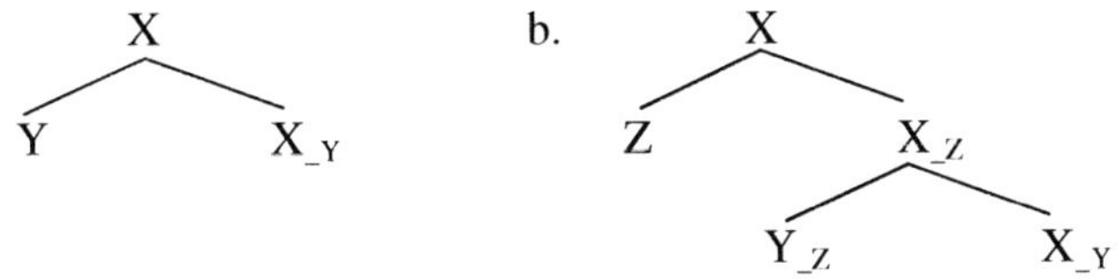

The Rule of Combination applies to lexical elements which are associated with the three types of subcategorization information shown in (14).

(14) a. Type of complement: N vs. V vs. . . .
b. Order of selection: left vs. right
c. Level of complement: X° vs. X^N

The grammar of a particular language is obtained by specifying this subcategorization information. Sample lexical specifications for German main verbs, modals and auxiliaries are given in (15). The direction of selection is specified by arrows.

(15) Sample lexical entries for verbs in German
a. Main verbs – V_{Main}:DP ←; V_{Main}: PP ←; V_{Main}: DP PP ←; . . .
b. Modal and auxiliary verbs – $V_{Mod|Aux}$: V←

The subcategorization frames shown in (15) all have in common that the direction of selection is uniformly to the left whereas the category of the selected element differs (DP and PP with main verbs, and V with modal and auxiliary verbs).

As discussed above (see (10)), auxiliary inversion in Standard German applies only to complex clusters whereas it applies across the board in Colloquial German. This is a kind of variation which cannot be captured by the subcategorization information given in (15). Bader and Schmid (to appear b) therefore make use of an additional complexity feature for verb clusters (adopted from Williams, 2003:184). This feature is shown in (16).

(16) Subcategorization feature for verb clusters: The *complexity* feature
a. Verb cluster: [VV-max]
b. Simple verb: [V°]

'VV-max' is to be understood as the maximal verb cluster selected by the verb at hand. This is the value of the complexity feature that we use to account for Standard German. It must combine two restrictions. First, inversion of the finite auxiliary occurs only in clusters of length three or greater. The feature 'VV-max' therefore requires a verb cluster as complement of the auxiliary, that is, a combination of at least two verbs ('VV'). Second, the auxiliary must invert to the cluster-initial position. This requirement is achieved by the maximality part of 'VV-max'. The auxiliary must be combined with a maximal verb cluster. In terms of the Rule of Combination, a maximal verb cluster is one in which all subcategorization requirements for verbs have already been saturated. In contrast to the first value of the complexity feature, the second one is quite simple. 'V°' requires that the auxiliary combines with a lexical head in the sense of X-bar theory.

The possibility of having complexity requirements as in (16) in the subcategorization frames of lexical items leads to three different systems of 3-verb clusters if only the complexity requirement is varied and order, type, and level specifications are kept the same. These three systems are shown in Table 2.

Table 2. Complexity Variations

V-orders	System 1: $\rightarrow \text{Mod}_{\text{VV-max}}$	System 2: $\rightarrow \text{Mod}_{\text{V}^{\circ}}$	System 3: $\rightarrow$ Mod
Aux-V-Mod	√	–	√
V-Aux-Mod	–	√	√

In System 1, in which a complex modal is selected to the right, only full inversion of the auxiliary is grammatical. This is what we find in Standard German. In System 2, the auxiliary selects a simple modal verb to the right, which results in partial inversion of the auxiliary only. This is the system of 3-verb clusters that has been described by Louden (1990) for Pennsylvania German. In System 3, finally, the complexity feature is dropped completely. As a consequence, auxiliary inversion is independent of complexity. This is exactly what we find in Colloquial German according to our experimental evidence.

The Standard German subcategorization frames for the perfect tense auxiliary *haben* may now be specified as in (17). Modal verbs are selected to the right and are subject to the complexity restriction described above. This ensures that auxiliary inversion only applies in verb clusters with at least three verbs, bringing the auxiliary always to the front of the cluster. All other verbs are selected to the left.

(17) Subcategorization frame for Standard German *haben* – V_{Aux}:

a. $\rightarrow \text{Mod}_{\text{VV-max}}$ b. $V \leftarrow$

The subcategorization frames for Colloquial German perfective *haben* are shown in (18). Modal verbs are again selected to the right, but this time independently of their complexity whereas all other verbs are selected to the left, as in Standard German.

(18) Subcategorization frame for Colloquial German *haben* – V_{Aux}:
a. →Mod b. V←

Applying the Rule of Combination to the subcategorization information in (17a) and (18a) derives the two trees for 3-verb clusters that are shown in (19).

(19) a. b.

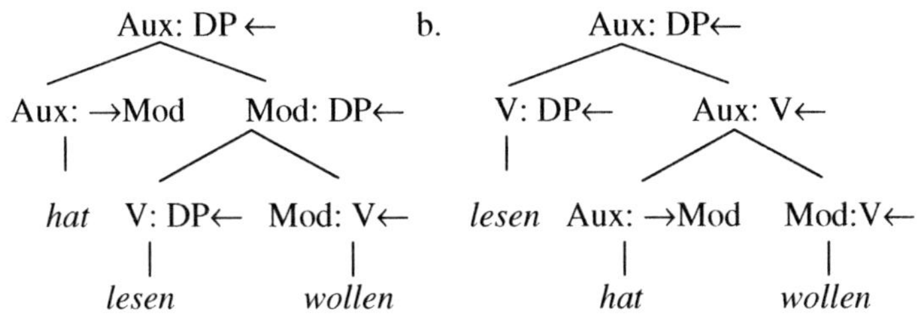

For Standard German, only tree (19a) can be derived because the complexity requirement of the perfect auxiliary is only fulfilled in this tree. When the complexity feature is dropped, as in (18a), both trees can be derived, and thus exactly the two verb orders that appear in Colloquial German according to our experimental evidence.

Optionality of auxiliary placement in Colloquial German therefore follows from the lack of an idiosyncratic complexity feature in the lexical entry of perfective *haben*. The verb cluster generalization given in (11) – auxiliary inversion is obligatory while the scope of inversion is underspecified – finds an adequate expression in the CAT-based approach. The variation between Standard and Colloquial German verb clusters involving modal verbs thus reduces to a small lexical difference – absence versus presence of the complexity requirement within the subcategorization frames of auxiliaries.

5. Experimental evidence from 5-verb clusters

In our work so far, we have investigated verb clusters ranging from two to four verbs. Here we report an additional experiment in which we investigated 5-verb clusters with the method of speeded grammaticality judgments. If the generalization is correct that modal-verb clusters in Colloquial German require the finite auxiliary to precede the modal verb but are otherwise unspecified with respect to the auxiliary's position, four versions of (20) should be accepted while only the version with the auxiliary in cluster-final position should be rejected. Note that the numbers in (20) refer to selection relations.

(20) (*Aux1*) V5 (*Aux1*) V4 (*Aux1*) V3 (*Aux1*) Mod2 (**Aux1*)

The 5-verb clusters were derived from the 4-verb clusters that formed the basis of the 4-verb cluster experiment in the preceding section in the following way. A sample sentence with a 4-verb cluster is repeated in (21).

(21) 4-verb clusters: Perf > Mod > [Pass > V]

…	*dass*	*das*	*Auto …*	*HAT*	*[*repariert	*werden*	***müssen]***
	that	the	car	has	repaired	be	must

'… that the car has had to be repaired.'

As indicated in (21), the inner layer of the 4-verb cluster contained a main verb in the passive voice, that is, a main verb plus a passive auxiliary ('to be repaired'). To obtain a 5-verb cluster, the passivized main verb was put into the perfect tense by inserting an additional perfect tense auxiliary ('to have been repaired'). The resulting sentence is shown in (22).

(22) 5-verb clusters: Perf > Mod > **Perf** > Pass > V

…	*dass*	*das*	*Auto …*	*HÄTTE*	*[*repariert	*worden*	*sein*	***müssen]***
	that	the	car	had	repaired	been	be	must

'… that the car should have been repaired.'

Intuitively, sentences as in (22) are somewhat complex but still fully comprehensible. Note in particular that the sentences under consideration differ in important respects from the sentences that were the topic of the seminal verb cluster study by Bach, Brown and Marslen-Wilson (1986). An example sentence with five verbs from Bach et al. is shown in 5.3).

(23)

[Ingrid]$_1$	*hat1*	*[Lotte]$_2$*	*[die*	*Bewohner]$_3$*	*[dem*	*Blinden]$_4$*
I.	has	L.	the	residents	the	blind person

[das	*Essen]$_5$*	*kochen5*	*helfen4*	*lehren3*	*hören2.*
the	food	cook	help	teach	hear

'Ingrid has heard how Lotte taught the residents to help the blind person cook the food.'

Sentences like (23) were shown to be basically incomprehensible, a finding which confirms the intuition one has when reading such sentences. Note, however, that in (23) NP arguments are not only introduced by the most deeply embedded main verb but by all other verbs too except the finite auxiliary. The sentence therefore contains four NP arguments in addition to its five verbs. Furthermore, sentence (23) contains several instances of shared semantic arguments; for example, the NP *dem Blinden* ('the blind person') is both the agent argument of *kochen* ('to cook') and the beneficiary argument of *helfen* ('to help') from which it also gets its case.

Neither of these complications is present in the sentences of the current experiment. NP arguments are only introduced by the most deeply embedded main verb, and argument sharing is accordingly not involved. In fact, due to the effect of passivization, the sentences of the current experiment contain just a single NP argument in addition to the verb cluster.

5.1. Method

Participants. 20 students of the University of Konstanz participated in the current experiment. Participants were either paid or they received course credits. All participants were native speakers of German and naive with respect to the purpose of the experiment.

Materials. 20 sentences were created with each sentence appearing in five versions according to the five positions that the finite auxiliary can occupy in a 5-verb cluster. An original experimental sentence is shown in (24). The five possible positions of the auxiliary, which would be *hätte* ('had') in (24), are indicated by the five numbered bullets. The bullet numbered 1 is the position required in Standard German.

(24) *Ich weiß, dass das Dokument im Laufe des Tages*
I know that the document in-the course of-the day
$\bullet_1$ *vernichtet* $\bullet_2$ *worden* $\bullet_3$ *sein* $\bullet_4$ *sollen* $\bullet_5$.
destroyed been-PASS be-PERF shall
'I know that the document should have been destroyed in the course of the day.'

As shown in (24), all sentences consisted of a main clause followed by an embedded clause introduced by the complementizer *dass* ('that'). The 5-verb cluster under investigation was always part of the embedded clause. Two modal verbs were used in ten sentences each: *müssen* ('must') and *sollen* ('shall').

From the total set of 20 sentences, four lists were created. Each list contained an equal number of sentences in each condition but no more than one version of any sentence appeared in a list. Each participant saw only a single list of experimental sentences. The order of presentation was randomized for each participant individually. The experimental sentences were embedded in a list of 110 filler sentences. The filler sentences represented a wide variety of grammatical and ungrammatical sentences and were partly taken from unrelated experiments.

Procedure. Sentences were presented visually using the DMDX software developed by K. Forster and J. Forster at Monash University and the University of Arizona. Participants were seated in front of a computer monitor. They were told

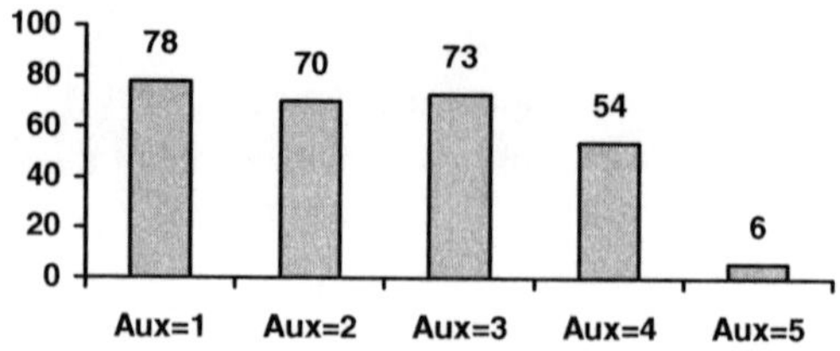

Figure 3. Percentages of judgments 'grammatical' for the five positions of the finite auxiliary that were tested in the current experiment

that they would be presented sentences on the screen and that their task was to judge the grammaticality of each sentence as quickly and as accurately as possible. The concept of grammaticality was explained by examples. Participants initiated each trial by pressing the space-bar which triggered three fixation points to appear in the center of the screen for 1050 milliseconds. Thereafter, the sentence appeared on the screen in a word by word fashion with each word appearing at the same position (mid-screen). Each word was presented for 225 msec plus additional 25 msec for each character to compensate for length effects. There was no interval between words. Immediately after the last word of a sentence, three red question marks appeared on the screen, signaling to participants that they now were to make their judgment. Participants indicated their judgment by pressing either the left or the right shift key on a computer keyboard. They used their right hand to indicate that a sentence was grammatical and their left hand to indicate that it was ungrammatical. If participants did not respond within 2000 milliseconds, a red warning "zu langsam" ('too slow') appeared on the screen and the trial was finished automatically.

Prior to the experimental session, participants received practice trials to ensure that they had understood the task. During the practice trials but not during the experimental session participants received feedback as to the correctness of their judgments.

5.2. Results

Figure 3 shows the percentages of responses 'grammatical' for the five auxiliary positions that were tested in the current experiment. One-way analyses of variance (ANOVAs) with either participants (F1) or items (F2) as random factor revealed a highly significant effect of the factor Auxiliary Position ($F1(4,76) = 34.30$, $p < .001$; $F2(4,76) = 22.72$, $p < .001$). Subsequent planned comparisons showed that the first three auxiliary positions did not differ from each other (all

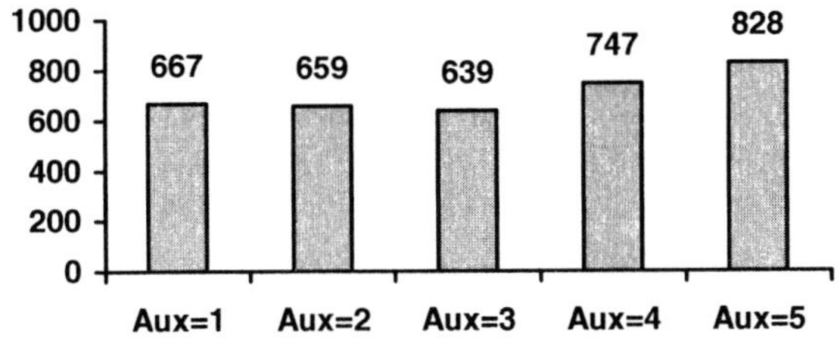

Figure 4. Mean reaction times in ms for judgments 'grammatical' for the five positions of the finite auxiliary that were tested in the current experiment

t-values < 1), but the fourth position differed significantly from the mean of the first three (54% versus 73%; t1 = 5.18, p < .01; t2 = 2.77, p < .01). The fifth position finally differed significantly from the fourth position (54% versus 6 %; t1 = 6.74, p < .001; t2 = 5.48, p < .001).

Mean reaction times for judgments 'grammatical' are shown in Figure 4. We do not present statistical analyses for reaction times because there would have been too many empty cells in the analysis. Numerically, the reaction time pattern is the inverse of the pattern of percentages of judgments 'grammatical'. The first three positions received the fastest reaction times; reaction times for the fourth position are about 90 ms slower, and reaction times for the fifth position are slower by additional 90 ms.

5.3. Discussion

The results of the current experiment provide a striking confirmation of the verb cluster generalization that we derived from our prior experiments with verb clusters containing two, three, or four verbs: For 5-verb clusters of the sort considered here, we see a clear distinction between the positions in which the auxiliary precedes the modal verb and the single position in which the auxiliary follows the modal verb. The first three auxiliary positions preceding the modal verb were accepted to a substantial degree. Judgments for the fourth position were significantly lower but still received a value above 50%. However, when the auxiliary verb followed the modal verb, the acceptance rate dropped sharply to a value only slightly above 0%.

The fact that no condition reached more than 78% judgments 'grammatical' can plausibly be attributed to the inherent complexity associated with a verb cluster containing 5-verbs. Although our results clearly argue that the sentences under consideration could be successfully processed – in contrast to the 5-verb sentences of Bach et al. (1986), as discussed above – it is nevertheless true that even the 5-verb clusters of the current experiment are complex. This is not only true in syntactic terms but also in semantic terms. Although four of the five verbs are function verbs which do not introduce thematic roles of their own – which makes the cluster much easier to process than the clusters investigated by Bach et al. (1986) – the high degree of stacking nevertheless seems to complicate the interpretation of the cluster. Crucially, even the cluster internal order that is considered to be grammatical in Standard German – the cluster with the auxiliary inverted to the front of the cluster – showed a somewhat reduced acceptability. In fact, the first three auxiliary positions received grammaticality values which were statistically not distinguishable from each other. The fourth auxiliary position was judged significantly worse than the first three but still much better than the fifth position in which the auxiliary follows the modal verb. While we do not have an explanation for the reduced acceptability of the fourth position, we can at least note that something similar has been reported for the Dutch verb-particle construction that was mentioned in the introduction. While all particle positions in front of the main verb are considered grammatical, some seem to be preferred over others in stylistic terms (see Evers 2003).

6. General Discussion

We have presented an experiment on auxiliary inversion in German 5-verb clusters. Extending earlier results on 2, 3- and 4-verb clusters, the results of the current experiment show that the rules of prescriptive grammar – according to which only verb clusters with fully inverted auxiliary are grammatical – are at odds with the grammar of verb cluster formation internalized by native speakers of German: As in Standard German, auxiliary inversion is obligatory for native speakers, but in contrast to Standard German, the scope of inversion is free. We therefore get optionality in our experimental data which we take to represent Colloquial German.

Since Standard German lacks this kind of optionality, the set of grammatical verb clusters is much smaller in Standard German than in Colloquial German. Standard German allows exactly one order for each cluster size whereas Colloquial German allows n-1 orders for each cluster of size n. For clusters of size 3–5, we thus get 3 grammatical variants for Standard German but 9 grammatical variants for Colloquial German. All orders which are grammatical in Standard German are also grammatical in Colloquial German, making Standard German a subset of Colloquial German.

While Standard and Colloquial German thus exhibit substantial differences in terms of surface strings, the underlying grammatical difference is only minimal according to the syntactic analysis presented here. Standard German imposes a complexity requirement on auxiliary inversion but Colloquial German does not. Given the apparently idiosyncratic nature of the complexity feature, the lack of such a feature in Colloquial German implies that the grammar of Colloquial German is less complex than the grammar of Standard German. This is a welcome result because Colloquial German represents native speakers' spontaneous grammaticality judgments. It therefore seems reasonable to assume that Colloquial German reflects a more natural grammar than Standard German which might be an artificial product of prescriptive pressure.

We are thus led to the hypothesis that the optionality found with auxiliary inversion in Colloquial German is something which follows without further stipulations from the correct syntactic analysis. Further evidence for this hypothesis comes from other cases of optionality found in the syntax of verb cluster formation. Chief among them is the phenomenon of Dutch particle climbing which was briefly mentioned in the introduction. The relevant data from example (1) are repeated in a schematic form in (25).

(25)	… ***[op***	*zou*	***op***	*willen*	***op***	*mogen*	***op***	*bergen*	****op]***
		would		like		be-allowed		put	away

On first sight, Dutch particle climbing and Colloquial German auxiliary inversion seem to be two quite different things. In particular, the 'moveable' element in Dutch, the particle, is a selected element which takes the lowest position in the selectional hierarchy of the verb cluster. In Colloquial German, in contrast, the 'moveable' element is a finite auxiliary which is the highest selecting element within the cluster. This difference notwithstanding, we will argue now that the two constructions share a range of properties which makes it possible to derive them by the same formal means.

First of all, in both cases there is a predominant direction of selection in the verb cluster domain. Typically, the direction of selection is to the right in Dutch but to the left in German, leading to a rigid left-to-right (Dutch) or right-to-left (German) linear order of the elements in the verbal cluster.[6] At the same time, however, a verb cluster may contain an element with exactly the opposite selectional requirement from the other cluster elements. In Dutch, this element is the main verb itself which selects non-verbal complements to the left and thus in the opposite direction from the other verbs of the verb cluster; in German, an auxiliary selecting a modal verb is associated with a reversed direction of selection. What we thus get is a verb cluster with inconsistent direction of selection, as shown schematically for Dutch in (26a) and for German in (26b).

(26) Inconsistent direction of selection:

a. Dutch: V1→ V2 → [*PAR4* ← V3]

b. German: *AUX1*→ [V4 ← V3 ← V2]

Configurations as in (26) give rise to verb-cluster internal optionality. Either the highest or the lowest element in the chain of selection may freely appear in any position inside the verbal cluster as long as it does not violate the direction of selection. In Dutch, this is the lowest element, namely the verb particle; in German, it is the finite auxiliary, the highest element. This difference between German and Dutch is a consequence of the fact that Dutch verb clusters are right-oriented whereas German verb clusters are left-oriented.

In the CAT-based analysis that we have presented above, the optionality that arises in (26a) and (26b) follows without further stipulation from the fact that the Rule of Combination allows the transmission of subcategorization information (functional composition). As has already been shown in (19) for German verb clusters, this makes it possible to insert the auxiliary in any position in front of the modal verb. In fact, a complex feature specification 'VV-max' was necessary to prevent the auxiliary from appearing in any position except the cluster-initial one.

Two illustrative syntactic trees for Dutch are shown in (27). For ease of exposition, we have omitted the subcategorization information pertaining to the DP arguments of the particle verb.

(27) a. b.

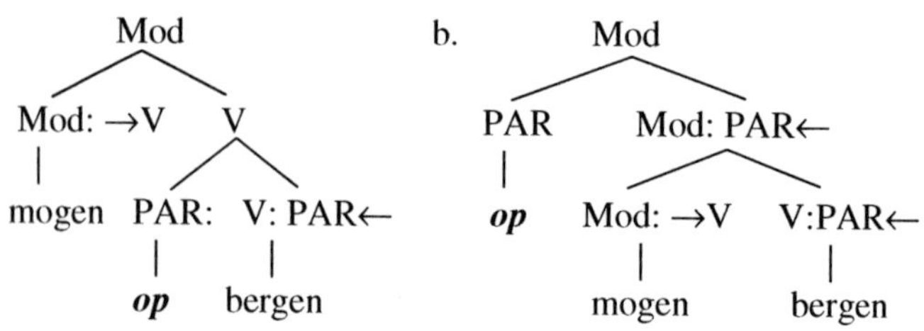

In (27a), the particle *op* combines immediately with the main verb by which it is subcategorized. In (27b), the main verb first combines with the modal verb *mogen*; the subcategorization feature 'PAR←' is inherited by the resulting syntactic node, and the particle combines with this node. Deriving the further positions of *op* in (25) works in a similar way.

Note finally, that for the kind of optionality that we have discussed above, mixed direction of selection is a prerequisite. If the direction of selection is consistent either to the right, as in a head-initial language like English (cf. (28a)), or to the left, as in a head-final language like Japanese (cf. (28b)), each element must appear exactly at the position in the syntactic tree which corresponds to its position in the chain of selection.

(28) Consistent direction of selection:
  a. English: V1 $\rightarrow$ V2 $\rightarrow$ V3 $\rightarrow$ [V4 $\rightarrow$ α]
  a. Japanese: [α $\leftarrow$ V4] $\leftarrow$ V3 $\leftarrow$ V2 $\leftarrow$ V1

As a concluding remark, let us consider the issue of optionality in verb cluster formation from the perspective of language acquisition. As is well-known from the pertinent literature (e.g., Guasti 2002), children acquire the basic word-order regularities of their native language quite early on. A child learning German or Dutch will therefore detect the basic OV nature of these languages at an early stage.

During this stage the child assumes that verbs always select their complements to the left. When acquiring German, the child will also realize soon that verbs selected by other verbs adhere to the OV nature of German too, making 'selected verb before selecting verb' the order normally obeyed by verb clusters. At some later point, the child will come to realize that there exists one exception with respect to the direction of selection in the verbal cluster: auxiliary verbs may select modal verbs to the right. As soon as the child detects such a case of selection in the "wrong" direction, a slight revision of the child's initial assumption about the general OV nature of German is necessary. The child will postulate a lexical entry specifying that auxiliaries select modal verbs to the right. In the absence of negative evidence to the contrary, the child will then be led to the further conclusion that the auxiliary may appear in every position inside the cluster as long as it selects its modal verb complement to the right. What the child will thus have acquired is the grammatical system of Colloquial German as described above.

Of course, this is not the system of Standard German because Standard German requires the additional feature VV-max. According to the analysis pursued in this paper, Standard German imposes an artificial restriction on the scope of auxiliary inversion, a restriction which can only be acquired by negative evidence. We were not able to find relevant information on this point in the acquisition literature. An ongoing corpus study revealed that in German newspapers verb clusters occur almost exclusively with the Standard German order, that is, with full inversion of the auxiliary. However, in a systematic web search we found that clusters with partial inversion of the auxiliary also occur with some regularity whereas clusters with no inversion at all are basically non-existent. Two illustrative examples containing a 4-verb cluster with the same main verb are given in (29). The finite auxiliary shows up in second position in (29a) and in third position in (29b).

(29) a. *Udo machte deutlich, dass ohne Frank dieses Festival*
U. made clear that without F. this festival
nicht in die Realität ***umgesetzt hätte werden können****.*
not into the reality put had been can
'Udo made clear that this festival could not have been realized without Frank.'
(Downloaded on 1.1.2008 – www.genesis-fanclub.de/archiv/petergabriel/interviews/koenixxtreffen.htm)

b. *Schröder wäre es bestimmt auch recht gewesen, wenn*
S. were it surely also right been if
es 1:1 ***umgesetzt werden hätte können****.*
it put been had can
'It would surely have been okay for Schröder if it could have been realized 1:1.'
(Downloaded on 1.1.2008 – www.stern.de/forum/showflat.php?Cat=0&Board=politikdeutschland&Number=1346410&page=3)

If the difference between language as used in newspapers and language as used in the internet can be corroborated, it suggests that we get optionality with respect to auxiliary inversion mainly with less formal registers. This in turn suggests to us that the lack of optionality in Standard German is indeed a matter of prescriptive influence, and that a grammar allowing the peculiar kind of optionality that is found in verb-cluster formation must be less complex than a grammar disallowing it.

Notes

* This work was supported by the Deutsche Forschungsgemeinschaft (SFB 471, Project D2). Thanks are due to the organizers and the audience of the *Linguistic Evidence Conference 2008*, as well as to Sam Featherston, Josef Bayer, Simon Hopp, Julia Henninger and Marianne Schmidt for lively discussions and helpful comments.

1. Bader and Schmid (to appear b) conducted a further experiment in which the past participle of modals was compared to the bare infinitive in 3-verb clusters. This experiment confirmed the obligatoriness of the bare infinitive (IPP).
2. Bader and Schmid (to appear b) transform their experimental results (% grammatical) into binary distinctions (assuming that the dividing line between grammatical and ungrammatical sentences is 50%). Since we are still not yet in a position to account for the gradience in the data we will follow this practice here.
3. This experiment contained a second factor "position of modal verb". The modal verb either followed the passivized verb, as in the examples considered here, or preceded it. For reasons of space, we omit the latter condition here.

4. Although we could not discuss the data concerning future tense verb clusters in the current paper, we have included the future tense in the generalization (11) for reasons of completeness.
5. For reasons of space, we can discuss neither similar nor dissimilar syntactic accounts of verb cluster formation. For comprehensive discussion and relevant references, see Bader and Schmid (to appear b).
6. For Dutch, this is a simplification because Dutch exhibits a much greater degree of optionality than we can describe here; see, e.g., Koopman and Szabolcsi (2000), Wurmbrand (2006), and references cited there.

References

Abraham, Werner
1995 *Deutsche Syntax im Sprachenvergleich. Grundlegung einer typologischen Syntax des Deutschen.* Tübingen: Narr Verlag.

Bach, Emmon, Colin Brown and William D. Marslen-Wilson
1986 Crossed and nested dependencies in German and Dutch: A psycholinguistic study. *Language and Cognitive Processes* 1: 249–262.

Bader, Markus and Jana Häussler
submitted Towards a model of grammaticality judgements. *Language.*

Bader, Markus and Tanja Schmid
to appear a CAT meets GO: 2-verb clusters in German. In: Jeroen van Craenenbroeck (ed.) *Alternatives to cartography.* Berlin: Mouton de Gruyter.

Bader, Markus and Tanja Schmid
to appear b Verb clusters in Colloquial German. *Journal of Comparative German Linguistics.*

Bennis, Hans
1992 Long head movement: The position of particles in the verbal cluster of Dutch. In: R. Bok-Bennema and R. van Hout (eds.), *Linguistics in the Netherlands*, 37–47. Amsterdam: John Benjamins.

Cowart, Wayne
1997 *Experimental Syntax: Applying Objective Methods to Sentence Judgments.* Thousand Oaks, CA: Sage Publications.

Evers, Arnold
2003 Verbal clusters and cluster creepers. In: Pieter A. M. Seuren and Gerard Kempen (eds.), *Verb Constructions in German and Dutch*, 43–89. Amsterdam: John Benjamins.

Fabricius-Hansen, Cathrine, Peter Gallmann, Peter Eisenberg and Reinhard Fiehler
2005 *Der Duden, Bd.4 : Die Grammatik.* Mannheim: Dudenverlag.

Featherston, Sam
2007 Data in generative grammar: The stick and the carrot. *Theoretical Linguistics* 33: 269–318.

Geach, Peter Thomas
1970 A programm for syntax. *Synthese* 22: 483–497.

Guasti, Maria Teresa
2002 *Language acquisition. The growth of grammar.* Cambridge, MA: MIT Press.

Koopman, Hilda and Anna Szabolcsi
2000 *Verbal complexes.* Cambridge, MA: MIT Press.

Lötscher, Andreas
1978 Zur Verbstellung im Zürichdeutschen und in anderen Varianten des Deutschen. *Zeitschrift für Dialektologie und Linguistik* 45: 1–29.

Louden, Mark L.
1990 Verb raising and the position of the finite verb in Pennsylvania German. *Linguistic Inquiry* 21: 470–477.

Radford, Andrew
1997 *Syntax. A minimalist introduction.* Cambridge: Cambridge University Press.

Sapp, Christopher D.
2006 Verb order in subordinate clauses from Early New High German to Modern German. Indiana University.

Schmid, Tanja
2005 *Infinitival syntax: Infinitivus Pro Participio as a repair strategy.* Amsterdam: John Benjamins.

Schmid, Tanja and Ralf Vogel
2004 Dialectal variation in German 3-verb clusters. *Journal of Comparative Germanic Linguistics* 7: 235–274.

Seuren, Pieter A. M.
2003 Verb clusters and branching directionality in German and Dutch. In: Pieter A. M. Seuren and Gerard Kempen (eds.), *Verb Constructions in German and Dutch*, 247–296. Amsterdam: John Benjamins.

van Riemsdijk, Henk
2002 The unbearable lightness of GOing. The projection parameter as a pure parameter governing the distribution of elliptic motion verbs in Germanic. *Journal of Comparative Germanic Linguistics* 5: 143–196.

Weiß, Helmut
1998 *Syntax des Bairischen. Studien zur Grammatik einer natürlichen Sprache.* Tübingen: Niemeyer.

Williams, Edwin
2003 *Representation Theory.* Cambridge, MA: MIT Press.

Wurmbrand, Susanne
2006 Verb clusters, verb raising, and restructuring. In: Martin Everaert and Henk van Riemsdijk (eds.), *The Blackwell companion to syntax*, 229–343. Oxford: Blackwell.

Clitic placement in Serbian: Corpus and experimental evidence

Molly Diesing, Dušica Filipović Đurđević and Draga Zec

1. Introduction

The focus of our paper is the distribution of the so-called "second-position" clitics. Languages of this type fall into three classes: those in which the sentential position for clitics is after the first word (1W), those in which clitics come after the first phrase (1P), and those in which clitics may come either after the first word or after the first phrase (1W/1P). This results in the following three-part typology:[1]

(1)

	First Word	First Phrase	Cases
Type 1	✔		Hittite, Croatian
Type 2		✔	Czech, Slovenian, Malagasy
Type 3	✔	✔	Serbian, Ngiyambaa, Warlpiri

Serbian thus emerges as a case of special interest, in that it allows both the first word and first phrase placement options. This in turn raises the question of what the status of the two placement possibilities are in the grammar of Serbian. That is, is the grammar exhibiting genuine optionality, or do the two possibilities encode some linguistically relevant difference? Much of the previous literature on South Slavic clitics (such as Browne 1974, Franks and Progovac 1994, and Progovac 1996, to cite just three examples) seems to at least imply the former – the two options are often given identical English glosses – but our own research brings us closer to the second conclusion. When the two sentences given below are uttered, they not only have very different intonational contours, but are felicitous in different contexts.

(2) a. *Taj zadatak **je** veoma važan.*
that task is-Cl very important
'That task is very important.'

b. *Taj **je** zadatak veoma važan.*
that is-Cl task very important
'That task is very important.'

Example (2a), with 1P placement, has unmarked intonation, and is acceptable in "out-of-the-blue" contexts. Example (2b) has a marked contour, and is only acceptable in contexts in which contrastive emphasis on "that" is appropriate. Our claim is that not only do we not find optionality unrestricted by grammar, but that clitic placement is dependent on both syntactic and pragmatic factors.

2. A proposal and its motivations

Current work on Serbian clitics has focused on whether to characterize the second position placement of clitics as being primarily a result of syntactic mechanisms (Franks and Progovac 1994, Progovac 1996), or essentially prosodic in origin (Halpern 1999, Radanović-Kocić 1996, Bošković 2001).[2] Within the prosodic perspective, Zec (2005), further provides a definition of the second position occupied by clitics in prosodic terms, accounting for facts unexplained within the syntactic approach. However, this work also shows that, while important, the prosodic approach alone cannot capture the distribution of clitics, which can only be fully captured by additionally invoking the structural approach.

As implied above, an initial point of failure in many of these accounts is in not recognizing that there are differences among types of sentences in terms of their "markedness". That is, it is not sufficient to judge the grammaticality of the sentences, but their appropriateness in a given context must also be gauged. Current research has also relied heavily on native speaker judgments that have been culled primarily from previously published work, or from interrogating native speaker linguists. While these are not uncommon methods in theoretical linguistics, it is well worth augmenting the database with other sources, in this case searches of corpus sources and a series of experiments designed to elicit judgments from naïve native speakers. This is essential not merely in order to settle the empirical questions regarding data, but also in regard to the larger theoretical questions concerning the structure of the grammar. If semantic/pragmatic factors indeed play a role in clitic placement, then the problem must be approached from a broader view of the "interfaces" involved.

Our initial hypothesis is that matrix declarative sentences containing second position clitics can be classified into four types, based on whether the initial constituent is an argument or a predicate, and whether the clitic in each case follows the first word (1W) or the first phrase (1P):

(3) a. *Taj zadatak* ***je*** *veoma važan.* 1P (Argument)
that task is-Cl very important
'That task is very important.'

	b.	*Taj*	***je***	*zadatak*	*veoma*	*važan*		1W	
		that	is-Cl	task	very	important			
		'That task is very important.'							
(4)	a.	*Veoma*	***je***	*važan*	*taj*	*zadatak.*		1W	(Predicate)
		very	is-Cl	important	that	task			
		'That task is very important.'							
	b.	*Veoma*	*važan*	***je***	*taj*	*zadatak*		1P	
		very	important	is-Cl	that	task			
		'That task is very important.'							

In the current literature the principal focus is on the argument cases, with very little discussion of the predicate cases (limited primarily to participle fronting). The literature also includes discrepant judgments and conclusions. For example, the 1W/1P alternation in clitic placement has been claimed to reduce to a dialectal split between Serbian and Croatian (Anderson 2005: 111).[3] To give another example of data disagreement, Bošković (2001) claims "that it is well known that very heavy constituents obligatorily delay clitic placement," citing the following contrast:

(5)	a.	*Njegovom*	*prijatelju*	*prodali*	***su***	*knjigu.*	
		his	friend.dat	sold	Cl-are	book.acc	
		'As for his friend, they sold (him) the book.'					
	b.	*Njegovom*	*prijatelju*	***su***	*prodali*	*knjigu.*	
		his	friend.dat	Cl-are	sold	book.acc	
		'To his friend, they sold the book.'					
(6)	a.	*Njegovom*	*najboljem*	*prijatelju*	*prodali*	***su***	*knjigu.*
		his	best	friend.dat	sold	Cl-are	book.acc
		'As for his best friend, they sold (him) the book.'					
	b.	**Njegovom*	*najboljem*	*prijatelju*	***su***	*prodali*	*knjigu.*
		his	best	friend.dat	Cl-are	sold	book.acc

Our consultants find all four examples in (5)–(6) to be grammatical, however, and we have found sentences like (6b) in our corpus. Thus, there is ample motivation for both expanding the database of examples and enriching the methodology of investigation in order to get a clearer picture of the facts and how best to explain them.

Our study proceeds in two phases. In the first we analyzed corpora of Serbian prose to assess the validity of our proposed four types of clitic placement. In the second phase we conducted a series of experiments which served both to verify the corpus data and to collect "live" native speaker judgments.

3. The corpus investigation

For the corpus study we utilized two sources, the first a corpus from the Serbian daily press compiled by Ebart Media Documentation (www.arhiv.co.yu). This consists of printed media, comprised of more than 700,000 texts, approximately 70 million words. The second corpus consisted of literary prose, the Corpus of Serbian Language (www.serbian-corpus.edu.yu). This corpus consist of approximately 11 million words ranging from the 12th century to contemporary times; the contemporary literary prose component from which we drew our samples comprises over 1 million words.

In selecting sentences from the corpora, we limited ourselves to declarative sentences containing auxiliary and pronominal clitics. We excluded main and subordinate clause beginning with question words, and various types of subordinate clauses: relative, temporal, conditional, comparative and consequential clauses. In all these cases there is no second position placement of clitics, and they are thus not relevant to our study. Following these principles of selection, we ended up with a total of 2993 sentences: 1323 sentences from the daily press and 1670 sentences from the literary prose corpus.

We analyzed and placed each of our sampled sentences into the four categories of our classification.

The results tabulated in Picture 1 show an interesting asymmetry between both the argument and predicate cases, and between the first word and first phrase placements. In the argument case, we see a large proportion of the 1P sentences, and a small proportion of the 1W sentences. The situation is reversed in the predicate case, where we find a large proportion of the 1W sentences and a miniscule proportion of the 1P sentences.

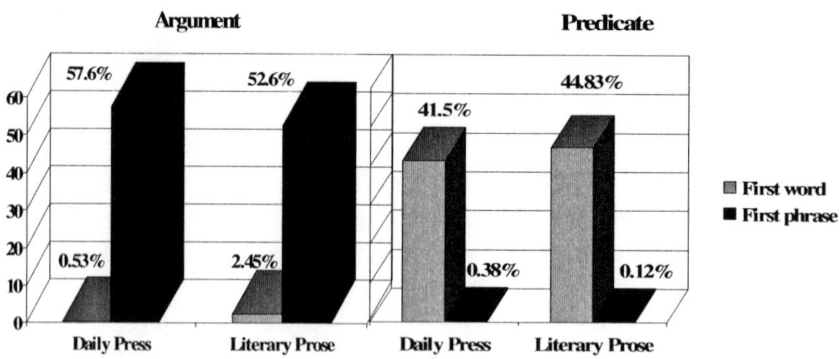

Figure 1. Percent of four sentence categories found in two corpora (percents calculated within a corpus).

The results we obtained are striking in several respects. First, we found support for all types of cases we predicted. More importantly, we found that the two types of cases, arguments and predicates, have different default positions for clitics: the "normal" position for clitics in the argument case is after the first phrase, and in the predicate case, after the first word. In fact the proportions of dispreferred cases are very small. This raises the possibility of alternative interpretations for their appearance such as errors in the data base, possibly being at the margins of grammar or even ungrammatical. We had access to an additional corpus of data from spoken Serbian, consisting of 40,000 words. A search of this yielded more tokens of the non-default type: 12 of the Argument/1W case and 1 of the Predicate/1P case. While encouraging, these are still small enough numbers that turning to an additional source of evidence seems warranted. Thus, we turn now to the second phase of our research, the psycholinguistic experiments.

4. Experiments

In order to test the results of the database study we conducted two psycholinguistic experiments. The first experiment was a paper and pencil questionnaire aimed at understanding the production of this language phenomenon, while the second experiment involved a computer based presentation of sentences. The purpose of the second experiment was to explore the on-line comprehension of these sentences.

We conducted both experiments using the same sentences. The sentences included two sets, 60 in each, one for the argument and the other for the predicate case. Within the set of argument sentences, there were three cases, each represented by 20 sentences, with the subject, object, and prepositional phrase arguments in preposed position (Serbian allows scrambling of constituents). An orthogonal further division within the set of argument sentences was the presence of either a determiner or an adjective within the argument noun phrase. The set of predicate sentences was divided into three groups, with 20 sentences in each, representing three types of predicates, adjectival phrase (AP), noun phrase (NP) and verb phrase (VP). The table in (7) summarizes the types of sentences used in the experiments:

(7) Types of sentences used in the psycholinguistic experiments

A. Argument		**60**	*B. Predicate*	**60**
	Determiner	Adjective		
Subject	10	10	AP	20
Object	10	10	NP	20
Prep Phrase	10	10	VP	20

4.1. Experiment 1

Method

Participants: Thirty-eight students from The Department of Psychology, at The Faculty of Philosophy, in The University of Novi Sad participated in the experiment. All of the participants were native speakers of Serbian, and had normal or corrected to normal vision.

Stimuli and design: One-hundred-and-twenty grammatical Serbian sentences were presented in the Roman alphabet. Half of the sentences were of the argument type, and half of the sentences were of the predicate type, with varied structures, as shown in (8). The critical clitic was omitted from each sentence, and the two positions of clitics (after the first word and after the first phrase) were replaced with a line, i.e. a blank to be filled in:

(8)	Argument sentence	Taj	__	zadatak	__	veoma	važan.
		/that	__	task	__	very	important/
	Predicate sentence	Veoma	__	važan	__	taj	zadatak.
		/very	__	important	__	that	task/

The dependent variable was participants' placement of a clitic in one of the two possible positions for each of the two sentence categories.

Procedure: Sentences were printed in a six-page booklet. There were three different random orders of sentences. Each participant was given a booklet with only one random order. Each booklet contained a detailed instruction asking the participant to fill in only one of the two blanks using only one of the listed clitics. The filling in was to be done in such a way to make the sentence sound as common as possible in the participant's native language. Participants took approximately twenty minutes to complete the task.

Results

The responses revealed a dramatic difference between clitic positions across two sentence categories. While 92.98% of participants placed a clitic after the first phrase in argument sentences, only 2.41% of participants placed a clitic after the first phrase in predicate sentences. Logistic regression performed on participants response revealed that the observed difference was significant: $\chi^2(1) = 1557.16$, $p < 0.0001$ (Picture 2).

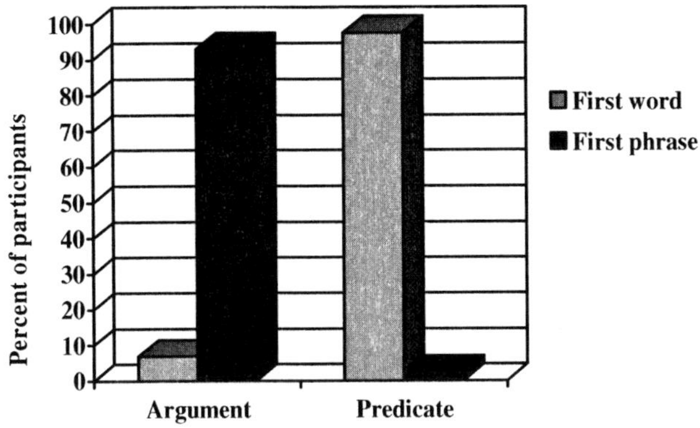

Figure 2. Percent of participants placing a clitic after the first word (light grey), and after the first phrase (dark grey) when completing argument (left), and predicate sentences (right) in experiment 1.

4.2. Experiment 2

In experiment 1 we were interested in the differences between the two possible clitic positions in argument and predicate sentences in sentence production. In order to investigate these differences at the level of language perception, or processing, as well, we conducted the second experiment using the sentence list presented in experiment 1 as a starting point.

Method

Participants: Forty-eight students from The Department of Psychology, at The Faculty of Philosophy, University of Novi Sad, participated in the experiment. All of the participants were native speakers of Serbian, and had normal or corrected to normal vision. Participants were randomly assigned to only one of the two experimental blocks.

Stimuli: One-hundred-and-twenty target sentences from experiment 1 along with additional 120 ungrammatical Serbian sentences (control sentences) were presented in the Roman alphabet. The ungrammatical control sentences were constructed to mirror the syntactic structure of the target sentences that were presented in the experiment. Ungrammaticality was achieved by choosing a clitic that fails to agree with the verb.

Design: Sentences were constructed to fit 2 × 2 factorial design. Half of the sentences were of the argument type, and half of the sentences were of the predicate type. For each sentence, the place of the clitic alternated between two possible positions: after the first word, and after the first phrase. Clitic position was balanced in a two block latin square design. Sentences that appeared with a clitic after the first word in one block, would have a clitic positioned after the first phrase in the second block, and vice versa. This way, all of the sentences appeared with a clitic in both positions, and all of the participants were presented with all of the sentences, and both clitic positions, but none of the participants was exposed to the same sentence twice.

Procedure: Stimuli were presented in a sentence acceptability judgment task. The participants were given instructions to judge whether the sentence appearing on the screen was acceptable in their language. They were told to base their answers on their intuitions as native speakers, and that there would not necessarily be right or wrong answers. Sentences were presented one-by-one, in a random order, on a computer screen. Prior to each sentence a fixation point was presented for 2000 ms. A sentence would remain on the screen until participant's response, but its duration was limited to 8 seconds. Participants were given twelve practice trials. Sentences appearing in the practice trials were not included in the analyses.

Results

All analyses were conducted on the responses to target sentences. Analysis of reaction times was performed only on responses marking the acceptance of a sentence. Reaction times attached to a rejection of a sentence, as well as reaction times out of the range of $\mp$ 2.5 standard deviation units were excluded from the analysis.

Logistic regression of yes/no answers in sentence acceptability task revealed a significant main effect of sentence type: $\chi^2(2) = 232.65$, $p < 0.0001$, a significant main effect of clitic position: $\chi^2(2) = 228.12$, $p < 0.0001$, and a significant interaction between the two: $\chi^2(1) = 181.24$, $p < 0.0001$. Argument sentences with a clitic positioned after the first phrase had higher acceptance probability then argument sentences with a clitic positioned after the first word, while predicate sentences with a clitic positioned after the first word had higher acceptance probability than predicate sentences with a clitic positioned after the first phrase (Picture 3).

Along the same lines, a mixed effect regression of reaction times with participants and sentences as random effects, and sentence type and clitic position as fixed effects, revealed a significant main effect of sentence type: $F(1, 4477) = 5.543$, $p < 0.05$, the main effect of clitic position: $F(1, 4477) = 13.543$, $p < 0.001$, and a significant interaction between the two: $F(1, 4477) = 174.521$,

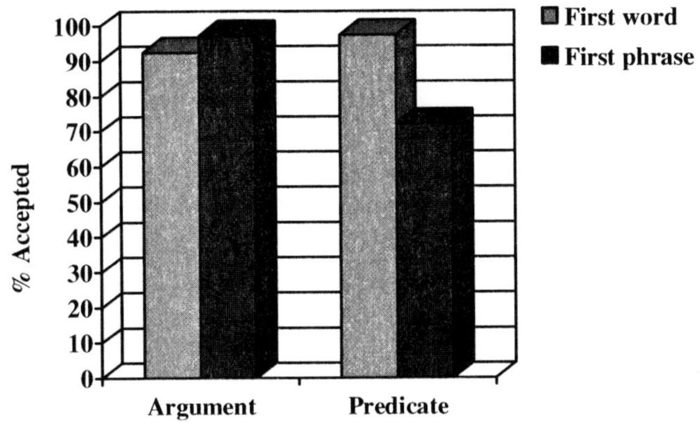

Figure 3. Mean acceptance rates for the argument (left), and predicate sentences (right) with a clitic positioned after the first word (light grey), and after the first phrase (dark grey) observed in experiment 2.

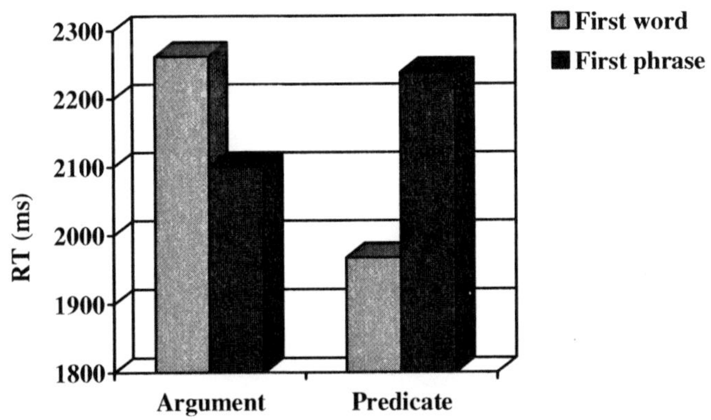

Figure 4. Mean reaction times for the argument (left), and predicate sentences (right) with a clitic positioned after the first word (light grey), and after the first phrase (dark grey) observed in experiment 2

$p < 0.0001$. Argument sentences with a clitic positioned after the first phrase were processed faster than argument sentences with a clitic positioned after the first word, while predicate sentences with a clitic positioned after the first word were processed faster than predicate sentences with a clitic positioned after the first phrase (Picture 4).

4.3. Discussion of experiments 1 and 2

The results of experiment 1 clearly establish that, in the argument case, the preferred position for clitics is after the first constituent, while in the predicate case, the preferred position is after the first word. The results of experiment 2 are more nuanced. Reaction times collected in Experiment 2 replicate the preferences found in experiment 1 (Picture 4). However, differences in acceptance probabilities between sentences with clitics after the first word and those after the first phrase are not very dramatic, and in the argument case, the difference is small (Picture 3). The relatively modest differences in high acceptance rates suggest that participants grant grammatical status to all four types of sentences.

Looking more closely at the argument type in both experiments, our results point at a correlation between clitic positioning after the first word and the presence of a (narrow) focus. We show this by presenting the sentences in (9)–(10) used in both experiments. Note that in (9) the sentence initial object argument consists of an adjective followed by a head noun, while in (10) the sentence initial object contains a demonstrative; (9)a and (10)a have clitics after the entire object argument, while in (9)b and (10)b the clitic appears after the first word.

(9) Object: adjective + noun

a. *Loše igrače ćemo izbaciti iz prve ekipe. 1st phrase*
bad players will-Cl kick out from first team
'Bad players will be kicked out from the first team.'

b. *Loše ćemo igrače izbaciti iz prve ekipe. 1st word*
bad will-Cl players kick out from first team
'BAD players will be kicked out from the first team.'

(10) Object: demonstrative + noun

a. *Ove igrače ćemo izbaciti iz prve ekipe. 1st phrase*
these players will-Cl kick out from first team
'These players will be kicked out from the first team.'

b. *Ove ćemo igrače izbaciti iz prve ekipe. 1st word*
these will-Cl players kick out from first team
'THESE players will be kicked out from the first team.'

What we found in experiment 1 is that argument sentences are more likely to be completed with the clitic after the first word if the first word is a demonstrative, as in (10)b, than if it is an adjective, as in (9)b, and this difference was statistically significant: $\chi^2(1) = 30.81$, $p < 0.0001$ (Picture 5).

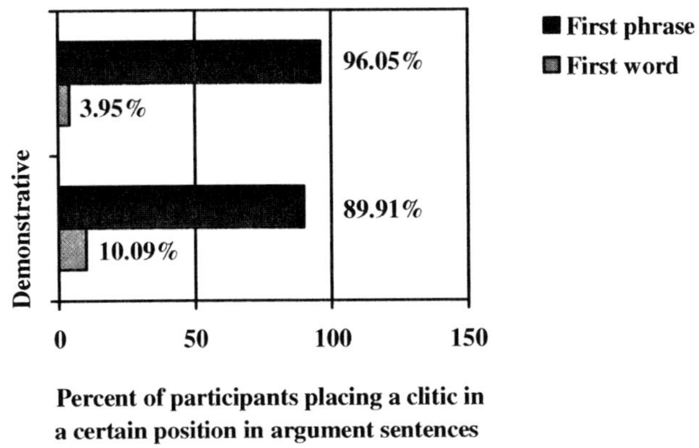

Figure 5. Percent of participants placing a clitic after the first word (light gray) and after the first phrase (dark grey) in argument sentences that contain adjective or demonstrative (experiment 1).

In the sentence acceptance task, in experiment 2, we found that object argument sentences were more likely to be accepted with the clitic after the first word if the first word is a demonstrative, the difference being statistically significant: $\chi^2(1) = 5.47$, $p < 0.05$ (Picture 6).

These findings suggest that the preferred status of demonstratives over adjectives as first word clitic hosts is due to potential differences in information

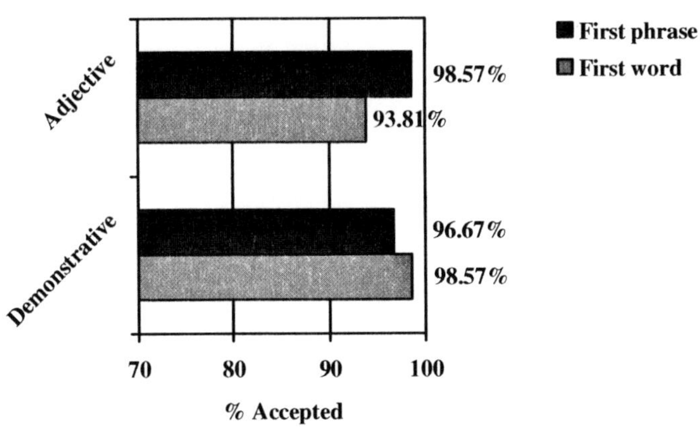

Figure 6. Percent of accepted argument sentences containing an adjective or a demonstrative, with a clitic positioned after the first word (light grey) or after the first phrase (dark grey) (experiment 2).

structure. In particular, a demonstrative (as a deictic and/or specific determiner in a language that does not otherwise have determiners) is more likely to be a point of contrast than an adjective. A broader hypothesis based on this finding is that the argument cases with the clitic after the first word supply a point of contrast in pre-clitic position consistent with either contrastive focus or contrastive topic interpretations. That this effect is found in experiment 2 only with object arguments correlates with their higher focusability.

5. Conclusions and directions for future research

We have clearly established preferred clitic placements in the two types of sentences. In the argument sentences, clitic positioning after the first phrase is more common in the corpus, and exhibits a higher percent of participants' placements, faster processing, and higher acceptance rates. By contrast, in predicate sentences, clitic positioning after the first word is more common in the corpus, and exhibits a higher percent of participants' placements, faster processing, and higher acceptance rates. We thus have clear indicators that this is not a case of structural optionality, whether syntactic or of some other sort.

However, factors that affect both preferred and dispreferred clitic placement in the two types of cases are yet to be established, and will be addressed in future research. Correlates of different clitic positionings, both within and across the argument and predicate types, will need to be identified by investigating a broad range of linguistic properties and their potential interactions. Our hypothesis is that clitic positioning is an interface phenomenon, in the broadest sense of the term, with at least prosody, syntax, and information structure contributing to the selection between the competing configurations in both the argument and predicate types. Syntax and its role in clitic positioning has had a central place in previous discussions about clitic placement. In addition, one aspect of the role of prosody has proven to be relevant: the first word, in both the argument and predicate types, has to be characterized in prosodic terms (Halpern 1995, Zec and Inkelas 1990, Zec 2005). We plan to address a further relevant role of prosody that has not yet been studied, namely, the characteristic intonational contours associated with the first word and first constituent cases in both the argument and predicate types. Furthermore, claims in the literature that the domain of clitic placement in Serbian corresponds to an intonational phrase (Radanović-Kocić 1996, Bošković 2001) have not been studied in prosodic terms or substantiated by acoustic evidence.

The least studied facet of clitic positioning is the impact of information structure, yet intuitively we feel that this is where the action is. In particular, differences between the four cases we have identified may well be correlated with different discourse conditions between the first word and first phrase positions within each category.

While the central concern of this paper is the bifurcation into the argument and predicate cases, the contrast between determiners and adjectives as first words in the argument case reported in section 4.3 is highly suggestive of the role for information structure that we envision. This hypothesis will be explored in future research by conducting further experiments that will directly address the correlations of the four cases of clitic positioning with differences in information structures, as well as with differences in intonational contours.

Acknowledgements. This research was supported by a seed grant from Mario Einaudi Center for International Studies at Cornell University. We also wish to thank Ružica Marinković for her help with corpus materials, as well as Aleksandar Kostić and Petar Milin of the Laboratory of Experimental Psychology, University of Belgrade, for their invaluable help in conceptualizing and realizing this project. Thanks also to Sam Featherston for his astute editorial comments, and to the organizers and participants of Linguistic Evidence 2008.

Notes

1. Sources for the typology in (1) are Garrett (1996) for Hittite; Katičić (1986) for Croatian; Toman (1986) for Czech; Golden and Sheppard (2000) for Slovenian; Paul (2001) for Malagasy; Donaldson (1980) and Klavans (1982) for Ngiyambaa; Legate (2008) and the references therein for Warlpiri.
2. While Halpern (1999) invokes prosody to characterize clitic placement after the first word, Bošković (2001) and Radanović-Kocić (1996) characterize the domain of clitic positioning in prosodic terms.
3. However, both types of clitic positioning are found in Croatian as well as in Serbian. The claim that clitic placement in Croatian is after the first word is based on prescriptive grammars such as Katičić (1986). As for Serbian, ample evidence for both types of clitic placement can be found throughout the literature, including this paper. The claim that clitics follow only the first constituent arise from theory-internal considerations, in which clitic placement is taken to be a result of syntactic movement only. First word placement is thus taken to be epiphenomenal, a result of so-called left-branch extractions. Anderson's claim is based in part on such analyses. For arguments against the purely syntactic approach see Bošković (2001) and Predolac (2007), among others.

References

Anderson, Stephen
2005 *Aspects of the theory of clitics*. Oxford: Oxford University Press.

Bošković, Željko
2001 *On the nature of the syntax-phonology interface*. Amsterdam: Elsevier.

Browne, Wayles
1974 On the problem of enclitic placement in Serbo-Croatian. In: Brecht, Richard and Catherine Chvany (eds.), *Slavic transformational syntax. Michigan Slavic Materials*, vol. 10: 36–52. Ann Arbor: University of Michigan

Donaldson, Tamsin
1980 *Ngiyambaa: The language of the Wangaaybuwan*. Cambridge: Cambridge University Press.

Franks, Steven and Progovac, Ljiljana
1994 On the placement of Serbo-Croatian clitics. In: G. Fowler, H. Cooper, and J. Ludwig (eds.), *Proceedings of the 9th Biennial Conference on Balkan and South Slavic Linguistics, Literature and Folklore*, vol. 7, 69–78. Bloomington: Indiana Slavic Studies.

Garett, Andrew
1996 Wackernagel's law and unaccusativity in Hittite. In: Halpern and Zwicky (eds.), 85–133.

Golden, Marija and Sheppard, Milena Milojević
2000 Slovene pronominal clitics. In: Beukema, Frits and den Dikken, Marcel (eds.), *Clitic Phenomena in European Languages*, 191–208. Amsterdam: John Benjamins

Halpern, Aaron
1999 *On the placement and morphology of clitics*. Stanford, CA: CSLI

Halpern, Aaron and Zwicky, Arnold (eds.)
1996 *Approaching second: second position clitics and related phenomena*. Stanford, CA: CSLI.

Katičić, Radoslav
1986 *Sintaksa hrvatskoga književnog jezika*. Jugoslavenska akademija znanosti i umjetnosti. Zagreb: Globus.

Klavans, Judith L.
1982 *Some problems in a theory of clitics*. Bloomington IN: Indiana University Linguistics Club.

Legate, Julie
2008 Warlpiri and the theory of second position clitics. *Natural Language and Linguistic Theory* 26: 3–60.

Paul, Ileana
2001 *Ve* as a second-position clitic. *Oceanic Linguistics* 40: 135–142.

Predolac, Nikola
2007 Against syntactic clitic placement in Serbian. Ms. Cornell University.

Progovac, Ljiljana
1996 Clitics in Serbian/Croatian: Comp as the second position. In: Halpern and Zwicky (eds.), 411–428.

Radanović-Kocić, Vesna
1996 The placement of Serbo-Croatian clitics: a prosodic approach. In: Halpern and Zwicky (eds.), 429–446.

Toman, Jindra
1986 Cliticization from NPs in Czech and comparable phenomena in French and Italian. In: H. Borer (ed.), *The syntax of pronominal clitics. Syntax and semantics 19.* New York: Academic Press.

Zec, Draga
2005 Prosodic differences among function words. *Phonology* 22: 77–112.

Zec, Draga and Inkelas, Sharon
1990 Prosodically constrained syntax. In: S. Inkelas and D. Zec (eds.), *The phonology syntax connection*, 365–378. Chicago: University of Chicago Press.

Explorations in ellipsis: The grammar and processing of silence

Lyn Frazier

1. Introduction

The grammar of ellipsis has been an exciting focus of linguistic research for a considerable time starting in the 1970s (Chao 1988, Grinder and Postal 1971, Hankamer and Sag, 1976, Sag 1976, Sag and Hankamer 1984, Webber 1978, Williams 1977) and continuing to the present (Dalrymple et al. 1991, Hardt 1993, Hardt and Romero 2004, Johnson 2008, Lobeck 1995, Merchant 2001, 2005, 2008a,b, Schwabe and Winkler 2003, Sheiber, Pereira and Dalrymple 1999, among many others). Many insightful approaches have been developed. The present paper provides an overview of an ongoing project with my colleague Charles Clifton designed to develop a theory of processing ellipsis. It also examines the implications of this processing theory for grammatical theories of ellipsis.

Crucially it will be assumed that it is the overall theory of language, the grammar plus theories of performance, that must account for linguistic intuitions. In other words, though linguistic intuitions form an important form of evidence about the grammar, those intuitions basically tell us whether a sentence sounds "good" (acceptable) or not. The notions "grammatical" or "ungrammatical" are not pre-theoretic but rather the consequence of devising a theory of language. Thus classifying sentences as grammatical/ungrammatical is the result of constructing the most explanatory overall theory of language, including a theory of grammar and theories of performance.

This paper will focus on the kinds of ellipsis that can cross sentence boundaries, primarily Verb Phrase Ellipsis (VPE), illustrated in (1), and Sluicing, illustrated in (2).

(1) *Josh laughed. Bella did ___ too.*

(2) *Lucy bought something. But I don't know what [ ].*

VPE elides a verb phrase following an auxiliary, *not* or *to*. In Sluicing, an interrogative clause is elided (Chung, Ladusaw and McCloskey 1995, Merchant 2001 among others). The interrogative binds a variable in a position corresponding to the position of an indefinite in the antecedent clause (*something* in (2)). Chung, Ladusaw and McCloskey (1995) dubbed *something*, the phrase in the antecedent clause that defines the position of the variable in the ellipsis clause, the "inner antecedent." Some examples of sluicing lack an inner antecedent. Such examples will be of special interest in Section 4.

Processing studies of ellipsis have shown a stronger parallelism effect for VPE ("surface anaphora") than for deep anaphora (especially Tanenhaus and Carlson 1990, Mauner,Tanenhaus and Carlson 1995) and sometimes "distance" effects, Murphy (1985), but also Martin and McElree (2008).

(3) a. *The garbage was taken out. John did last night.*
b. *The garbage was taken out. John did it last night.*

These studies support the view that there is an important distinction between anaphora and ellipsis.

The present paper is organized into three sections. It takes up information structure constraints on ellipsis first. Various processing effects suggest that focus expectations influence ellipsis resolution. Further, it is argued that at least one discourse constraint on ellipsis should be captured in the theory of processing, not in the grammar. The next section takes up elided constituents with "flawed" antecedent clauses which do not perfectly match the syntax of the elided clause. It is argued that, although ungrammatical, they are acceptable under particular circumstances – specifically, under circumstances where the processor can repair the antecedent at LF using its normal repair mechanisms. The third section turns to island constraints. Several observations can be explained if it is assumed, in stark contrast with all work on sluicing since that of Ross (1967,1969), that even sluicing may technically be subject to island constraints. It is argued that Sluicing island violations are technically ungrammatical, but acceptable when an overt inner antecedent is present. Taken jointly, the three sections are an attempt to provide rather broad coverage of the empirical data on ellipsis without complicating either the grammar or the theory of processing.

2. Information structure

It is clear that information structure influences the acceptability of ellipsis. The antecedent of an elided constituent must be already given (Rooth 1992, Merchant 2001). Further focus influences the choice of preferred antecedent in cases of ambiguity (see in particular Carlson 2002, for evidence in a wide-range of structures.)

2.1. Focus

Frazier and Clifton (1998a) tested ambiguous sluicing sentences with an inner antecedent in either the matrix clause (*some tourist*) or the embedded clause (*someone*), as in (4) below. In an eye movement recording study, they found that ambiguous sentences like those in (4) were read more quickly than counterparts disambiguated to the matrix subject inner antecedent (not illustrated here).[1] They proposed that the matrix subject interpretation was dispreferred, and read more slowly than the object antecedent interpretation, because the matrix subject is not an expected location for informational focus. Assuming that focused inner antecedents are preferred over unfocused antecedents, this could explain the eye movement results. To test this conjecture, in an auditory comprehension study, they placed a prominent accent on either the embedded object (4a) or the matrix subject (4b).

(4) a. *Some tourist suspected that the hotelkeeper was hiding SOMEONE. Guess who?*

b. *Some TOURIST suspected that the hotelkeeper was hiding someone. Guess who?*

There was a significant effect of accent placement. More object antecedent interpretations were chosen when the object was accented (4a) than when the subject was accented (4b) (72% vs 48%). This was predicted by the hypothesis that perceivers prefer analyses where the inner antecedent is focused – either explicitly with a pitch accent as in the auditory study or implicitly by occurring in a position (late in the sentence) where informationally-focused constituents typically occur.

Carlson et al. (2008) provided further evidence that both overt pitch accents and the expected location of informational focus influence the interpretation of an elided constituent. In sluicing examples like those in (5) a prominent (L+H*) accent was placed on the subject of the antecedent clause (5a), the object (5b), both (5c) or only on the verb (5d).

(5) a. Subject Accent: *The CAPtain talked with the co-pilot, but …*
(we couldn't remember who else.)

b. Object Accent: *The captain talked with the CO-pilot, but …*

c. Both Accent: *The CAPtain talked with the CO-pilot, but …*

d. Verb Accent: *The captain TALKed with the co-pilot, but …*

Subject accent sentences (5a) received fewer object interpretations than both accent (5c) or verb accent (5d) sentences, which in turn received fewer object interpretations than object accent sentences (5b).

The findings discussed so far in this section might suggest only that overt pitch accents matter, and direct object antecedents are preferred to subject antecedents. To test whether it is really the expected position of informational focus that matters, the examples in (6) were tested in an auditory study. In (6) the potential inner antecedents in English are either the direct object or the object of the preposition. (Note that in languages without preposition stranding, the sentences in (6) are expected to unambiguously require the direct object interpretation, see Merchant (2001)). But in (6), unlike in the earlier examples, it is the prepositional phrase which occurs in clause final position. Thus the object of the preposition should be the most likely constituent in (6) to receive informational focus and the most likely phrase to be chosen as the inner antecedent. Carlson et al. (2008) manipulated the position of an overt accent and found that it was the later constituent, the object of the preposition, that was the preferred antecedent overall, and especially when that constituent was accented.

(6) a. Object Accent: *Lucy bought some PRESent for some occasion, but I don't know what.*

b. PP Accent: *Lucy bought some present for some oCCASion, but I don't know what.*

When the prepositional phrase was accented (6b), there were 72% prepositional object responses. This decreased significantly to only 60% prepositional object responses when the direct object was accented.

A clefted constituent is contrastively focused and thus, for example, requires an exhaustive interpretation. In a self paced reading study where readers had to choose a paraphrase of a sentence after reading it, an effect of both contrastive focus (what constituent was clefted) and expectations about informational focus were observed: When the object was clefted there were 75% object responses, but when the subject was focused there were only 39% object responses.

(7) a. *It was Lisa who Patty praised at the ceremony,/ but I don't know who else.*

b. *It was Patty who praised Lisa at the ceremony,/ but I don't know who else.*

Paraphrases:

a. *I don't know who else Patty praised.* (object antecedent)

b. *I don't know who else praised Lisa.* (subject antecedent)

Not surprisingly, reading times for object clefts were longer than for subject clefts, as has been found in many previous studies.

Information structure effects of the same sort just discussed have also been found in other languages, modulo differences in the way focus is expressed in those languages. See in particular Stolterfoht et al. (2007) for an investigation of German, and Biezma (2008) for an investigation of Iberian Spanish.

The studies discussed above show rather clearly that focus-structure plays a role in processing, by influencing ambiguity resolution. Other aspects of information structure also play a role in processing ellipsis. Antecedents which are part of the main assertion of an utterance are preferred, especially across sentence boundaries (Frazier and Clifton 2005). For example, in a written questionnaire, the ambiguous sentences in (8) were tested.

(8) a. *John said Fred went to Europe and Mary did too.*

b. *John said Fred went to Europe. Mary did too.*

In (8), if the matrix VP is chosen as antecedent, then Mary too said Fred went to Europe; if the embedded VP is chosen as antecedent, then Mary too went to Europe. When the antecedent and ellipsis were in the same sentence, as in (8a), matrix antecedents were chosen only 40% of the time. The lower (embedded VP) antecedent was often chosen (60% of the time) presumably in part because the syntactic representation is still highly salient when the elided constituent occurs in the same sentence as the antecedent. In the syntax, recent material is highly salient and local dependencies are generally preferred. Across sentence boundaries, however, as in (8b), significantly more matrix antecedents were chosen, presumably because the discourse representation becomes relatively more salient across sentence boundaries, and in the discourse representation it is information-structure notions, like main assertion, that capture salience relations.

In a further test of the main assertion hypothesis, elided verb phrases with either main clause or subordinate clause antecedents were tested in a self paced reading study where each item was followed by a question probing its interpretation. The main assertion hypothesis predicts that main clause antecedents will be preferred to subordinate clause antecedents.

(9) a. *Mary laughed after she made a joke about the supervisor. Then Tina did too.*

b. *After Mary laughed she made a joke about the supervisor. Then Tina did too.*

Independent of clause order, roughly three quarters of the time readers selected the main clause VP antecedent, i.e., in both (9a) and (9b) with no significant difference between them.

In another test of the main assertion hypothesis (also reported in Frazier and Clifton 2005), sentences with potential "epistemic" clauses such as (10a) were tested to check that indeed it is the main assertion of an utterance that matters, not tree geometry per se.

(10) a. *I think Mary smokes. Sam does too.*
b. *The teacher thinks Mary smokes. Sam does too.*

In (10a) the highest clause is open to an epistemic interpretation where it only conveys the degree of certainty with which the speaker makes the assertion in the embedded clause. On the epistemic interpretation, the matrix clause could simply be replaced by an adverb, e.g., by *apparently* in (10a). The matrix clause of (10b), by contrast, contains a third person subject and is not open to an epistemic interpretation. Thus the main assertion hypothesis, but not a generalization based on tree geometry, predicts fewer matrix antecedents for the elided VP in (10a) than in (10b). That is exactly what was observed. Sentences open to an epistemic interpretation received fewer matrix VP antecedents (32%) than sentences not open to an epistemic interpretation (10b), which received 50% matrix interpretations. A control study tested first person versus third person subjects with verbs like *announce,* which are not open to an epistemic interpretation. In the control study, there was no difference in the number of matrix antecedents chosen for sentences with first person subjects versus third person subjects, as expected if the effects reported for (10) were in fact due to the effect of the epistemic interpretation on what the perceiver takes to be the main assertion of the sentence.

2.2. Syntactic vs. discourse constraints

The main assertion hypothesis predicts that elided verb phrases with an antecedent in a conditional sentence should provide a catch-22 for the processor. In a conditional sentence, neither the antecedent clause nor the consequent clause is asserted (or entailed). What is asserted is the conditional relation. So an elided verb phrase with an antecedent in a conditional, e.g., (11a) below, should be only marginally acceptable. This was confirmed in a speeded acceptability judgment task, where hypothetical conditional sentences like (11a) were accepted only 52% of the time.[2,3]

In a written paraphrase selection study (Clifton and Frazier (submitted)), sentences like those in (11) were tested to assess the interpretations people assign to elided constituents with a conditional antecedent. In the two sentence examples (11a,b), a conditional sentence was followed by a sentence containing an ellipsis. In the three sentence examples (11c,d), a lead-in sentence was added. The lead-in essentially established the information described in the first clause of the conditional sentence. The idea was that the lead-in sentence might prompt the processor to cancel out the antecedent clause of the conditional sentence, because it would no longer present new information. In effect, the consequent clause would become the assertion of the second sentence, and thus a more tempting antecedent for the elided constituent, according to the main assertion hypothesis.

(11) a. *If John went to the store, he bought Twinkies. George did too.*
b. *If John went to the store, he bought Twinkies. George too.*
c. *Mary is sure that John went to the store. If John went to the store, he bought Twinkies. George did too.*
d. *Mary is sure that John went to the store. If John went to the store, he bought Twinkies. George too.*

Paraphrase selection:

(12) a. *It's also true of George that he bought Twinkies.*
b. *It's also true of George that if he went to the store he bought Twinkies.*

In sum, focusing on the VPE examples (11a,c), the prediction of the main assertion hypothesis was that they would receive a substantial number of full conditional responses, indicated by selection of the paraphrase in (12b), **but** the full conditional response would be chosen less often when the antecedent clause of the conditional conveyed only discourse-given information (making the consequent clause the main assertion), as in (11c), than when it conveyed new information, as in (11a). Both predictions were confirmed. Sentences like (11a), without a lead-in, received 58% full conditional responses. Examples like (11c), with a lead-in sentence, received significantly fewer (only 43%) full conditional responses. This is expected if the antecedent of the conditional tended to be canceled out when it expressed already given information.

The results discussed in this section are readily explained if the processor as well as the grammar is taken into account. Information structure notions play a role in processing ellipsis, influencing preferred antecedents in examples which are open to more than one grammatical analysis. Imperfect examples of ellipsis with an antecedent inside a conditional become more acceptable when the information in a discourse conspires to allow both syntactic and discourse constraints to be satisfied, e.g., by canceling out the antecedent of a conditional. Accounting for these results is straightforward in a theory of processing, which is inherently dynamic, involving incremental integration of information, but it is less straightforward to account for them in the theory of grammar, assuming the grammar is stated in a static format.[4]

3. Acceptable ungrammaticality

In this section, I will assume that the grammar of ellipsis requires an elided constituent and its antecedent to match syntactically (certain morphological details aside). Following Arregui et al. (2006) and Frazier (2008), I will argue that certain examples that violate this constraint are nevertheless acceptable under specific conditions, namely, when the antecedent can be repaired at LF using the parser's normal repair mechanisms, and when the syntactic mismatch is one likely to have been produced by the production mechanisms responsible for syntactic blends.[5]

3.1. The recyclying hypothesis

The hypothesis that flawed antecedents are acceptable when they may easily be repaired at LF was dubbed the "Recycling hypothesis" (Arregui et al. 2006, see too Tanenhaus, Carlson and Seidenberg 1985): When an elided VP has a flawed antecedent, the processor repairs the antecedent. If this can be done easily, using only grammatical operations for which there is evidence, then the ellipsis will be relatively acceptable (on a par with syntactic reanalysis of garden path structures).[6] Evidence in support of the hypothesis came from an acceptability judgment study showing progressively degraded acceptability (fewer "yes" responses in a speeded acceptability judgment study) going from (13a), with a matching VP antecedent, to (13b) with a VP in subject position, to (13c) where a trace must be replaced by its ultimate binder, to (13d) where the verb heading the desired VP antecedent is available only by going inside a word.

(13) a. *None of the astronomers saw the comet, /but John did.*
(Available verb phrase)

b. *Seeing the comet was nearly impossible, /but John did.*
(Embedded verb phrase)

c. *The comet was nearly impossible to see, /but John did.* (Verb phrase with trace)

d. *The comet was nearly unseeable, /but John did.* (Negative adjective)

Further support for the recycling hypothesis came from a similar study showing that elided verb phrases with an antecedent in a verbal gerund (14a,b) were judged significantly more acceptable than those with an antecedent in a nominal gerund (14c,d).

(14) a. *Singing the arias tomorrow night will be difficult / but Maria will.* (Verbal, -mod)

b. *Singing the arias slowly tomorrow night will be difficult / but Maria will.* (Verbal, mod)

c. *Tomorrow night's singing of the arias will be difficult / but Maria will.* (Nominal, -mod)

d. *Tomorrow night's slow singing of the arias will be difficult / but Maria will.* (Nominal, +mod)

Further the presence of a modifier in a verbal gerund tended to increase acceptability a bit (14b) and the presence of a modifier (adjective) in the nominal modifier tended to hurt acceptability a bit (14d), though these latter effects were small and not significant. Further work is needed to determine whether these small effects are reliable. But notice that the presence of an adverb may help to flag the presence of a VP thus facilitating VPE whereas the presence of an adjective would only make recycling of the source antecedent more difficult. Thus the direction of the possible effect fits with the recycling hypothesis.

3.2. The role of the speaker

If examples of ellipsis without matching antecedents are ungrammatical, and just patched up by the parser, as argued here, then the question arises why speakers would ever elide a phrase under circumstances where it would produce an ungrammatical sentence? The idea behind the recycling hypothesis is that speakers often produce syntactic blends, as well as other speech errors, and the listener may automatically correct those errors. Indeed, speakers may utter an antecedent clause in a passive form, for example, and then later when they plan the ellipsis clause, forget that the antecedent was passive and produce an active ellipsis clause. Memory errors of this general sort have been studied for some time. Mehler (1963) showed that passives are misrecalled as actives more often than actives are misrecalled as passives. On the present "acceptable ungrammaticality" account of elided constituents with flawed antecedents, this predicts that ellipsis examples with a voice mismatch should be more acceptable when the antecedent is passive and the ellipsis clause active than vice versa. This was tested in a written acceptability judgment task. It was also predicted that examples containing a presupposition trigger (*already*, *too*) would be judged more acceptable than examples without a presupposition trigger. The presence of a presupposition trigger might indicate to the listener/reader that the speaker was assuming that a matching antecedent was already available in context. Specifically, the experiment tested examples like those in (15) and (16).

(15) a. *The dessert was praised by the customer after the critic did already.*
b. *The dessert was praised by the customer and the critic did.*
c. *The customer praised the dessert after the appetizer was already.*
d. *The customer praised the dessert and the appetizer was.*

(16) a. *The student was praised by the old schoolmaster, and the advisor did too.*
b. *The student was praised by the old schoolmaster, and the advisor did.*
c. *The advisor praised the student, and the old schoolmaster was too.*
d. *The advisor praised the student, and the old school master was.*

Examples with a passive-active mismatch were rated more acceptable than examples with an active-passive mismatch. Examples containing a presupposition trigger were rated more acceptable than those without a presupposition trigger, especially examples containing the presupposition trigger *already* (perhaps *too* was less effective because the presupposition of *too* is difficult to accommodate). In sum, the predictions of the recycling hypothesis were confirmed.

The evidence summarized here supports an approach which treats ellipsis examples with flawed antecedents as examples of acceptable ungrammaticality. For evidence that we independently need to recognize the notion of acceptable ungrammaticality, see Otero (1972), Staum and Sag (2007), and discussion in Frazier (2008). For evidence that we independently need a theory of reanalysis/repair in the theory of processing, see Fodor and Ferreira (1998), Frazier and Clifton (1998b). The recycling account of 'flawed' ellipsis exploits independently required mechanisms to explain a fairly subtle pattern of acceptability. The account does not really need to add anything new to either the theory of grammar or the theory of processing.

Before leaving this section, note that the hypothesis that syntactic mismatches between an antecedent clause and ellipsis clause give rise to ungrammaticality explains why simple unadorned voice mismatch examples such as (17) don't sound acceptable.

(17) *The kitchen was cleaned. The janitor did.*

On the present view, they are ungrammatical. Given how simple the examples are, it seems unlikely the speaker has made a syntactic blend. Thus the examples are also unacceptable. It is more complicated examples that typically show up in corpus studies (attested examples like *This problem was to have been looked into, but nobody did*, cited by Kehler, 2002).

3.3. Nonactuality implicatures

Attested examples of ellipsis with a mismatching antecedent often have antecedents that support a non-actuality implicature, i.e., an implicature that the state of affairs described is not actual, as illustrated in (18b). In contrast to (18a), uttering (18b) implies that no trip is already planned for August.

(18) a. *A trip is planned for August.*
b. *A trip should be planned for August.*

The importance of non-actuality implicatures may be that they provide an implicit contrast between the state of affairs described by the antecedent clause and the actual state of affairs. This contrast may serve to focus the content of the clause, making it highly accessible and thus facilitating recycling and increasing the acceptability of flawed ellipsis. Further, the nonactual (desired or goal) state may organize discourse, helping to link individual events/states together, and it may implicitly introduce a potential question under discussion. Thus, a variety of considerations point to the beneficial impact of nonactuality implicatures on the acceptability of flawed ellipsis. Frazier and Clifton (in progress) tested the hypothesis that nonactuality implicatures facilitate mismatched ellipsis, using sentences like those in (19) and (20). In (19) the elided verb phrase in the final sentence may take as its antecedent either the more prominent main clause verb phrase of the first sentence (*chastised a worker*) or the less prominent relative clause verb phrase (*brought production to a halt*).

(19) a. *The supervisor chastised a worker who brought production to a halt. Fred did recently.*

b. *The supervisor chastised a worker who would have brought production to a halt. Fred did recently.*

The non-actuality implicature added to the relative clause in (19b) should increase the number of relative clause antecedents, according to the non-actuality implicature hypothesis. In a written comprehension study, this prediction was confirmed.

Examples like those in (20) provide a test of the hypothesis that nonactuality implicatures increase the acceptability of mismatched ellipsis.

(20) a. *A trip is planned for August, but Anne didn't.*
b. *A trip must be planned for August, but Anne didn't.*

Sentences like those in (20) were tested in a written acceptability judgment study. As predicted, examples like (20b) with the nonactuality implicature were rated as being significantly more acceptable than examples like (20a). On an account where voice mismatches are completely grammatical (Merchant 2007, 2008b), it is not clear why simple voice mismatch examples should be bad nor is it clear why adding a nonactuality implicature should increase the acceptability of the example.

To summarize, it's been suggested here that the grammar should be kept highly restrictive, by explaining the acceptability of some ungrammatical ellipsis examples in the theory of processing. Specifically, assuming that antecedents with a voice mismatch are ungrammatical but at times acceptable can help explain:

- the unacceptability of many instances of voice mismatches in the simplest unadorned examples.
- the asymmetry between passive-active and active-passive mismatches shown in Arregui et al. (2006).
- the correlation between the unacceptability of such examples and repair difficulty.
- the greater acceptability of flawed antecedents when a non-actuality implicature is present than when it is not.

One challenge for the present account of voice mismatches, pointed out by Merchant (2007), is explaining why voice mismatches[7] in sluicing sound worse than in VPE. I suspect this is because a sluiced constituent contains a variable. When a VPE example contains a variable, then a voice mismatch sounds worse than it otherwise would (e.g., *Every room will have been cleaned that the janitor will*). Hence, elided constituents with a variable in them may just be fussier about the syntactic matching condition than examples where the elided constituent does not contain a variable.

We turn now to another area where perhaps the grammar may be kept maximally restrictive once the grammar is embedded in a theory of language processing, namely, the area of island constraints.

4. Acceptable ungrammaticality: Island violations

Since the earliest discussions of sluicing (Ross 1967,1969), it has been observed that sluicing may violate islands. For example, (21a) seems quite acceptable compared to it's non-sluiced counterpart (21b).

(21) a. *Ina watched the boy who ate something weird but she didn't know what.*

b. **What did Ina watch the boy who ate x ?*

In the literature, it has generally been assumed that extraction out of islands is grammatical in sluicing sentences, at least in examples with an overt inner antecedent (Chung, Ladusaw and McClosekey 1995, Merchant 2001). Indeed in recent work, Merchant (2008a) has focused on the reason why sluicing may violate islands when VP ellipsis may not. His account is intriguing. He assumes that an island-violating trace is marked with an asterisk indicating its ungrammaticality. In sluicing all asterisked traces are deleted, whereas in VP ellipsis an asterisked trace will remain. On this account, clearly island-violating movements in sluicing sentences are grammatical, not just acceptable.

An alternative view is that all island violations are technically ungrammatical, even in sluicing. But sometimes island violations are acceptable. It is this position that will be explored here. On this alternative view, extraction out of islands is syntactically prohibited even for sluicing. But it is acceptable if the discourse processor can substitute a variable of type e for an existing phrase in the syntactic representation (Frazier and Clifton 2005). In other words, similar to intrusive pronouns (Sells 1984) and binding chains (as opposed to antecedent government chains, Cinque 1986), the idea is that a relation between the interrogative and a syntactic position may be established by the discourse processor rather than by the syntactic processor.

In what follows, as elsewhere, I'll assume the existence of syntactic structure in the ellipsis site. Considerable linguistic evidence supports this view. Evidence comes comes from examples with traces in the elided constituent, Fiengo and May (1992), parasitic gaps, Kennedy (2003), scope, Lasnik (2001), missing antecedents, Grinder and Postal (1971), and the distribution of preposition stranding in sluicing, Merchant (2001), for example. Psycholinguistic evidence also supports the assumption of linguistic structure in the elided constituent, Frazier and Clifton (2005). As in other work, I'll also assume that the syntactic processor assigns minimal structure as it goes, and it doesn't violate strong islands. The discourse processor integrates new material relying on information-structure notions, including the notion of "main assertion."

Several predictions of the 'acceptable-but-ungrammatical' approach to sluicing island violations have been tested. They suggest at very least that the common view that sluicing island violations are grammatical, rather than merely acceptable, may be less firmly established than has previously been assumed.

4.1. D-linking

On the assumption that sluicing island violations are ungrammatical, the examples must be rescued by the discourse processor setting up a dependency between the interrogative constituent and a syntactic position that is interpreted as a variable. Given the discourse processor's involvement, we might expect d-linked sluicing examples to be more acceptable than examples with indefinite interrogatives (see Frazier and Clifton (2002) for evidence showing a preference for d-linked antecedents for intrusive pronouns inside islands). The expected preference for d-linked interrogatives was confirmed in a written acceptability judgment study, using sentences like those in (22).[8] Sentences were rated on a 5-point scale where "5" indicated a perfectly normal sentence that a native speaker might say or hear. Examples with a d-linked interrogative (22b) were rated as better than examples with an indefinite interrogative (22a).

(22) a. *John met someone who witnessed a terrible accident today but he didn't say what.* 3.17

b. *John met someone who witnessed a terrible accident today but he didn't say which one.* 3.69

However, it should be noted that d-linked interrogatives may be more acceptable than non-dlinked interrogatives in all forms of sluicing, even without an island violation. Consequently, while the acceptability judgment data are reassuring for the present approach, they may not truly discriminate among the theories under consideration.

4.2. Sprouting

Chung, Ladusaw and McCloskey (1995) dub sluicing examples that do not contain an overt inner antecedent examples of "sprouting." Because the antecedent clause does not contain an overt constituent in the position corresponding to the variable in the elided clause, a position for the variable must be created ("sprouted") rather than being copied from the antecedent clause. For example, a direct object position must be created in the elided clause in (23a) and a position for the locative adjunct must be created in (23b).

(23) a. *John ate but I don't know what.*

b. *John slept but I don't know where.*

For present purposes, what's interesting about sprouting in islands is that neither the syntactic nor discourse processor can create the variable that's needed: the syntactic processor can't go inside an island, and the discourse processor can't create syntactic structure. Thus island violations in sprouting examples should be ungrammatical and unacceptable, since the examples can't be rescued by the discourse processor.

In a written acceptability judgment study (Frazier and Clifton 2005, Experiment 8a), sluicing examples with island violations were tested. Participants were instructed to rate each sentence on a 5-point scale. They were informed that capitalized words would be spoken with stress. Each sentence had three forms. One with no overt inner antecedent in the relative clause (24a), one with an overt inner antecedent (24b) and one with the inner antecedent capitalized (24c).

(24) a. *Frederica listened to some tenor who was singing but she didn't say what.* 3.07

b. *Frederica listened to some tenor who was singing something but she didn't say what.* 3.39

c. *Frederica listened to some tenor who was singing SOMETHING but she didn't say what.* 3.73

The prediction was that acceptability of the examples should systematically increase from (24a) to (24c). Although all three are technically ungrammatical on the present account, in (24a) the example should also be unacceptable because the discourse processor cannot step in and replace a constituent with a variable (because there *is* no constituent and the discourse processor can't build syntactic structure). In (24b) the discourse processor must replace the inner antecedent with a variable, but it gets little help identifying the position of the variable whereas in (24c) the stress on the inner antecedent should help to make clear the intended position of the variable. The results confirmed the predictions with a significant main effect of structure; in pairwise tests, (24c) was rated significantly better than the other two forms.

Comparable effects were obtained for subject island violations, as illustrated in (25). Again each sentence had three forms: one with no overt inner antecedent (25a), one with an overt (uncapitalized) inner antecedent (25b) and one with a capitalized inner antecedent (25c).

(25) a. *We know to win is possible but we don't know what.* 2.49

b. *We know to win something is possible but we don't know what.* 2.97

c. *We know to win SOMETHING is possible but we don't know what.* 3.18

As expected, acceptability increased from (25a) to (25c), with a significant main effect of structure. In pairwise tests, (25a) was rated significantly less acceptable than the other two forms.

In a speeded acceptability judgment study (Frazier and Clifton 2005, Experiment 8b), island violation examples were compared to their main clause (no island) counterparts, as illustrated in (26). The present account predicts an interaction: sprouting examples relative to their overt inner antecedent counterparts should be particularly unacceptable when they are in an island, because they cannot be rescued by the operation of the discourse processor.

(26) Relative clause (Island):

a. *They hired someone who won but I can't remember what.* 58.3% acceptable

b. *They hired someone who won something but I can't remember what.* 79.4% acceptable

c. *They hired someone who won SOMETHING but I can't remember what.* 80.5% acceptable

Main Clause (No island):

d. *Someone won but I can't remember what.* 70.2% acceptable

e. *Someone won something but I can't remember what.* 83.3% acceptable

f. *Someone won SOMETHING but I can't remember what.* 86.3% acceptable

In terms of the acceptability judgments, there was a main effect of inner antecedent, a main effect of relative clause/main clause, and an interaction of these two factors (fully significant by subjects, marginal by items). The results suggest that indeed the penalty for sprouting examples relative to their overt inner antecedent counterparts is larger in island-violation examples than in no island examples. This is not really expected if sluicing can freely violate islands. It is expected if violating islands in sluicing examples is ungrammatical but can be rescued under some circumstances, namely, when an overt inner antecedent is present.

4.3. Avoiding island violations

If sluicing examples like (27) are ambiguous between two grammatical readings, we might expect focus to influence which interpretation readers select. On the other hand, if only one interpretation is fully grammatical, we might expect that even when focus favors the island-violation analysis it would not predominate since a fully grammatical interpretation is available.

Frazier and Clifton (in progress) tested sentences like those in (27) in a self paced reading task with a following question after each sentence. Particpants read the sentence. Then they read the question and answered it by choosing one of two paraphrases provided (by pressing the key under that response).

(27) a. *John said something nasty about the girl who won something/ but I can't remember what.*

b. *John said SOMETHING nasty about the girl who won something/ but I can't remember what.*

c. *John said something nasty about the girl who won SOMETHING/ but I can't remember what.*

d. *John said something nasty about the girl who won/ but I can't remember what.*

Question: *What can't I remember?*

1. *What John said.* 2. *What the girl won.*

Normal	37%RC
1st Capitalized	30%RC
2nd Capitalized	46%RC
Sprouting	21%RC

Relative clause antecedent answers never predominated, were never a majority of the responses, even in the condition where focus favored the relative clause antecedent, as in (27c). Sentences like (27a) and (27c) received significantly more relative clause responses than sentences like (27d); sentences like (27b) also received significantly more relative clause responses than sentences like (27c). If the relative clause responses are technically ungrammatical, there is a clear reason for avoiding the relative clause response even when the focus was contained inside the relative clause. If the relative clause responses are fully grammatical, then it is less clear why when focus favored this response, it was nevertheless not the dominant response.

4.4. Further avoidance of island violation: Coordinate structures and sluicing

In Frazier and Clifton (2005), sentences like those in (28) were investigated (along with their conjoined clause counterparts, and counterparts where the order of conjunct was switched). For present purposes what's interesting is the interpretation that people report for sentences like (28). As pointed out to me by Kathryn Pruitt, the interpretation assigned to (28) seems to be *but he didn't tell me what he studied,* not the island (Coordinate structure constraint) violating interpretation *but he didn't tell me what he slept and studied.*"

(28) *Michael slept and studied but he didn't tell me what.*

Although I have not conducted a formal experiment, the native speakers I have checked have all agreed with Pruitt's intuition. This suggests that the processor recycles the antecedent in (28) into a grammatical form, avoiding the island violation.

4.5. Adjunct islands

A visual on-line acceptability judgment task was used to test adjunct island violations in wh-questions (29b), in sluicing (29d) and in declarative controls (29f), see Experiment 3, Frazier and Clifton (2005).

(29) a. *What lecture was Sally impressed with?*
3807 ms, .831 Ok

b. *What lecture was Sally impressed after?*
3974 ms, .611 Ok

c. *Sally was impressed with some lecture, but I don't remember what.*
2746 ms, .651 Ok

d. *Sally was impressed after some lecture, but I don't remember what.*
2775 ms, .519 Ok

e. *Sally was impressed with some lecture.*
3579 ms, .838 Ok

f. *Sally was impressed after some lecture.*
3886 ms, .833 Ok

Each adjunct example was paired with a corresponding (no violation) argument example. The percent acceptability differed significantly among the three syntactic forms, with the declarative control sentences accepted most frequently and the sluicing sentences least frequently. Argument sentences were accepted more frequently than adjunct sentences, but crucially the interaction with syntactic form was also significant. Simple t-tests indicated that argument extraction was accepted more often than adjunct extraction ($t(47) = 4.48$, $p < .001$) and *argument sluicing was accepted more often than adjunct sluicing* ($t(47) = 2.98$, $p < .01$), *even though the difference between the argument control and the adjuncdt control sentences did not approach significance* ($t > 1.0$). In short, sluicing examples with an adjunct island violation are rated less acceptable than their no island violation (argument extraction) counterparts, and this penalty cannot be attributed to a general disadvantage for adjuncts relative to arguments since it does not appear in the control sentences (29e,f). This outcome is expected if sluicing cannot violate islands.

4.6. Why do island violations often seem less severe in sluicing than in overt cases?

Intuitions suggest that island violations in sluicing are less severe than in overt island violation examples, e.g., compare (21a) and (21b). Similarly, in the adjunct island study reported in Section 4.5, the acceptability penalty for an island violation was significant for sluicing, but smaller than it was for ordinary wh-questions. Why should the size of the penalty differ?

Generally, we expect a larger impact of a violation in focused material than in unfocused material because perceivers allocate more attention to focused material than to unfocused material (e.g. Cutler and Fodor 1979) and more attention to material in prominent positions than material in less prominent positions (Sanford and Sturt 2002). Being overt may be one form of being prominent.

4.7. A conceptual problem

One proposed account for why island violations are permitted in sluicing is based on the insight that all asterisked traces would be elided in sluicing (Merchant 2008a). This account is in some ways appealing. But it remains unclear why it should matter if "*trace" has been elided (= not pronounced) if the syntactic representation is still present. Given theories where syntactic structure is present in the elided constituent, an asterisked trace will be contained in the syntactic representation of the constituent even if the constituent is not pronounced. So both the grammatical account and the processing account of sluicing island violations need to appeal to the notion that not pronouncing a constituent influences the severity of a violation.

5. Conclusions

Both syntactic conditions and discourse conditions constrain ellipsis. Dynamic processing of language may disguise the (un-)grammaticality of some instances of ellipsis under circumstances where the syntax of the antecedent has already undergone some relevant discourse operation (canceling out of the antecedent of a conditional, computing a non-actuality implicature) or because the antecedent undergoes a repair at LF.

The grammar may define ideal sentences. When speakers often fail to fully conform with the ideal in a particular (systematic) way, and hearers easily and correctly identify the intended structure/meaning of the sentence, this may produce ungrammatical but relatively acceptable sentences, especially when supported by a clear contrast implied by a non-actuality implicature. This approach explains why passive-active mismatches are more acceptable than active-passive mismatches, why passive-active mismatch examples are not perfect, and therefore why presupposition triggers or non-actuality implicatures should help the examples. On an approach where voice mismatches are grammatical, one would not expect asymmetries between passive-active and active-passive order. All voice mismatches should be fully grammatical and not in need of rescuing.

Sentences with island violations in elided constituents may be ungrammatical but acceptable under circumstances where the discourse processor may step in and supply a variable. The absence of an overt acoustically detectable violation may make such sentences sound more acceptable than sentences with overt island violations. This processing approach to island violations in ellipsis explains why they are not possible with sprouting (where neither the syntactic processor nor discourse processor may supply the variable for the interrogative to bind), and why acceptability judgments are degraded for sluicing out of adjunct islands (though not as sharply as for overt adjunct island violations). It also explains why sluicing island violations are reconstructed without an island violation when that option is available, either when an antecedent is interpreted as a single conjunct to avoid a coordinate structure violation, or when an island violating analysis is avoided in cases of ambiguity where focus preferences would favor the island-violating analysis.

Many approaches to ellipsis have been pursued in the grammatical literature. One issue (Schwabe and Winkler 2003) is whether ellipsis ("deletion") can be unified with movement ("copy" and "deletion"). If ellipsis structures are constrained by islands, as movement is, this may remove one obstacle to treating them as "delete copy." There remain issues, however, about whether this unification is real and whether it is desirable (e.g., see Gullifer 2008[9]).

The overarching theme of the present paper is that assessing the implications of linguistic data requires consideration of both the grammar and theories of language performance. In order to arrive at the best theory of language we must consider various possibilities for where to place constraints on language: often they may belong in the grammar, but other times they may best be placed elsewhere. Various superficial properties of constraints may hint at cases where it is particularly important to consider both grammatical accounts and processing accounts of particular data or constraints. For example, it may be especially important to consider processing alternatives to grammar-only accounts in cases where the constraints at issue are dynamic, or when the same structure shows great variability in its acceptability depending on factors known to play a role in language processing, or when violations are sensitive to information structure, which is known to determine how attention is allocated and how likely it is that violations are detected. In the end, of course, it is the simplest most explanatory overall theory that will determine the status of constraints. But getting to the best theory may require considerable flexibility and open-mindedness in our assumptions about which sub-theory should explain the data.

Acknowledgements. This work was supported by NIH grant HD-18708.I am very grateful to an anonymous reviewer for insightful comments. I also wish to thank Chuck Clifton, Kyle Johnson, Angelika Kratzer, Jason Merchant, and Chris Potts for discussion of the ideas presented here.

Notes

1. In the eye movement study, none of the words appeared in all capital letters.
2. In the case of Bare Argument Ellipsis, the sentences are also degraded. One possible reason is that the variable-creation mechanism must violate an island. This should be easier if the variable is already part of the alternatives defined by the focus structure of the sentence. This predicts that (i), where the subject is focused should be more acceptable than examples without a contrastive accent on *John*.
   (i) *If JOHN went to the store, he bought twinkies. FRED too.*
3. Although antecedents in hypothetical conditionals (Edgington 2003) are at best marginally acceptable, antecedents in counter-factuals seem to be acceptable (see Garnham, Oakhill and Cain 1998). See Frazier and Clifton (in progress) for evidence that adding a nonactuality implicature or entailment to a hypothetical conditional antecedent makes the antecedent more acceptable. As we'll see below, non-actuality implicatures also help ellipsis in examples with flawed antecedents.
4. An anonymous reviewer raised the question of where information structure is placed on this view. It seems likely from my perspective that information structure plays a role in sentence grammar and 'discourse grammar,' i.e., the linguistic knowledge native speakers of a language have about the regularities governing the distribution of sentences in context.
5. Readers familiar with Frazier 2008 may wish to skip this section since it is largely a recap of that paper.
6. An anonymous reviewer asked why it is the antecedent that is repaired and not the elided constituent. On a structure-sharing view, these possibilities probably cannot be distinguished. However, if one thinks of copying as being distinct from structure sharing, then repair of the copied antecedent is what is at issue.
7. Examples of voice mismatches in sluicing don't always strike me as being completely unacceptable (e.g., *A famous politician told an obvious lie last night on national tv. I bet you can guess by which scumbag.*) Nevertheless, they do typically seem worse than corresponding VPE examples with voice mismatches, perhaps for the reason suggested in the text (the presence of a variable).
   Merchant (2008b) points out that pseudogapping does not tolerate voice mismatches (i), and notes that pseudogapping and VPE must target constituents at different levels, given that VPE can support quantifier float (ii) but pseudogapping (iii) cannot.
   (i) *Roses were brought by some and others did lilies.
   (ii) ***Many** of them have turned in their assignment already, but they haven't yet **all**.*
   (iii) ***Many** of them have turned in their take-home already, but they haven't yet their paper.* (****all***).

   These arguments are difficult to assess for me because most instances of pseudogapping, including the active form of pseudogapping (*Some brought roses and others did lilies*), are already highly degraded according to my own intuitions.

8. An anonymous reviewer, a native speaker of German, supplied the German counterparts to (22) given below in (i), along with the intuitions specified. I have checked the intuitions with two other native speakers of German, who agree that *was* is terrible, the non-island violating *wen* is perfect, and the d-linked interrogative *welchen* is intermediate. Thus, apparently the German facts are very similar to those in English.

   (i) Hans hat jemanden getroffen, der heute einen schrecklichen Unfall gesehen hat, aber er hat nicht gesagt *was ('what')/??welchen ('which one')/ wen ('who').

9. Gullifer (2008) presents the results of a self-paced reading study comparing the processing of filler-gap sentences and closely related cataphoric sluicing examples, illustrated in (i).

   (i) a. *I'm not sure who my Uncle is getting engaged to.*
   b. *I'm not sure who, but my Uncle is getting engaged to someone.*

   (ii) a. *I can't remember what,/ but the fisherman/* ***fitted something to his boat*****\n** *upon arriving/ at Old Crystal Lake.*
   b. *I can't remember what,/ but the fisherman/ who always wore the bright orange hat/* ***fitted something to his boat/n*** *upon arriving/ at Old Crystal Lake.*
   c *I can't remember what/ the fisherman/* ***fitted to his boat*****\n** *upon arriving/ at Old Crystal Lake.*
   d. *I can't remember what/ the fisherman/ who always wore the bright orange hat/* ***fitted to his boat*****\n** *upon arriving/ at Old Crystal Lake.*

   (The "/"s in examples mark presentation regions and "\n"s mark line breaks.) For the critical fourth region (bolded in (ii)), reading times were longer for the filler-gap sentences where the filler and gap were separated by a lot of material than for the 'short' filler-gap sentences, whereas the long sluicing sentences took no longer to read than their short counterparts. This shows that the two dependencies are processed differently, and presumably should not be given a grammatical treatment which unifies them.

Table 1. Average reading times in ms for regions of each version of the sentence. The critical region in the analysis is region 4, the region that contains the main verb phrase of the sentence.

Region	*1*	*2*	*3*	*4*	*5*	*6*
Short Sluice (SSI)	1001	878	1288	753	866	
Long Sluice (Lsl)	970	1083	1471	1208	778	848
Difference (LSI-SSI)	–32	205	1471	**–80**	24	–18
Short Filler-Gap (SFG)	886	638	975	733	800	
Long Filler-Gap (LFG)	891	984	1528	1060	706	829
Difference (LFG-SFG)	5	347	1528	**84**	–26	29

References

Arregui, Ana, Charles Clifton, Lyn Frazier, and Keir Moulton
2006 Processing elided VP s with flawed antecedents. *Journal of Memory & Language* 55: 232–246.

Biezma, Maria
2008 Subject preferences in Spanish replacives (tentative title).

Carlson, Katy
2002 *Parallelism and Prosody in the Processing of Ellipsis Sentences*. New York: Routledge.

Carlson, Katy, Michael W. Dickey, Lyn Frazier, and Charles Clifton
To appear Information structure expectations in sentence comprehension. *Quarterly Journal of Experimental Psychology.*

Chao, Wynn
1988 *On Ellipsis*. New York & London: Garland Publications.

Chung, Sandra, William Ladusaw, and James McCloskey
1995 Sluicing, and Logical Form. *Natural Language Semantics* 3: 239–282.

Cinque, G
1986 Bare quantifiers, quantified NPs and the notion of operator at S-structure. *Rivista di Grammatica* 11: 1–63.

Clifton, Charles, and Lyn Frazier
Submitted Imperfect ellipsis: Antecedents beyond syntax?

Cutler, Anne, and Jerry A. Fodor
1979 Semantic focus and sentence comprehension. *Cognition* 7: 49–59.

Dalrymple, Mary, Stuart Sheiber and Fernando C. N. Pereira
1991 Ellipsis and Higher-Order Unification. *Linguistics and Philosophy* 14: 399–452.

Edgington, D.
2003 What if? Questions about conditionals. *Language and Mind* 18(4): 380–401.

Fiengo, Robert and Robert May
1992 The eliminative puzzles of ellipsis. In: *Proceedings of the Stuttgart Ellipsis Workshop* (reported in Johnson, 1996).

Fodor, Janet D. and Fernanda Ferreira
1998 *Reanalysis in Sentence Processing*. Dordrecht: Kluwer Academic Publishers.

Frazier, Lyn and Charles Clifton
1998a Comprehension of sluiced sentences. *Language and Cognitive Processes* 13: 499–520.
1998b Sentence reanalysis, and visibility. In: Janet D. Fodor and Fernanda Ferreira (eds.), *Reanalysis in Sentence Processing*. Dordrecht: Kluwer Academic Publishers.

2005 The syntax-discourse divide: Processing ellipsis. *Syntax* 8(2): 121–174.

2008 Processing ellipsis: A processing solution to the undergeneration problem. In: Charles Chang and Hannah Haynie (eds.), *Proceedings of WCCFL* 26. Cascadilla Press.

In progress Non-actuality implicatures in ellipsis.

Garnham, Alan, Jane Oakhill and K Cain

1998 Selective retention of information about the superficial form of text: Ellipses with antecedents in main and subordinate clauses. *Quarterly Journal of Experimental Psycholoy* 51A: 19–39.

Grinder, John and Paul M. Postal

1971 Missing antecedents. *Linguistic Inquiry* 2: 269–312.

Gullifer, Jason

2008 Processing reverse sluicing: A contrast with processing filler-gap dependencies. Poster presented at CUNY Conference on Human Sentence Processing, Chapel Hill.

Hankamer, Jorge and Ivan Sag

1976 Deep and surface anaphora. *Linguistic Inquiry* 7: 391–428.

Hardt, Daniel

1993 Verb Phrase ellipsis: Form meaning, and processing. Ph.D. dissertation, University of Pennsylvania.

Hardt, Daniel and Maribel Romero, M.

2004 Ellipsis and discourse structure. *Journal of Semantics* 21: 375–414.

Johnson, Kyle

1996 When verb phrases go missing. *Glot International* 2(5): 3–9.

2008 *Topics in Ellipsis*. Cambridge: Cambridge University Press

Kennedy, Chris

2003 Ellipsis and syntactic representation. In: K Schwabe and S Winkler (eds.), *The interfaces: Deriving and Interpreting Omitted Structures*. John Benjamins Pub. Co.

Lasnik, Howard

2001 When can you save a structure by destroying it? In: Min-Joo Kim and Uri Strauss (eds.), *Proceedings of the North Eastern Linguistic Society 31* Volume 2: 301–320, GLSA: Amherst, MA.

Lobeck, Anne

1995 *Ellipsis: Functional Heads; Licensing and Identification*. Oxford: Oxford University Press.

Martin, Andrea and Brian McElree

2008 A content-addressable pointer mechanism underlies comprehension of verb phrase ellipsis. *Journal of Memory and Language* 58: 879–906.

Mauner, Gail, Michael Tanenhaus and Gregory Carlson, G.

1995 A note on parallelism effects in processing deep and surface verb-phrase anaphora. *Language and Cognitive Processes* 10: 1–12.

Mehler, Jacques
1963 Some effects of grammatical transformations on the recall of English sentences. *Journal of Verbal Learning and Verbal Behavior* 2: 346–351.

Merchant, Jason
2001 *The Syntax of Silence*. Oxford: Oxford University Press.
2005 Fragments and ellipsis. *Linguistics and Philosophy* 27: 661–738.
2007 Voice and ellipsis. University of Chicago manuscript.
2008a Variable island repair under ellipsis. In: Kyle Johnson (ed.), *Topics in Ellipsis*. Cambridge University Press: Cambridge.
2008b An asymmetry in voice mismatches in VP-ellipsis and pseudogapping. *Linguistic Inquiry* 39 (1): 169–179.

Murphy, G
1985 Psychological explanations of deep and surface anaphora. *Journal of Pragmatics* 9: 171–198.

Otero, Carlos
1972 Acceptable ungrammatical sentences in Spanish. *Linguistic Inquiry* 3: 233–242.

Rooth, Mats
1992 A theory of focus interpretation. *Natural Language Semantics* 1: 117–121.

Ross, John R.
1967 Constraints on variables in syntax. MIT doctoral dissertation.
1969 Guess who? In R Binnick, A Davison, G Green, and J Morgan (eds) *Proceedings of CLS* 5: 252–286.

Sag, Ivan
1976 Deletion and Logical Form. MIT doctoral dissertation. [Published by Garland Press, 1980.]

Sag, Ivan and Jorge Hankamer
1984 Toward a theory of anaphoric processing. *Linguistics and Philosophy* 7: 325–345.

Sanford, Anthony J. and Patrick Sturt
2002 Depth of processing in language comprehension: not noticing the evidence. *TRENDS in Cognitive Sciences* 6 (9): 382–386.

Schwabe, Kerstin and Susanne Winkler
2003 *The interfaces: Deriving and Interpreting Omitted Structures*. John Benjamins Publishing Company.

Sells, Peter
1984 Syntax and semantics of resumptive pronouns. University of Massachusetts doctoral dissertation.

Shieber, Stuard, Fernando C. N. Pereira and Mary Dalrymple
1999 Interaction of scope and ellipsis. In. S. Lappin and E. Benmamoun (eds.), *Fragments: Studies in Ellipsis and Gapping*. Oxford: Oxford University Press.

Staum, Laura and Ivan Sag
2007 Multiple *That*: A strategy for reducing integration costs. Poster presented at CUNY 2007, La Jolla, California.

Stolterfoht, Britta, Angela Friederici, Kai Alter and Anita Steube
2007 Processing focus structure and implicit prosody during reading: Differential ERP effects. *Cognition* 104 3: 565–590.

Tanenhaus, Michael and Gregory Carlson
1990 Comprehension of deep and surface verb phrase anaphors. *Language and Cognitive Processes* 5: 257–280.

Tanenhaus, Michael, Gregory Carlson, and Mark Seidenberg
1985 Do listeners compute linguistic representations? In: David Dowty, Laurie Karttunen and Arnold Zwicky (eds.), *Natural Language Parsing: Psychological, Computational and Theoretical Perspectives*, 359–408. Cambridge University Press.

Webber, Bonnie
1978 A formal approach to discourse anaphora. Harvard University doctoral thesis.

Williams, Edwin
1977 Discourse and Logical Form. *Linguistic Inquiry* 8: 101– 39.

Comparatives and types of *þonne* in Old English: Towards an integrated analysis of the data types in comparatives derivations*

Remus Gergel

1. Introduction

This chapter investigates the syntax of comparative structures, concentrating on one potential trigger of syntactic operator structures in Old English (OE), namely the word *þonne* ('than','then'). The study seeks to combine different types of linguistic evidence to support a simple analysis of comparative inversion (CI), which is at odds with the requirement that an English sentence have a subject raised to Spec,TP.

As a first description, CI is an optional process that constitutes a register-bound and often marked derivation for many speakers of Present Day English (PDE); see Emonds (1970: 7). It is nonetheless notably still licensed, as e.g. in (1), or in the example in (2), natural in a written register.

(1) *She hasn't bought as many souvenirs as has her husband.*

(2) *The Rochester scientists have now shown that parthenolide is in fact more selective at stopping cancer through apoptosis than was the standard drug cytarabine. (Townsend Letter for Doctors and Patients, July, 2005)*

The syntactic basics at stake are simply stated. A linearization with the subject after the finite, as is the case in a surfacing CI string, could be underlyingly caused by two major derivations. The standard analysis assumes that the auxiliary is in C and the subject in Spec,TP. The analysis to be defended here, on the other hand, reconstructs the assumed A-movement and refrains from movement to C. We will propose that the auxiliary is just in T, with the subject stranded even lower. This alternative option is parsimonious, but the dilemma it induces is real given the force of the EPP (theoretically, but also empirically – see most English sentences).

The line of argument for the alternative proposal will be that the step it involves is worth taking once enough data types are considered since their totality would remain unexplained otherwise. My main data come chiefly from diachronic syntax but I also present some synchronic syntactic arguments and preliminary arguments rooted in the information structural notion of contrast in a historical context.

Within its diachronic core area, the chapter equally weighs up evidence of different types. I begin comparing the results of a corpus-based syntactic investigation (see Gergel 2008 for a more detailed analysis) with the results of a study based on selected textual material (here particularly *Beowulf*) to test for syntactic and contrast properties in comparatives more generally.

The paper is structured as follows. In section 2, I highlight the main differences between the standard analysis and the current proposal. The article then discusses several types of evidence, starting out from the suggestions in Culicover and Winkler (2008) and Gergel (2008): In section 3, I discuss synchronic arguments. Section 4 gives an overview of the historical development of the construction and its next of kin drawing on the Penn-Helsinki Corpora of English. Section 5 presents a specialized case study investigating the role of *þonne* in early Old English more closely. Section 6 gives an interpretation of the way in which the types of evidence revolving around CI relate to one another.

2. Two possibilities for comparative inversion: A V2 perspective

A first analysis of the construction might seem to necessitate the head C as the landing site of the finite auxiliary and the Spec,TP stranded behind in the standard position hosting the subject (see Merchant 2003, Potts 2002, Gergel, Gengel, and Winkler 2007, among others, for discussions). Such a derivation is sketched in (3).

(3) C-based analysis of comparative inversion (genuine V2)

$[_{CP} \ldots$ **C (verb, Aux, etc.)** $[_{TP}$**Subj.** **T** $[_{VP}\ t_{subject}\ t_{finite\ verb} \ldots]]]$

The C-based analysis given in (3) involves a classical V2 derivation (see, e.g., den Besten 1983). It has certain theoretical virtues including a parallel analysis to, say, questions in English or broader V2 effects in the other Germanic languages (even though it already appears in an unexpected corner of the grammar from the Germanic perspective, namely comparatives). Further, it would also comply with the EPP feature of PDE without further ado, the subject position being filled structurally high, in Spec,TP.

A simpler alternative, however, is *not* to move, as shown in (4), where the auxiliary is not displaced to C and the subject stays in situ, i.e. in Spec,VP.

(4) T-based analysis of comparative inversion

$[_{CP} \ldots \text{C} \ [_{TP} \_ \ \textbf{T (verb, Aux, etc.)} \ [_{VP} \ \textbf{Subj.} \ t_{\textit{finite verb}} \ldots]]]$

The T-based analysis schematized in (4) is an English-type of V2 (see Haeberli 2002; Speyer forth.; Kroch 2007 for such proposals; for introductory purposes: It is not a genuine V2 effect in the sense going back to den Besten 1983, but one targeting solely the Infl-domain, specifically T here, and giving a "fake" impression of V2 in a subset of the cases).

I pointed out the lack of movement above because the only movement that might occur in (4) is orthogonal to the analysis of CI in and by itself (even though it needs to be controlled for). The lower movement schematized above, that is the one from V to T, is an independent process that has to do with the V-to-I/T property of a language or stage of a language (see e.g. Kroch 1989, Roberts 1993). Its presence can be disregarded here (for arguments in favor of its independence see Gergel 2008).

All in all, the derivation in (4) has the advantage of being economical from a theoretical point of view, but at the cost of violating the EPP. It is hence opportune to argue for it first, as I shall try to do next.

3. Synchronic arguments against a genuine V2 effect

Even though the standard analysis allows us to capture certain tendencies concerning various ellipsis types from a grammatical point of view (see, for example, Merchant 2003, Park and Niinuma 2004 for suggested implications regarding VP-ellipsis and pseudogapping), it can be improved in terms of both explanatory and descriptive adequacy in other respects.[1]

A first theoretical argument that makes the standard analysis problematic comes from the fact that it would achieve subject-auxiliary inversion by moving the auxiliary from T, a characteristic of root transformations (see Emonds 1970), but without being obligatory, as is usually the case with such transformations. Further, a comparative is not a root clause.

A direct empirical argument against it can be drawn from sequences of multiple auxiliaries, as in (5) drawn here from the Cambridge Grammar (see Huddleston and Pullum 2002).

(5) *It is no more expensive than would be the system you are proposing.*

Such examples make a V2 implementation implausible. It is not the case that residual V2 effects involving complex heads are unimaginable or unattested by themselves. In fact, they appear in various guises and conditioned in contexts that differ from the standard ones known from Germanic (cf. Legendre 2000 for recent discussion of Basque, or Hegarty 2005: Chapter 2 on Tohono O'odham, and references cited in both sources). But the nature of such residual V2 patterns is also quite different from the English phenomenon of stacked auxiliaries in a number of respects. In such cases there is typically independent syntactic evidence for complex heads or clustering properties, unlike in English, where a run of the mill V2 (in PDE this is almost necessarily a question or it involves, e.g., negative preposing) cannot accommodate two auxiliaries.

Next, recall that a theoretically and empirically important alarm seems to come from the EPP. But if the data are considered in more detail, it turns out that comparative clauses in fact allow violations of this constraint in more contexts. This special lexical property (in the sense of Borer 1984), which can be projected in comparatives, is instantiated in several classes up to the present, as shown in the subjectless free relative in (6), drawn from the British National Corpus.

(6) *Besides, meanwhile, I'm still smoking more than __ is good for me.* (BNC - CAG 1423)

Culicover and Winkler (2008) and Gergel (2008) discuss additional synchronic tests, which are purported to exclude the C-derivation and support the English type of V2. Due to lack of space for laying out all the background, I refer to those contributions for the syntactic reasoning. What is particularly relevant here is that an additional type of data is used in each study – focus on the one hand, diachronic-comparative data on the other.

Let me then solely mention one particular and central fact discussed by Culicover and Winkler, given that it involves a different type of evidence, viz. the one rooted in the information-structural component (see Winkler 2005 for architectural suggestions in this domain). The claim is that CI arises as a condition of contrastive focus, i.e. the construction (in their account also in a more technical sense) requires a contrastive focus reading. An example in point is (7).

(7) *ANNA ran much faster than could have any of her FRIENDS.*

Culicover and Winkler show that the subject of the comparative clause in (7) in particular is contrastively focused.

The contrast observation is of special interest since it raises the question whether this condition has always held true from a historical perspective and whether it has always had the same predictive power in the grammar of CI (along the lines of 'Only use CI under contrast conditions'). In the next section, I give an overview of the historical developments to lay out what is at stake in structural terms in the diachronic analysis of CI. I then return to the question of contrast placed in the diachronic context, and in OE in particular, within the qualitative case study developed in section 5.

4. The syntax of comparative inversion in the context of Old English

In this section, I sketch what I take to be the basic development of CI at the main historical stages of the language with focus on OE. To this end, I have made use of the Penn-Helsinki Corpora of Historical English (Kroch, Santorini, and Delfs 2004; Kroch and Taylor 2000; Taylor, Warner, Pintzuk, and Beths 2003) and follow the argumentation discussed in more detail in Gergel (2008).

The grammar of OE provides a useful diagnostic to distinguish between classical V2 and the English type of V2 derivations (see Pintzuk 1991; Fischer et al. 2000; Kroch et al. 2000; Haeberli 2002, among others). Genuine V2 and the English-type of V2 with the verb ending in the Infl-domain are primarily distinguishable on the basis of the position of subject pronouns. Thus, with full DPs, the appearance of V2 can be caused either by movement of the verb to T or to C. With pronoun subjects, however, only the types of verb movement that are generated by genuine V2 (i.e. to C) can display the verb left-linearized relative to the subject. This has to do with the relative high position of the pronouns that is well known for the OE stage of the language (with which this chapter is concerned; see, for example, Fischer et al. 2000 for extensive discussion of the facts regarding this point). An example of the former, high-landing type of movement is a question operator; an example of the latter is topicalization (cf. in particular Kroch, Taylor and Ringe 2000). These two types are illustrated in (8) and (9), respectively.

(8) C-based (genuine) V2: e.g., the case of wh-questions
hwi sceole we oþres mannes niman? (AELS 24.188)
why should we another man's take

(9) T-based "V2" in OE: e.g., the case of topicalization:
a. *& of heom twam is eall manncynn cumen* (WHom 6.52)
and of them two is all mankind come

b. *scortlice ic hæbbe nu gesæd ymb þa þrie dælas*
briefly I have now spoken about the three parts
(Or 9.18)

Next, we can test whether the scope of the movement involved in CI was T or C since OE also had subject-finite inversion in comparative clauses, as illustrated below.

(10) hwæt is atelicor geðuht ... [þonne is ðæs hreoflian lic ...]?
what is more-horrible seemed than is the leper's body
What seems more horrible than does the leprous body?
(cocathom1, ÆCHom_I,_23:370.157.4656)

In (10), then, the finite verb *is* inverts with the subject *ðæs hreoflian lic*.

I next describe how the test can be constructed in conjunction with what is known about verb movement to T vs. C, as evidenced from examples such as (8) and (9) above, now transferred to comparatives. The idea is to determine whether the inversion of the type shown in (10) in OE could also invert pronoun subjects. Call this the pronoun test: Either the finite verb in a comparative can raise past a pronoun subject, or it cannot. The test makes a clear prediction for OE: If CI also inverts pronouns in OE, it will have the verb in C, patterning with (8). If it does not, it exhibits the finite verb in the Infl-domain (under current assumptions in T), patterning with (9).

Let me now turn to the main result of the corpus study regarding the qualitative aspect of the pronoun test, which was conducted by checking clauses that had both an overt finite element and an overt subject. While inversion is attested in comparatives in general, as mentioned, the historical evidence also indicates that inversion in such cases could not displace a verb to the left of a pronoun (i.e. structurally higher to the C position) during the OE period. In particular I could not find the configuration in (11) in the OE database and assume that it was unproductive at best. (For discussion of the Middle English developments in the context of the changes in V2, see, for example, Kroch, Taylor, and Ringe 2000).

(11) Old English pronoun restriction for CI:
*[COMPARATIVE CLAUSE [FINITE-VERB] [SUBJECT-PRONOUN]]

In addition to this qualitative test, the corpora also allow us to obtain estimates on the general development of comparative clauses in the language. Estimates such as the ones given in (12) were obtained.

(12) Overview of inverting clausal comparative structures

OE:	223/5114 =	4.36%
ME:	135/1639 =	8.23%
EModE:	31/2497 =	1.24%

The estimates in (12) might have to be taken with some caution since we are dealing with a construction that is sensitive to syntax but also extra-syntactic factors in a changing environment. But they are not entirely accidental. If fact, they are explained if we add two more diachronic ingredients. First, I assume that ModE only allows the Spec,TP filled by a null-expletive (Haeberli 2000) as an archaic and marginal possibility, as evidenced in the CI cases and corroborated from other special cases in comparative clauses. Hence the dramatic dip towards ModE. Second, assuming with Pintzuk (1991) that the directionality of the TP was in the relevant cases roughly evenly split between the head-final and head-initial option in OE, but not in ME, we can explain the doubling of the incidence of CI during ME as follows. Nearly half of the comparative clauses of OE that have the underlying derivation to generate inversion (that is, via movement to T and leaving the subject lower) will not show it on the surface because they happen to be in a head-final TP, i.e. in a [VP T] structure. This offers an explanation for the basic numerical trends on the currently defended T-based version of V2. This particular prediction borne out on the T-based analysis fails on a C-based analysis of CI. An explanation based on putative variation in the headedness of the CP (instead of the TP, as proposed) is not available because the CP domain is head-initial at both stages of the language and the numerical change could not be explained in the same way.

To summarize: There are emerging arguments stemming from two different data types, diachronic data and information-structural data, that support a simpler analysis of CI (see Culicover and Winkler 2008 and Gergel 2008). A rather clear result from the point of view of the corpus-based investigation was that a movement to C in the context of OE runs counter not only to economy but also to the most important test developed for verb movement at the time, the pronoun test. We observed that there is indeed a pronoun ban on CI in OE. Therefore CI does not pattern with C-based inversion. Further, the numerical patterns are more adequately explained on an analysis that assumes the finite element to be just in the T-domain.

5. An investigation of þonne in the Old English of Beowulf

In this section, I discuss the results of a specialized case study concerned with *þonne* (together with its spelling variants in OE). On the one hand, here we will test for its operator behavior in comparative contexts. The section thus complements the data types discussed above by conducting detailed analysis from one lexeme rather than from an annotated corpus. The aim is, just as above, to decide on the most appropriate syntactic representation by using different types of data. To do so, we will in a second step also look contrastively at instances of *þonne* that did not introduce comparative clauses, but which provide additional testing ground for the two types of inversion discussed above (viz. T-based and C-based). Given that, for instance, the comparative and the temporal type of *þonne* were originally related (see Mitchell 1985), we will further investigate whether comparative *þonne* already had outstanding syntactic properties compared to temporal *þonne* in the earliest comprehensive records of English.

To this end, I conducted this study on the material available in the poem of *Beowulf*. The edition I have used as a primary textual source is Jack (1994). In conjunction with it, I have used the electronic version of the poem made available by the University of Toronto, which in turn draws on further sources; cf. Dobbie (1953). I will mostly have to leave further philological issues regarding the text aside. I simply point out relevant issues for the linguistic task at hand when they become relevant.[2] After an introduction, the section analyzes the types of *þonne* that might have behaved as operators according to several criteria. Recall from section 4 that an operator-type of movement (such as the one in questions) displaces the finite verb to C, i.e. a classical (C-based) V2 structure. I use the term operator in this simple sense here, meaning a syntactic configuration that triggers movement to C (see Fischer et al. 2000). The concrete question will be how *þonne* behaves in regard to inversion in the grammar of *Beowulf*. In addition, I will address the question whether and how comparative *þonne* might have introduced contrast in the text of the poem.

5.1. Motivating and describing the data source

Why choose *Beowulf* and textual work to investigate a syntactic phenomenon? While this case study does not allow larger-scale overviews comparable to the ones based on the more systematic estimates of the previous section, it has potential advantages in complementary respects from the point of view of the data types involved (cf. Pintzuk and Kroch 1989 for a similar case study on the headedness of VP). A specific advantage of choosing *Beowulf* stems from the possibility of investigating CI at a stage of the language that was closer to the other Germanic languages also in its syntactic features. This is of interest from a comparative perspective for two reasons. First, both the philological and the syntactic tradition have agreed on classifying *Beowulf* as reflecting an early stage of OE based on oral epic poetry (see Klaeber 1922; Pintzuk and Kroch 1989, among others). Second, since we can observe that Continental West Germanic – to which OE has often been also syntactically likened (see e.g. van Kemenade 1987's seminal study) – does *not* have comparative inversion, we are interested to see whether the early OE syntax of *Beowulf* did, or whether it rather converged with a language like German, which lacks the possibility of inversion constructions in comparatives.

Let me also mention a few additional points for choosing textual data-work of this type for syntactic purposes: A text-based investigation allows one to control for each token of the database individually in an easily practicable manner. Similarly, it allows us to control for context quickly. To a certain degree, the metrical organization of the poem finally also enables one to investigate properties pertaining to the contrast of the standards of comparison and focus-based syntactic isolation of the compared material (see Culicover and Winkler 2008; Gergel et al. 2007; Merchant 2003; Winkler 2005).

5.2. The overall distribution of *þONNE*

I next describe the pool of tokens that were extracted by beginning with a superset of the potential spelling variants. I then analyze the actual occurrences of the operator along with its attested variants with regard to several criteria continuing the discussion into the following subsections.

To begin, the Oxford Dictionary of English (OED) mentions no less than fifteen variants for *þonne* throughout the history of English, which were to lead up to *than* through a final step of spelling correction. The correction consisted in distinguishing the comparative operator – orthographically, that is – from the temporal one (corresponding to *then* in current English) during the seventeenth century. In view of their earlier history, the similarity of *then* and *than* is not entirely accidental, however. Nonetheless, I will argue that syntactically they present some differences even when they are largely identical in form, as in archaic OE. They instantiate distinguishable types of inversion triggers. I analyze their common ancestors in order to put to the test the diachronic inversion patterns inspected in the previous section and analyze factors such as pronoun syntax and contrast in various types of comparatives and non-comparative structures.

Let me first describe the distribution of forms. I searched the poem for all variants given in the OED. Of the 15 variants, not surprisingly, only 3 are attested in *Beowulf*, an early OE text. There were a total of 73 instances of ÞONNE in the poem. Of these, 57 tokens had the form *þonne*, 15 tokens involved the variant *ðonne* and there was one (relevant) comparative token of the reduced form *þon*.[3] I have disregarded occurrences of additional items that are orthographically overlapping with potential variants of *þonne* but which are grammatically irrelevant items for immediate purposes. Specifically, determiners have been disregarded. The standard example of a determiner at issue here is *ðone*, which in OE could be a spelling variant of both the comparative operator and an accusative masculine determiner or a relative pronoun. What has been taken into account, on the other hand, is the homophonous but temporally or discourse-functioning *þonne,* again together with its spelling variants, in particular *ðonne*, as well as adverbs going by the same names. All of these could have been potential operators, and hence inversion triggers. (In what follows, all relevant spelling variants are meant when I use ÞONNE.) I will further mention a few additional items that are independent lexically but related either syntactically or semantically as we go along, but in essence this part of the study is one concerned with ÞONNE in the manner described.

Let me next give an overview in the distribution of meaning. A clear comparison involving degree semantics was involved in 17 pertinent tokens. The originally temporally flavored ÞONNE is thus the numerically predominant item used in the text of the poem. (A more detailed view of the taxonomy in meaning is given below since not all non-comparatives are temporal, not all temporal tokens behave the same, etc.) Given that ÞONNE could be an operator in comparative and temporal contexts, I next describe both types and then a few derivative subtypes. I then focus on the syntactic patterns obtaining in the comparative and temporal contexts. Finally, I compare the types of inversion in the various contexts with the aim of checking whether this study correlates with our previous conclusions.

5.3. First potential operator uses of ÞONNE (non-comparative)

The majority of the non-comparative uses of ÞONNE have relatively clear temporal readings. Typically they are rough equivalents of 'when' and sometimes 'while', or a quantificational reading such as 'whenever'. (Current-English *while*, originally a noun, showed sporadic signs of grammaticalization only later on during the OE and the early ME period; cf. Mitchell 1985 and Eckardt 2007). Examples in point for ÞONNE are given in (13).

(13) Temporal subordinator interpretations of ÞONNE

a. ***þonne*** *he swulces hwæt secgan*
when he of-such-a matter something tell
wolde (B. 880)
wanted
'when he wanted to say something about these matters'

b. *weaxeð ond wridað,* ***þonne*** *se weard*
grows and flourishes while the guardinan
swefeð (B. 1741)
sleeps

c. *Swa sceal man don* ***þonne*** *he æt guðe gegan*
so shall man do whenever he at battle gain
þenceð (B. 1535)
thinks
'So man shall do whenever he wishes to win in war.'

At the same time however, not all non-comparative uses of ÞONNE can be categorized as unambiguous temporal subordinators. For one, the label subordinator does not yield an adequate characterization with respect to the full range of data. There is evidence that some of the clauses introduced by ÞONNE had the status of main clauses. This ties in with the general status of many partial subordinators in the OE period that could also be used as introducers of main clauses and the use of correlative constructions in various domains including the temporal one.[4] An example of such a temporal main clause introduced by the adverb ÞONNE is given in (14).

(14) ***þonne*** *cwið æt beore se ðe beah*
then speaks at (the) beer-drinking who (the) precious-object
gesyhð (B. 2041)
sees
'Then speaks at beer-drinking the one who sees the precious object.'

A combination of the main-clause and the subordinate-clause use in a typical correlative construction is illustrated in (15).

(15) ***Ðonne*** *wæs þeos medoheal on morgentid, drihtsele*
then was this mead-hall at morning, noble hall
dreorfah, ***þonne*** *dæg lixte, …* (B. 484)
blood-stained, when day shone forth
'Then this mead-house and noble hall was stained with blood in the morning, when the daylight broke.'

Even beyond the subordination issue, not all *non*-comparative clauses are however properly characterized as temporal either. First, there is the possibility of ambiguity, e.g. commonly between a temporal and a conditional reading (but potentially also between others), cf. (16).

(16) *þonne wig cume,*
if/when war comes

Second, ÞONNE as an introducer of the consequent in conditional sequences was grammaticalized by the OE period; (17).

(17) ***gyf*** *þonne Frysna hwylc frecnan spræce ðæs morþorhetes*
if then Frisian anyone audacious speech the deadly feud
myndgiend wære, ***þonne*** *hit sweordes ecg seðan scolde.*
reminding were, then it sword's edge settle should
(B. 1104)
'If any Frisian, moreover, by audacious speech, should remind of that murderous feud, then by sword's edge must it be settled.'

Third, there are a series of examples in which non-comparative *þonne* is used with an adverbial discourse function rather than a temporal one; (18).

(18) *Næs þæt þonne mætost mægenfultuma* (B. 1455)
neg-was that then the least powerful-helps
'Nor was that then the least of powerful helps'

Finally, the question is how the potential operator ÞONNE behaves with respect to verb movement and inversion. What can be observed is that the non-comparative ÞONNE as a temporal adverb can, rather expectedly for the period, trigger movement that reaches C; cf. (19).[5]

(19) ***ðonne*** *wene* ***ic*** *to þe wyrsan geþingea.* (B. 525)
then expect I for you worse outcome
'Then I expect a worse outcome for you.'

Recalling the pronoun test, the reason why the verb in (19) must have reached the head C is that it inverts with a pronoun subject (see Fischer et al. 2000; Kroch et al. 2000; Pintzuk 1991; a.o.).

5.4. Back to comparative *þONNE*

This subsection is divided into two. In the first part, I address the overtly clausal comparatives in the poem and compare them to the corpus data of section 4. In the second part, examples that are reduced on the surface will be analyzed with the goal of testing contrast properties in the standard of comparison.

Despite the fact that fully sentential comparative structures in *Beowulf* are scarce, they are attested in some forms (cf., e.g., (20)). The example in (21) further shows that a full-DP subject could undergo inversion in a comparative.[6]

(20) a. *Scyld wel gebearg life ond lice læssan hwile*
The shield well protected life and body a shorter while
mærum þeodne þonne his myne
for the renowned prince than his purpose
sohte, (B. 2570)
required.

b. *bat unswiðor þonne his ðiodcyning þearfe*
(and) bit less strongly than its noble king
hæfde (B. 2578)
had need of

(21) *Næfre ic maran geseah eorla ofer eorþan ðonne is*
never I greater saw of warriors on earth than is
eower sum (B. 247)
of-you one
'I have never seen a greater warrior on earth than is one of you.'

The fact that comparatives can invert with a finite element already in the earliest comprehensive sample of the language is significant from a grammatical point of view. For one, it illustrates a crucial difference from West Germanic comparatives, which do not generate CI (perhaps also due to their more consistent head-final structures than those of OE; see section 4 and the next point). Recall that the text of *Beowulf* has been shown to exhibit predominantly head-final order in the VP (Pintzuk and Kroch 1989). But the directionality does not prove to be as strongly head-final within the TP. CI also shows just this, because in a uniquely head-final TP it would not be visible, as discussed in section 4 above. While the competition view (Kroch 1989; Pintzuk 1991) allows the variation between T-VP and VP-T orders, a different question remains as to what may drive the discrepancy (and the time lag) between the headedness-developments in the two domains (VP and TP). A possible answer to this question can be found in the directionality of syntactic change proposed in Biberauer et al. (2008) and related work. Developing earlier observations of A. Holmberg, Biberauer et al. propose an account of how linearization interacts with language change phrased in terms of the Final-Over-Final-Constraint. The bottom line of the constraint (arguably the constraint itself being derived from phase theory) is that a change within head-final phrase structures must start at the top (and not at the bottom) of the syntactic tree.

Applying the proposal to the language state in *Beowulf*, the directionality observation just mentioned explains why the syntax of the poem might be less conservative in TP headedness than in VP headedness, since a change in the former must precede a change in the latter. That means that while the structure of the VP still has the (conservative) head-final version (Pintzuk and Kroch 1989; Fischer et al. 2000), the headedness of the TP is already mixed. In fact, it must have been so, before a directionality change within the VP could have occurred.

But what about inversion with pronouns in comparatives? There was no occurrence of subject-auxiliary inversion involving a pronoun subject here either, i.e. as in the OE study based on the parsed corpus. This might be a fact about the comparatively small size of the sample, but notice that there is neither a lack of pronouns, nor of stressed pronouns (as I show next specifically for comparative phrases). We therefore draw the intermediate conclusion that there was a syntactic basis for CI in *Beowulf*, in that the poem patterns unexceptionally within the context of OE syntax as far as the pronoun restriction and CI are concerned. In order to show the properties of pronouns and of the compared material more generally, we next need to consider so-called phrasal comparatives.

Apparent phrasal comparatives come in various sorts depending on the types (and sizes) of ellipsis which they license. I say 'ellipsis' on the assumption that most of the material in phrasal comparatives is a reduced Spell-Out from the sentential cases (Lechner 2004). This is a matter of taxonomical convenience here. (Arguments are also available for the view in languages like English, though certainly not universally.[7]) The more significant points for current purposes, however, are (i) to determine what types of structure can be stranded after *ÞONNE*; (ii) whether there is any common characteristic that they share; and (iii) whether the examples and what they might have in common can shed any light on the relationship between comparatives and focus structure.

A first empirical point here is that the phrasal comparatives following *ÞONNE* display a broad range of possibilities. A sample is given in (22), illustrating (non-exhaustively) some of the categories: bare nouns, contrastive full DPs, PPs, and arguably gapped or reduced VPs, respectively (we may remain agnostic on whether the latter involve internal ellipsis – the question is orthogonal here; cf Johnson 2006, Winkler 2005, among others).

(22) a. *Deað bið sella eorla gehwylcum þonne edwitlif!* (B. 2890)
death is better warrior each-one than life of disgrace
'Death is better for all warriors than a life of disgrace.'

b. *þæt ic merestrengo maran ahte,... ðonne ænig oþer man* (B. 533)
that I strength in the sea more had than any other man

c. *oftor micle ðonne on ænne sið* (B. 1579)
oftener far than (on) an only time

d. *No ic me an herewæsmun hnagran talige guþgeweorca, þonne Grendel hine* (B. 677)
neg I me in vigour-in-war poorer tally warlike-deeds than Grendel himself
'Of vigour in war no poorer I count me, in war-like deeds, than Grendel (counts) himself.'

A second point in terms of the derivations involved: a technical possibility that comes to mind is that the stripped standards of comparison in such examples have been evacuated to edge positions outside the clausal domain and survived the deletion of their sister structures (see Winkler 2005 for discussion). Notice in particular that pronouns could naturally also be the complement of *ÞONNE*; cf. (23) for an illustration with a simple and an intensified pronoun, respectively (even though, recall, pronouns are not attested in the poem with a following finite element in comparative clauses).

(23) a. *se wæs betera ðonne* ***ic***. (B. 469)
he was better than I

b. *forþon þe he ne uþe þæt aenig oðer man æfre mærða þon ma middangeardes gehedde under heofenum þonne* ***he sylfa***: (B. 503)
because he not allowed that any other man ever glorious deed the more (on) earth heeded under heavens than he himself.
'Because he did not grant that any other man cared more about ever glorious deeds under the heavens than himself.'

Finally, there is a potentially interesting property that is shared by all phrasal comparatives that are complements of *ÞONNE* in the poem (pronouns and non-pronouns alike). They are exceptionlessly verse-final. This also makes it likely that they were focused and complements the findings in that it shows how focus is a necessary condition in all the pertinent comparative contexts even though pronouns did not invert with T in the OE comparatives. This fact is in line with other types of T-based, and not C-based, V2 contexts in the language.

On the whole, we have seen in this section that syntactically distinct types of *þONNE* make themselves visible in the OE database inspected and that the comparative bears some of the syntactic features characteristic for CI that were identified in the previous sections. A final question is what the grammatical connection might be between the original adverbial uses of *þONNE* and the latter head that could select a comparative clause. Syntactically, an answer lends itself to the question from what has been proposed by Elly van Gelderen on grammaticalization and economy in a series of contributions (see, e.g., van Gelderen 2004). The key observation is that adverbs can grammaticalize to higher positions first as phrasal entities, and they can subsequently reanalyze to heads. This ties in with the status of the relevant *than* as a complementizer (Hankamer 1973). That the first step is upward is derivable from more general principles about movement dependencies applying in language change (see also Roberts and Roussou 2003 in particular). Possible motivation for the second reanalysis step may lie in the tendency towards a leaner structure, once more following van Gelderen's work on economy.

6. Concluding remarks: the relationship of the data types involved

Synchronic investigation for the purposes of syntactic analysis is the main place where linguistic investigations can best be conducted in general. But the case of archaic phenomena such as CI also makes it useful to look for additional data types and see how they relate to one another. In this connection, the paper discussed both quantitative and qualitative aspects chiefly based on two types of diachronic sources. It analyzed clausal comparative structures based on a corpus study and lexically extracted data based on the OE poem of *Beowulf*. While the first type of data is best suited to yield a possible estimate on the overall developments, the second has been an initial step to shed light on the history of one of the main potential syntactic operators in comparative clauses and the contrast properties in introduced. As conclusions of the current investigation, we can note:

(i) CI was available from the earliest OE records. This opens up the genesis question in relationship to Proto-Germanic for future research, and is grammatically significant because it lends credence to the proposal that the phenomenon patterned in a special way from the beginning of the extensive records in English, namely with the so-called English (T-based) type of V2, which is independently known in the history of the language.

(ii) The hypothesis of the T-based English-type of V2 effects was confirmed on a larger scale by the corpus work and by probing both quantitatively and qualitatively for the most plausible type of derivation.

(iii) Given the focus-structural basis of the phenomenon in current English together with the way it dovetails with the syntactic options of early English, an additional track has been opened. That is whether, for instance, an earlier option that was originally hard-wired has developed into a focus construction. This would be in itself interesting since it is a time-honored idea that *syntax* is but a fossilization of information structure. However, the idea of such a trend must be qualified for the case at hand, specifically in both potential directions (syntax > focus, focus > syntax). Plainly put, there seems to be a good share of syntax *and* information structure involved in CI at both stages of the language. Deeper investigation into the focus facts of early English is required to clear our understanding in comparatives as well, but from this preliminary investigation into the matter, I cannot see one entirely "over-ranking" the other in the constructions that I considered. In the latter connection I have illustrated two basic things: The syntactic basis of the phenomenon is not broken anywhere in the poem (no violation the pronoun restriction in OE, i.e. no auxiliary inversion with pronouns even though pronouns could be stressed at the time – this can be contrasted in further work with later Middle English examples. At the same time, it is plausible to assume that the comparatives that were analyzed here included a type of focus contrast – projecting up to various phrases (DPs, VPs, TPs) and including stressed pronouns in the phrasal comparatives.

A final question concerns the theoretical advantages that correlate with this incursion into various data types. A conspicuous historical argument consisted in excluding the C position. Next, if we accept the conclusion that the finite element does not move to C, then the strongest argument based on contrast properties (Culicover and Winkler 2008) that I illustrated here consisted in forcing the subject to stay lower than Spec,TP due to its contrast properties. Notice that if the auxiliary stays under T and *at the same time* the subject is contrasted and supposed to be isolated at the right-edge of a phonological phrase, then the subject must not comply with the EPP, in that it cannot bypass T and get to Spec,TP (or else it would not comply with its right-edge isolation). And the two results, namely of keeping both the auxiliary and the subject lower than standardly assumed, constitute the essence of the proposal that has been defended.

Notes

* This study is an attempt to reconcile the conclusions from the historical data in comparatives, for which it draws on Gergel (2008), with the insight from the information-structural conditions of inversion (see especially Culicover and Winkler 2008). For comments that helped improve the present chapter I remain particularly grateful to S. Featherston and S. Winkler. All remaining errors are my responsibility, of course.

1. While ellipsis is not the concern of this paper, it has also not been shown that the generalizations about ellipsis proposed could *not* be phrased at a lower structural height. In particular in the spirit of Merchant's (2001) E-feature, one could assume that anything can be deleted if the structure in question satisfies certain conditions, such as contrast (see Winkler 2005 for suggestions).
2. One place where the edition makes a difference is the following:

   (i) *þone yldo bearn æfre gefrunon*
   which men children ever should hear of
   'which the children of men should hear of forever.' (B. 70)

   In the edition I follow, the subordinate is rendered as a relative clause, but in others it is given as a comparative (including the online edition mentioned). I follow Jack's line of reasonsing (Jack 1994: 32) and his sources on this point noting that there is no comparative adjective in the surrounding context for the comparative clause to be licensed. While it is not impossible to have comparatives without an adjective in the comparative form, in OE this is not a known strategy of expressing gradable constructions.
3. I use the term 'reduced' here in a descriptive phonological, not a historical-chronological way. It is a matter of debate whether the reduced or the expanded form was available on a comparative reading first (Mitchell 1985: 619).
4. Notice the use of correlative strategies in constructions also semantically related to varieties ÞONNE such as *swa* and *þa*, respectively.
5. This is partly reminiscent of the operator *þa* (which often shares the meaning). I leave *þa* aside since its behavior is much better studied than ÞONNE.
6. Though further examples of ÞONNE triggering inversion are attested, I believe (21) is the only genuinely comparative one among them, which also shows the inversion overtly and properly. For non-comparative examples of ÞONNE see above. For an example of a comparative, which does at least descriptively not show proper inversion (using a trick of a resumptive *þa* in the higher position and an extraposed heavy relative), cf. example (i) below.

   (i) ... *þon þa dydon þe hine æt frumsceafte forð onsendon* (B. 43)
   than those had done that him at the beginning forth had sent

7. See, for example, Lechner (2004) and Bhatt and Takahashi (2007) for recent discussions. While the arguments are subject to cross-linguistic variation, one of the major empirical arguments of the purely phrasal analysis in PDE is not verified in OE. Instead of the case-variation between the predicate-ellipsis (*Mary is taller than I*

am) and the phrasal comparative (*Mary is taller than me*), the only pattern I was able to find in OE had the nominative in both ellipsis types (i.e. *ðonne ic/he* etc.), unless a different case was (orthogonally) imposed by a governing verb or preposition. I thank A. Kroch for raising a question that prompted this argument.

References

Beck, Sigrid
2007 Comparatives and superlatives. Ms. Universität Tübingen.

den Besten, Hans
1983 On the interaction of root transformations and lexical deletive rules. In: Werner Abraham (ed.), *On the Formal Syntax of the Westgermania*, 47–131. Amsterdam/Philadelphia: John Benjamins.

Bhatt, Rajesh and Shoichi Takahshi
2007 Direct comparisons: Resurrecting the direct analysis of phrasal comparatives. *Proceedings of SALT 17*, Ithaca, NY. CLC Publications.

Biberauer, M. Theresa, Anders Holmberg, Glenda Newton, Michelle Sheehan and Ian G. Roberts
2008 On impossible changes and borrowings: The Final-Over-Final-Constraint. Paper presented at the workshop *Continuity and Change in Grammar*. University of Cambridge.

Borer, Hagit
1984 *Parametric Syntax. Case Studies in Semitic and Romance Languages*. Dordrecht: Foris.

Culicover, Peter W. and Susanne Winkler
2008 English focus inversion constructions. Ms. Ohio State University and Universität Tübingen.

Dobbie, Elliott V.K.
1953 *Beowulf and Judith*. (The Anglo-Saxon Poetic Records 4.) London: Routledge and Kegan.

Eckardt, Regine
2007 Grammaticalization and semantic reanalysis. Semanticsarchive.net.

Emonds, Joseph E.
1970 *Root and structure preserving transformations*. Indiana University Linguistics Club: Bloomington.

Fischer, Olga, Ans van Kemenade, Willem Koopman and Wim van der Wurff
2000 *The Syntax of Early English*. Cambridge: Cambridge University Press.

Gelderen, Elly van
2008 *Grammaticalization as Economy*. Amsterdam/Philadelphia: John Benjamins.

Gergel, Remus
2008 Comparative inversion: a diachronic study. Ms. Universität Tübingen.

Haeberli, Eric
2002 Inflectional morphology and the loss of verb second in English. In: D. Lightfoot (ed.), *Syntactic Effects of Morphological Change*, 88–106. Oxford: Oxford University Press.

Hankamer, Jorge
1973 Why there are two 'than's in English. *Proceedings of the 9th Annual Meeting of the Chicago Linguistics Society*. Chicago, IL., 179–191.

Hegarty, Michael
2005 *Feature-Based Functional Categories: The Structure, Acquisition, and Specific Impairment of Functional Systems*. Berlin/New York: Mouton de Gruyter.

Huddleston, Rodney and Geoffrey K. Pullum (eds.)
2002 *The Cambridge Grammar of the English Language*. Cambridge: Cambridge University Press.

Jack, George
1994 *Beowulf: A student edition*. Oxford: Oxford University Press.

Johnson, Kyle
2006 Gapping is not (VP) ellipsis. Ms. University of Massachusetts at Amherst.

Kemendade, Ans van
1987 *Syntactic Case and Morphological Case in the History of English*. Dordrecht: Foris.

Klaeber, Friedrich
1922 *Beowulf and the Fight at Finnsburg*. Boston: Heath.

Kroch, Anthony S.
1989 Reflexes of grammar in patterns of language change. *Language Variation and Change* 1: 199–244.

Kroch, Anthony S. and Ann Taylor
2000 *The Penn-Helsinki Parsed Corpus of Middle English*. UPenn.

Kroch, Anthony S., Ann Taylor and Donald Ringe
2000 The Middle English verb-second constraint: A case study in language contact and language change. In: Susan Herring, Pieter van Reenen, and Lene Schoesler (eds.), *Textual Parameters in Old Language*, 353–391. Amsterdam/Philadelphia: John Benjamins.

Kroch, Anthony S., Beatrice Santorini and Lauren Delfs
2004 *The Penn Parsed Corpus of Early Modern English*. UPenn.

Lechner, Winfried
2004 *Ellipsis and Comparatives*. Berlin/New York: Mouton de Gruyter.

Legendre, Géraldine
2000 For an OT Conception of a Parallel Interface: Evidence from Basque V2. In: M. Hirotani, A. Coetzee, N. Hall, and J.-Y. Kim (eds.), *Proceedings of the 30th Conference of the North East Linguistic Society*, GLSA Publications.

Merchant, Jason
2001 *The Syntax of Silence: Sluicing, islands, and the theory of ellipsis.* Oxford: Oxford University Press.
2003 Subject-auxiliary inversion in comparatives and PF output constraints. In: Kerstin Schwabe and Susanne Winkler (eds.), *The Interfaces: Deriving and Interpreting Omitted Structures*, 55–77. Amsterdam/Philadelphia: John Benjamins.

Mitchell, Bruce
1985 *Old English Syntax*. Oxford: Clarendon.

Niinuma, Fumikazu and Myung-Kwan Park
2004 A case for head movement at PF: SAI in comparatives. In: Anne Breitbarth and Henk van Riemsdijk (eds.), *Triggers*, 431–450. Berlin/New York: Mouton de Gruyter.

Pintzuk, Susan
1991 Phrase Structures in Competition: Variation and Change in Old English Word Order. Ph.D. thesis, University of Pennsylvania.

Pintzuk, Susan and Anthony Kroch
1989 The rightward movement of complement and adjuncts in the Old English of Beowulf. *Language Variation and Change* 1: 115–143.

Potts, Christopher
2002 The syntax and semantics of 'as'-parantheticals. *Natural Language & Linguistic Theory* 20: 623–689.

Roberts, Ian G.
1993 *Verbs and Diachronic Syntax. A Comparative History of English and French.* Dordrecht: Kluwer.

Roberts, Ian G. and Anna Roussou
2003 *Syntactic Change. A Minimalist Approach to Grammaticalization.* Cambridge: Cambridge University Press.

Taylor, Ann, Anthony Warner, Susan Pintzuk, and Frank Beths
2003 *The York-Toronto-Helsinki Parsed Corpus of Old English Prose.*

Winkler, Susanne
2005 *Ellipsis and Focus in Generative Grammar*. Berlin/New York: Mouton de Gruyter.

Context effects in the formation of adjectival resultatives

Helga Gese, Britta Stolterfoht and Claudia Maienborn

1. Introduction

Stative constructions denoting the result of a preceding event are quite common cross-linguistically (Nedjalkov 1988). In languages like English or French these resultative constructions are expressed by the same grammatical means (i.e. with the same auxiliary) as eventive passives. Thus a sentence like *The letter is opened* has an eventive as well as a stative reading and will only be disambiguated by the context. In German, by contrast, resultative constructions and eventive passives are formally distinct: whereas the eventive passive in (1) is built with the auxiliary *werden* ('to become'), the respective resultative construction (traditionally dubbed "adjectival" or "stative passive") in (2) consists of a form of *sein* ('to be') combined with a participle II. This makes German a particularly well-suited language to study the formation and interpretation of resultatives.

(1)	*Der*	*Brief*	*wird*	*geöffnet.*	Eventive passive
	The	letter	becomes	opened	
	'The letter is opened.'				

(2)	*Der*	*Brief*	*ist*	*geöffnet.*	Adjectival resultative
	The	letter	is	opened	
	'The letter is opened.'				

Constructions of type (2) were traditionally analysed as a second kind of verbal passive, viz. a so-called "stative passive" (e.g. Helbig 1983, 1987). From this perspective, it was only natural to see them as being tightly related to and dependent on the eventive passive. Yet, in more recent times authors like Rapp (1997, 1998), von Stechow (1998, 2002), Kratzer (2000), Maienborn (2007) have argued convincingly that these constructions do not belong to the verbal paradigm but should rather receive an adjectival analysis: on this view, sentence (2) contains a form of the copula *sein* ('to be') in combination with an adjectivized verbal participle. In the following we will adopt this adjectival analysis for constructions of type (2), which we will dub "adjectival resultatives". For further discussion see

Gese et al. (2008). Stolterfoht et al. (2008) provide additional psycholinguistic evidence (based on a self-paced reading study) in favor of the adjectival analysis.

Once adjectival resultatives are not longer considered to be the "little brother" of eventive passives, the question which verbs admit the adjectival resultative formation appears within a different light. It is clear that transitive resultative verbs like *öffnen* 'to open' in (2) are perfectly suited for building adjectival resultatives. But what about unaccusative verbs? Authors like Helbig (1987) and Wunderlich (1997) exclude them categorically. The rationale behind this is that the formation of adjectival resultatives is only available for a subset of those verbs that form the eventive passive. As exemplified in (4) unaccusatives do not meet this restriction, hence there should be no adjectival analysis available for a construction like (3). Sentence (3) has only an eventive reading with *sein* as perfect tense auxiliary under this view.

(3) *Die Blumen sind verwelkt.*
The flowers are wilted
'The flowers are/have wilted.'

(4) **Die Blumen werden verwelkt.*
The flowers become wilted

However, if we adopt the adjectival analysis there is no reason to assume that there is an a priori link between adjectival resultatives and eventive passives. The admissibility of adjectival resultatives is not necessarily related to or dependent on the eventive passive formation. Hence, the question of whether unaccusatives do enter the adjectival conversion process has to be asked anew. In fact, some remarks on the existence of adjectival resultatives based on unaccusative verbs can be found in von Stechow (1998), Kratzer (2000) and Nogami (2000).

This is where the present paper enters the discussion. We will provide different kinds of evidence for the existence of an adjectival reading of sentences like (3) besides the present perfect reading. In section 2, we will summarize the empirical evidence presented in Gese, Maienborn and Stolterfoht (2008) showing that there is at least a subset of unaccusatives that has the potential to build adjectival resultatives. In section 3 we will develop the hypothesis that adjectival resultative formation is not rigidly limited to this subgroup of unaccusatives but rather controlled by extra-grammatical, pragmatic factors. This hypothesis is tested in section 4. We will present two rating studies on the acceptability of adjectival resultatives under different kinds of contextual variation. The results of these studies corroborate the assumption that the adjectival resultative formation is available in principle to all unaccusatives, always provided they get the right pragmatic support.

2. Empirical evidence for adjectival conversion with unaccusatives

In Gese, Maienborn and Stolterfoht (2008) we provided empirical evidence from corpora as well as from psycholinguistic experiments in support of the assumption that adjectival resultative formation is not limited to (some subset of) transitive verbs but may also include unaccusatives, for instance. That is, a sentence like (3) above would in fact be ambiguous on this view. Besides a present perfect (hence: eventive) reading it may have also an adjectival (hence: stative) reading. This evidence will be summarized below.

2.1. Evidence from corpora

In the discussion of the morphosyntactic status of the participle II in adjectival resultatives the following diagnostics proved to be good tests for adjectivehood (cf. in particular Höhle (1978), Litvinov and Nedjalkov (1988), Lenz (1994), Rapp (1997, 1998), Maienborn (2007)).

(i) Adjectival negation
(ii) Adjectival gradation
(iii) Coordination with genuine adjectives
(iv) Adjectival word formation
(v) Modification by temporal adverbials

In (6a) to (9a) below, the application of these diagnostics to the typical case of adjectival resultatives based on a transitive resultative verb reveals their adjectival status. Now, if we conduct the very same tests with the participles of unaccusative base verbs like the ones in the (b)-sentences we observe basically the same behavior. There appears to be no categorial difference between unaccusatives and transitive resultative verbs in this respect: Participles of either of them pass the tests for adjectivehood. This is briefly illustrated by the corpus data below. (The examples stem from corpora of written German, viz. the morphosyntactically annotated corpus TIGER 1.0 (http://www.ims.uni-stuttgart.de/projekte/TIGER) and the COSMAS II corpus from the IDS Mannheim (http://www.ids-mannheim.de/cosmas2) as well as from newspaper archives. For further details see Gese, Maienborn and Stolterfoht (2008).

(i) Adjectival negation

Unlike its English counterpart, the German prefix *un*-synchronically only combines with stems of category [+N], i.e. with adjectives and nouns but never with verbs (cf. Lenz 1994). As is shown in (5a) and (5b) the participles of both transitive resultative and unaccusative base verbs combine with *un*-. That means that the verbal participle must have been adjectivized.

(5) a. *Oft waren diese Regeln ungeschrieben,* [...]
Often were these rules unwritten
'These rules were often unwritten' (TIGER s11406)

b. *Die Farben sind praktisch unverblasst.*
The colours are practically un-faded
'The colours are practically unfaded.' (*Spiegel-Online*, 4.3.2008)

(ii) Adjectival gradation

Adjectival gradation is a sufficient criterion for the adjectival status of a word, although not a necessary one, cf. absolute adjectives. The existence of the regularly formed comparative forms in (6) clearly points to the adjectival status of the participles involved.

(6) a. [...] *man ist einfach abgelenkter.*
one is just distract-COMP
'one is just more distracted.' (COSMAS M00/MAR.05611)

b. *Der Dom ist verfallener, denn je.*
The cathedral is decayed-COMP than ever
'The cathedral is more decayed than ever.'
(COSMAS N92/DEZ.45715)

(iii) Coordination with genuine adjectives

Coordination is a popular means of testing the morphosyntactic identity of words (cf. Lang 1984). In order to combine with a genuine adjective as in (7a) and (7b), a verbal participle must have been adjectivized first. Only then will the two conjuncts be of the same morphosyntactic type.

(7) a. *Entlassungen seien weder geplant noch nötig.*
Dismissals are neither planned nor necessary
'Dismissals are neither planned nor necessary.' (TIGER s3166)

b. *Infarktpatientinnen, die vereinsamt und besonders*
Infarct-patients who grown-lonely and especially
depressiv sind, [...]
depressive are
'Infarct patients that are lonely and particularly depressive'
(COSMAS O98/AUG.82091)

(iv) Adjectival word formation

A further adjectival property of the participles in adjectival resultatives is their ability to form compounds with nouns as non-heads. There is no analogous word formation available to verbs. Thus, the respective participles in (8) must have been adjectivized before the complex adjectival was built.

(8) a. *Sonnenbeschienen wie Hauff war,* [...]
Sun-illuminated like Hauff was
'As "sun-lit" (i.e. privileged) as Hauff was'
(COSMAS H86/UA3.00526)

b. *Poiger und Cerny sind grippeerkrankt.*
Poiger and Cerny are flu-sickened
'Poiger and Cerny are sick with the flu.'
(COSMAS O95/MAR.22600)

(v) Modification by durational adverbials

Adjectival resultatives combine regularly with durational adverbials like *seit zwei Stunden* ('for (lit. since) two hours') but do not accept positional adverbials like *vor zwei Stunden* ('two hours ago'); cf. (9a)/(9c) vs. (9b). *Vor*-adverbials serve to locate the verbal referent before the utterance time. Therefore they are incompatible with present tense; cf. (9b). A legitimate combination of a participle of an unaccusative verb with a *vor*-adverbial as in (9d) requires *sein* to be analyzed as a perfect tense auxiliary. Sentence (9d) cannot be analyzed as adjectival.

(9) a. *Die Leichtathletik-Saison ist seit kurzem eröffnet* [...]
The athletics season is since shortly opened
'The athletics season is open as of recently'
(slightly simplified COSMAS K99/MAI.33770)

b. **Die Leichtathletik-Saison ist vor kurzem eröffnet.*
The athletics season is before shortly opened

c. *Bürgermeisterin Eva-Maria* Tempelhahn *(SPD) und ihr*
Mayor Eva-Maria Tempelhahn (SPD) and her
Team sind schon _seit_ _November 1995_ *ins*
team are already since November 1995 in the
benachbarte Goldschmidtshaus _umgezogen_.
neighboring Goldschmidt-house moved
'Mayor Eva-Maria Tempelhahn (SPD) and her team are relocated in the neighboring Goldschmidt-house already since November 1995.'
(*Frankfurter Rundschau*, 11.2.1997)

d. *Die Bürgermeisterin ist vor zwei Wochen umgezogen.*
The mayor is before two weeks moved
'The mayor moved two weeks ago.'

In short, these corpus data show that the same diagnostics that have proven to furnish solid evidence for the adjectival nature of the participles involved in standard adjectival resultatives can be carried over to the case of unaccusatives. The results of all diagnostics that we presented here consistently point towards the ability of at least some unaccusatives to build adjectival resultatives.

2.2. Rating study

As shown in (9a) and (9b) above, copula sentences with adjectivized participles combine with durational adverbials like *seit zwei Stunden*. They do not combine with positional adverbials like *vor zwei Stunden* in present tense; *sein*-perfects, on the other hand, do not combine easily with *seit*. Modification with *seit* vs. *vor* can thus be used as a means of disambiguating between the stative construction (adjectival resultative) and the eventive construction (present perfect) of an ambiguous sentence like (10). In the following we will use this distributional difference of *seit*- and *vor*-adverbials as a diagnostic means to tell apart stative vs. eventive constructions with unaccusatives.

(10) *Meine Nachbarin ist verreist.* ambiguous

a. *Meine Nachbarin ist seit zwei Wochen verreist.*
My neighbor is since two weeks left
'My neighbor is gone since two weeks ago.'[1]
adjectival resultative

b. *Meine Nachbarin ist vor zwei Wochen verreist.*
My neighbor is before two weeks left
'My neighbor left two weeks ago.' present perfect

The corpus data presented above provide first evidence that unaccusatives may form adjectival resultatives. It might however be that the corpus evidence renders a distorted view of the linguistic data, reflecting only marginally acceptable and/or highly context-dependent uses. To exclude this possibility we conducted an acceptability rating study; cf. Gese, Maienborn and Stolterfoht (2008). We investigated the question of whether people accept adjectival resultative constructions from unaccusative base verbs devoid of contextual support.

In the rating study we tested the hypothesis that there is at least a subset of unaccusative verbs that have the ability to undergo an adjectival conversion process, and are thus ambiguous when combined with *sein* ('to be'); cf. (10). Sentences with these verbs should exhibit similar ratings when modified by durational (10a) and by positional adverbials (10b). Both types of modification should be acceptable.

We presented two groups of items containing the participles of the following unaccusative verbs:

(11) Unaccusative1
wachsen ('to grow'), welken ('to wilt'), verreisen ('to go off on a journey'), verschwinden ('to vanish'), ablaufen ('to expire'), verstreichen ('to elapse'), versinken ('to sink'), erlöschen ('to die down'), anlaufen ('to start'), schwellen ('to swell'), wegfallen ('to drop out'), vergehen ('to pass by'), abwandern ('to migrate'), entbrennen ('to break out'), weichen ('to give way'), einkehren ('to stop for a bite to eat'), verstummen ('to fall silent'), abreissen ('to pull down'), steigen ('to rise'), sinken ('to fall')

(12) Unaccusative2
entstehen ('to arise'), erscheinen ('to appear'), kommen ('to come'), fliehen ('to run away'), zusammentreffen ('to meet'), fallen ('to tumble'), umkommen ('to perish'), platzen ('to burst'), sitzenbleiben ('to remain seated'), hochspringen ('to jump up'), explodieren ('to explode'), geschehen ('to happen'), auftauchen ('to show up'), einsteigen ('to board'), gelingen ('to succeed'), anreisen ('to arrive'), eintreten ('to enter'), erfolgen ('to take place'), bekannt werden ('to emerge'), passieren ('to come about')

For the condition "unaccusative1", we used participles of unaccusative base verbs that occurred in the COSMAS corpora in combination with *seit*-adverbials, whereas for the condition "unaccusative2", we took unaccusative verbs that were not found with *seit*-modification in the corpora. The materials manipulated the type of unaccusative verb and the type of adverb (*seit* vs. *vor*).

We predicted better ratings for sentences like (10a) than for (13a). For pairs of sentences like (10a) and (10b), we predicted similar ratings for the two types of modification.

(13) a. *#Die Skulptur ist seit zwei Monaten entstanden.*
The sculpture is since two months came about

b. *Die Skulptur ist vor zwei Monaten entstanden.*
The sculpture is before two months came about
'The sculpture came about two months ago.'

We used a six-point rating scale ('1' = good, natural sentence, '6' = unacceptable sentence). The results are shown in Figure 1. For further details of this experiment, see Gese, Maienborn and Stolterfoht (2008).

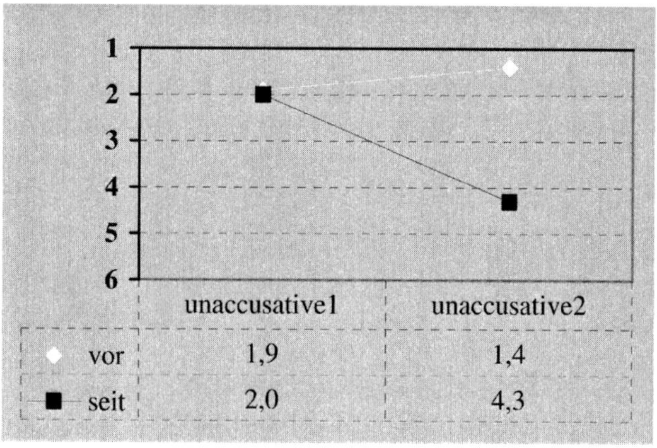

Figure 1. Acceptability ratings (scale 1–6; 1 = good/natural, 6 = bad) for sentences with *seit*- and *vor*-modification

Our results showed a significant effect of adverb type only for sentences like (13). No effect was found for sentences like (10): For these sentences the adjectival resultative reading and the perfect reading were judged as equally acceptable. Sentences of the type (10a) got better ratings than sentences of type (13a). We interpreted this result as evidence that there is indeed a group of unaccusative verbs (like *verreisen* 'to make a journey' in sentence (10)) that form the adjectival resultative besides the perfect, whereas a second group of unaccusatives (like *entstehen* 'to come about' in sentence (13)) forms only the perfect. Our rating study thus offers independent corroboration of the grammaticality of the corpus data presented above.

3. The flexibility of adjectival resultative formation

The rating study presented above provided evidence that some unaccusative verbs are able to form adjectival resultatives. But what about the unaccusatives of group "unaccusative2" such as *entstehen* in sentence (13)? Are they really excluded from this construction type? Put in other words: What are the criteria for the adjectival resultative formation in German? Do they split up the class of unaccusatives into two groups? Or are there other factors outside of the grammar that drive the adjectival resultative formation?

In the few existing papers on "adjectival passives" which mention unaccusatives, two sorts of constraints have been put forward: Von Stechow (1998: 27) claims that only non-causative achievement unaccusatives enter the adjectival conversion process. Nogami (2000: 98), on the other hand, restricts adjectival resultative formation to unaccusatives with incremental theme. The results of our rating study disprove both of these claims.

First, there are unaccusatives without incremental theme among the items that admit adjectival resultative formation. For instance, the following sentences (14)–(16) got similar (good) ratings for both types of temporal modification, although their base verbs do not contain an incremental theme:

(14) *Der Kontakt ist seit /vor Jahren abgerissen.*
The contact is since /before years severed
'Contact is severed since years ago / was severed years ago'

(15) *Meine Nachbarin ist seit /vor zwei Wochen verreist.*
My neighbour is since /before two weeks left
'My neighbor is gone since two weeks ago / left two weeks ago.'

(16) *Der Verfassungsstreit ist seit /vor einem Jahr*
The constitutional debate is since /before one year
entbrannt.
broken out
'The constitutional debate is conflagrant since a year ago / broke out one year ago'

Second, adjectival resultative formation of unaccusatives does not appear to be limited to non-causative achievements but also includes accomplishments; cf. (17) and (18)

(17) *Die Leuchtreklame ist seit Monaten erloschen.*
The neon signs are since months out
'The neon signs are out since months ago.'

(18) *Die Kritik ist seit ein paar Tagen verstummt.*
The criticism is since a few days silent
'Criticism is silent since a few days ago.'

And, conversely, not all non-causative achievements in our experiment show up among the unaccusatives that build adjectival resultatives. Sentences (19)–(21) contain participles of non-causative achievements, but were judged inacceptable in combination with *seit* in our experiment.

(19) *Der Junge ist *seit /vor zehn Minuten gefallen.*
The boy is since /before ten minutes fallen
'* / The boy fell ten minutes ago.'

(20) *Der Soldat ist *seit /vor zwei Monaten umgekommen.*
The soldier is since /before two months died
'* / The soldier died two months ago.'

(21) *Der Luftballon ist *seit /vor zwei Minuten geplatzt.*
The air balloon is since /before two minutes burst
'* / The balloon burst two minutes ago.'

In fact, the two sets of unaccusative verbs – those that admit adjectival resultatives and those that do not – constitute two fairly heterogeneous groups. No genuine lexical distinction seems to be involved. We thus conclude that group membership is not determined by proper semantic constraints on the verb. This then raises the question whether there could be a pragmatic explanation for the different behavior of unaccusatives with respect to the admissibility of the adjectival resultative formation.

In fact, closer inspection of the verb's linguistic context yields a first hint towards such an explanation: Most of the subjects in the sentences with bad ratings for *seit*-modification denote concrete objects; cf. e.g. (19)–(21). By contrast, the group that exhibits the perfect/adjectival resultative-ambiguity contains several abstract subjects as e.g. *Frist* ('deadline'), *Vertrauen* ('confidence'), *Produktion* ('production'), *Terrorgefahr* ('threat of terror'), *Kritik* ('criticism'), *Kontakt* ('contact'), *Verfassungsstreit* ('constitutional debate'), *Haltbarkeitsdatum* ('date of expiry') and *Zeit* ('time') (see appendix B for a full list of the test items.)

What could be the pragmatic impact of the use of an abstract object as the subject of these sentences? Why should the acceptability of the adjectival resultative formation improve? A possible explanation could be that abstract subjects often call for a figurative or metaphoric use of the participle that is predicated of them. Figurative use in turn requires more costly interpretation which has to be legitimized properly, e.g. by some gain in informativity. That is, the property expressed by the adjectivized participle should be of particularly high relevance. Thus, the reason behind a higher acceptability of adjectival resultative formation in figurative use would be that the resultant state is necessarily of particular salience under these conditions.

Our hypothesis is thus that the adjectival resultative formation depends on the salience of the resultant state expressed by the participle. This salience can be provided by the participle itself, or it can be triggered by the inner- or extrasentential context.

In the case of transitive, resultative verbs (e.g. *öffnen* 'to open') the content of the resultant state is already made explicit within their lexical meaning. Consequently, these verbs do not need additional pragmatic support to legitimize adjectival resultative formation. Sentence (2) repeated here as (22) is perfectly acceptable without any context.

(22) *Der Brief ist geöffnet.*
The letter is opened
'The letter is opened.'

Other verbs, as for example a transitive activity verb like *streicheln* ('to pet'), do not specify a resultant state at all. There is no proper content that we could associate a priori with a resultant state of being petted. In the case of an unaccusative like *platzen* ('to burst'), the verb's lexical content includes a resultant state of being burst. Yet this resultant state has no content on its own that would suffice to highlight it thereby evoking a contrast with potential alternatives. This is what prevents these verbs from entering the adjectival conversion process without any additional pragmatic support.

(23) ??*Die Katze ist gestreichelt.*
The cat is petted
'The cat is petted.'

(24) ??*Der Luftballon ist seit zwei Minuten geplatzt.*
The air balloon is since two minutes burst
'The balloon is burst since two minutes ago.'

But if the context provides the adequate kind of pragmatic support, i.e., if there is a plausible resultative interpretation of the predicate, or if the subject triggers an interpretation with a particularly prominent resultant state, adjectival resultative formation becomes possible.

Rapp (1998: 243) and Kratzer (2000: 4) pointed out that for activity verbs, a suitable context providing a resultative interpretation of the participle is a "job is done" or "that's over" interpretation which defines the fulfillment of the activity as a contextually salient target that has to be achieved. A natural setting for an adjectival resultative use of *ist gestreichelt* 'is petted' would thus be (25); cf. Maienborn (2007) for further details.

(25) *Anna hat ihre Nachbarspflichten erfüllt: Der Briefkasten ist*
Anna has her neighbor-duties fulfilled: The mail-box is
geleert, die Blumen sind gegossen und die Katze ist
emptied the flowers are watered and the catis is
gestreichelt.
petted
Anna has done her neighborly duties: the mailbox is emptied, the flowers are watered and the cat is petted.'

What has not been noted yet in the literature is that adjectival resultative formation of activity verbs may also be improved by a subject that triggers a figurative use of the participle; compare (26) with (23).

(26) *Meine Seele ist gestreichelt.*
My soul is petted
'My soul is caressed.'

Sentence (26), although perhaps not perfectly acceptable, seems nevertheless much better than (23). While (23) definitely needs a resultative context such as (25) in order to be rescued from ill-formedness, the subject in (26) triggers a reading of the predicative participle which establishes a sufficiently relevant resultant state. Hence, (26) requires less pragmatic support by the surrounding context.

The situation is exactly the same for our class of unaccusatives that seem to resist adjectival resultative formation; cf. section 2. Within the right intra- or extra-sentential context the respective adjectival resultative constructions improve considerably.

Take for instance *platzen* ('to burst'): Without contextual information, sentence (24) is extremely bad. Yet, if we chose another subject, one which, in combination with the participle, yields a predication that according to our world knowledge describes a resultant state with enough content to evoke significant alternatives, the sentence improves considerably; cf. (27).

(27) *Die Aktienblase ist seit gestern geplatzt.*
The stock bubble is since yesterday burst
'The stock bubble is burst since yesterday.'

The same result can be achieved by embedding sentence (24) within an appropriate context that provides the relevant motivation for highlighting the resultant state of the balloon being burst; cf. (28).

(28) This year the opening of the festival will be signaled by bursting a balloon. A visitor asks: "Is the festival opened already?" –
„Ja, der Ballon ist seit fünf Minuten geplatzt."
Yes the balloon is since five minutes burst
'Yes the balloon is burst since five minutes ago.'

If this intuition is right, then the bad ratings one group of unaccusatives received with *seit* are not due to any grammatical or lexical constraints on the adjectival resultative formation, but could be given a pragmatic explanation: The participles of these unaccusatives just happened to lack the right subject and/or context that would provide the required pragmatic support for the adjectival resultative formation.

From this perspective the question of which verbs enter the adjectival conversion process would be not so much an issue of the grammar but rather of pragmatics. Given the right pragmatic support even such suboptimal candidates as transitive activity verbs or unaccusatives of group 2 (cf. the list under (12)) are potential candidates for building adjectival resultatives.

4. Experimental evidence for contextual constraints on the adjectival resultative formation

With the following two rating studies we wanted to substantiate the claim put forward in the previous section, according to which adjectival resultative formation is principally open to any unaccusative, including those which got bad ratings in our first rating study, given the right sentential or extrasentential context. We tested the hypothesis that the context has an impact on the acceptability of adjectival resultative sentences with these 'suboptimal' unaccusative base verbs. We examined both kinds of contextual variability discussed above: variation of the extrasentential context and variation of the intersentential context, i.e. the subject triggering a figurative or non-figurative use of the participle.

4.1. Experiment 1: Context variation

We tested whether the admissibility of the adjectival resultative formation can be increased by a suitable context. By comparing sentences like (29a) and (29b) within two types of context: a neutral one and one that makes the resultant state denoted by the participle particularly salient. In order to keep the two contexts comparable, we made them equally long and equally plausible and used similar lexical material.

neutral context

(c1) *Schichtwechsel in der Kardiologie-Abteilung des Krankenhauses. Der Arzt, der gerade anfängt, erkundigt sich bei seinem offensichtlich aufgeregten Kollegen, was in der letzten Schicht mit dem Herzinfarkt-Patienten geschehen sei. Dieser antwortet:*

Change of shifts in the cardiology department of the hospital. The doctor that is taking over is asking his visibly agitated colleague, what happened to the cardiac patient. The colleague answers:

(29) a. *"Der Herzstillstand ist seit zehn Minuten eingetreten."*
The cardiac arrest is since ten minutes commenced
'The cardiac arrest is commenced since ten minutes ago.'

b. *"Der Herzstillstand ist vor zehn Minuten eingetreten."*
The cardiac arrest is before ten minutes commenced
'The cardiac arrest set in ten minutes ago.'

resultative context

(c2) *Wie jeder Arzt weiß, sind Wiederbelebungsmaßnahmen nur selten von Erfolg, wenn ein Herzstillstand länger als fünf Minuten anhält. Bei der Ankunft eines Herzinfarktpatienten erkundigt sich der diensthabende Arzt beim Rettungssanitäter, ob denn noch Hoffnung bestehe. Der Sanitäter verneint und fügt hinzu:*

Every doctor knows that resuscitation attempts are rarely successful in cases when cardiac arrest lasts more than five minutes. As a cardiac patient is brought in, the doctor on duty asks the paramedic whether there is any hope. The paramedic says no and adds:

(29) a. *"Der Herzstillstand ist seit zehn Minuten eingetreten."*
The cardiac arrest is since ten minutes commenced
'The cardiac arrest is commenced since ten minutes ago.'

b. *"Der Herzstillstand ist vor zehn Minuten eingetreten."*
The cardiac arrest is before ten minutes commenced
'The cardiac arrest set in ten minutes ago.'

The following hypotheses can be formulated for Experiment 1:

(H1) Sentences with a *seit*-adverbial (cf. 29a) should get better ratings when embedded in a resultative context (c1) than in a neutral one (c2). There should be no rating differences for sentences with a *vor*-adverbial like (29b) in the two types of contexts.
(H2) All four narratives should be judged equally plausible.

Method

Participants
48 undergraduate students of the University of Tübingen participated for course credit. All were native speakers of German.

Materials
The materials manipulated the type of adverb (*seit* vs. *vor*) and the type of context (*neutral* vs. *resultative*); (see examples (29); the full set of experimental sentences is provided in Appendix A). Adverb type and context were manipulated within items. The target sentences comprised the 20 items of the rating study presented in section 2.2 which received bad ratings in combination with a *seit*-adverbial (for further details see Gese, Maienborn and Stolterfoht 2008). In order to extend the list of items we added four sentences which did not occur with *seit*-modification in the COSMAS corpora.

The 24 experimental items were combined with 24 filler items which covered a range of structures, all modified either by a *vor*-adverbial or by *seit*. The 48 items as a whole contained an equal number of (more or less) grammatical as well as (more of less) ungrammatical sentences. Four presentation lists were created and randomized in parallel two times. Each participant saw only one version (*seit* or *vor*) of each of the target sentences embedded in one type of context *(resultative* or *neutral*), counterbalanced across the four conditions.

Procedure
The questionnaires were distributed by email to students in an introductory linguistics class. Participants had one week to complete the questionnaire. They were told to read the narratives carefully and to rate the acceptability of the last sentence on a scale from 5 to 1. If the sentence was easy to understand, if it

made sense and seemed to be good, natural German, then they should rate this sentence with '5'. If the sentence didn't make sense to them or they thought it is a bad German sentence, then they should rate it '1'. To control for effects of plausibility differences between the two contexts, we additionally asked participants to rate the plausibility of the whole stories ('5' = very plausible … '1' = very implausible).

Results

The results are presented in Tables 1 and 2.

Table 1. Mean ratings (scale 5–1; 5 = good/natural, 1 = bad) for the acceptability judgment task

Adverb type	context type	
	resultative	neutral
seit	2,1	1,8
vor	4,2	4,2

For the acceptability rating task, a repeated measures ANOVA revealed a highly significant main effect of adverb type (F1 (1,47) = 391.43, $p \leq .001$; F2(1,23) = 329.57, $p \leq .001$) whereas the effect of context type was only significant in the subject analysis (F1 (1,47) = 4.937, p = .03; F2 (1,23) = 2.40, p = .13).

More importantly, we found an interaction of adverb type and context type which was only marginally significant in the subject analysis, but fully significant in the item analysis (F1(1,47) = 3.391, p = .072; F2(1,23) = 4.815, $p \leq .05$). The conventional 2 × 2 analysis of variance provides some evidence that sentences with *seit*-modification were rated better in the resultative context, whereas sentences with *vor*-modification did not show any rating difference between the two types of contexts.

Since this pattern of results was predicted, we performed more focused tests, comparing sentences with *seit* and *vor* in the two contexts. The ratings for the two context types differed significantly for sentences with *seit* (F1 (1,47) = 8.20, $p \leq .01$; F2 (1,23) = 6.24, $p \leq .05$) but not for those with *vor* ($F < 1$). Sentences with a *seit*-adverbial (cf. (26a)) got better ratings when embedded in a resultative context (c1). This finding confirms our hypothesis (H1).

The analysis of the plausibility ratings (repeated measures ANOVA) revealed no significant main effects of context or adverb type and no interaction between these factors ($F < 1$). The results confirm hypothesis (H2): Both types of contexts with the two types of target sentences were judged equally plausible.

Table 2. Mean ratings (scale 1–5; 5 = plausible, 1 = very implausible) for the plausibility judgment task

Adverb type	context type	
	resultative	neutral
seit	3,9	3,9
vor	4,0	4,0

The results of Experiment 1 confirm our two hypotheses: We found better ratings for sentences with a *seit*-adverbial embedded in a resultative context than in a neutral one. We found no context effect for sentences with *vor*-adverbials. This effect cannot be explained by the plausibility of the narratives: All narratives were judged equally plausible.

These results show clearly that the context has an impact on the acceptability of the adjectival passive with unaccusative verbs. In our second experiment, we tested whether a comparable effect can be observed with the variation of sentence subjects.

4.2. Experiment 2: Subject variation

In our second rating study, we tested the hypothesis that the type of subject is able to improve the admissibility of the adjectival resultative formation via a context that is prototypically associated with the predication of the sentence. For constructing our material, we used the target sentences with *seit* (cf. (25a)) from Experiment 1 and manipulated the subjects of these sentences (cf. (30a) and (30b)).

(30) a. **Der Junge ist seit zehn Minuten gefallen.*
The boy is since ten minutes fallen

b. *Die Grenzen sind seit zwei Tagen gefallen.*
The borders are since two days fallen
'The borders are open since two days ago.'

In section 3 above, we developed the hypothesis that the acceptability of adjectival resultatives depends on the salience of the resultant state. In some cases, this salience is warranted by the lexical content of the base verb itself (cf. unaccusatives like *verreisen* ('to make a journey')), in other cases it has to be established by the context (cf. experiment 1). If this is right – and provided that a participle in figurative use generally denotes a resultant state which is particularly salient – the following hypothesis can be formulated for Experiment 2:

(H3) Sentences with a *seit*-adverbial should get better ratings when the subject of the sentence admits a figurative use of the unaccusative participle (cf. 30b).

Method

Participants
28 students of the University of Tübingen were paid for their participation. All were native speakers of German.

Materials
The materials consisted of 12 target sentences from Experiment 1 with the following modifications: For the condition "concrete" the subject NPs were changed in six cases to a more concrete noun, e.g. *Der Herzstillstand ist seit zehn Minuten eingetreten* ('The cardiac arrest is commenced since ten minutes ago.') was replaced by *Der Freund ('the friend') ist seit fünf Minuten* eingetreten. For the condition "figurative" the subject NPs were chosen to admit the figurative use of the participle cf. (30b). All in all, we had 12 pairs of sentences with unaccusative verbs. The materials manipulated the type of subject NP (*concrete* vs. *figurative*) within items; see examples (30a) and (30b). The full set of experimental sentences is provided in Appendix B.

The 12 experimental items were combined with 58 filler sentences covering a range of grammatical and ungrammatical structures. Two presentation lists were created and randomized in parallel two times. Each participant saw only one version (*concrete* or *figurative*) of each of the sentences, counterbalanced across the two groups of sentences.

Results
The results are presented in Figure 2.

A repeated measures ANOVA revealed a highly significant main effect of subject type ($F1\ (1,27) = 50.97, p \leq .001$; $F2\ (1,11) = 21.06, p \leq .001$). Sentences with a subject which allows for a figurative use of the participle were rated better than sentences with a concrete use of the participle (3.1 vs 2.0). These results confirm hypothesis (H3).

Discussion

The goal of our two rating studies was to find out whether adjectival resultative formation is in principle open to all unaccusative verbs. Given the findings in Gese, Maienborn and Stolterfoht (2008) which proved the acceptability of an

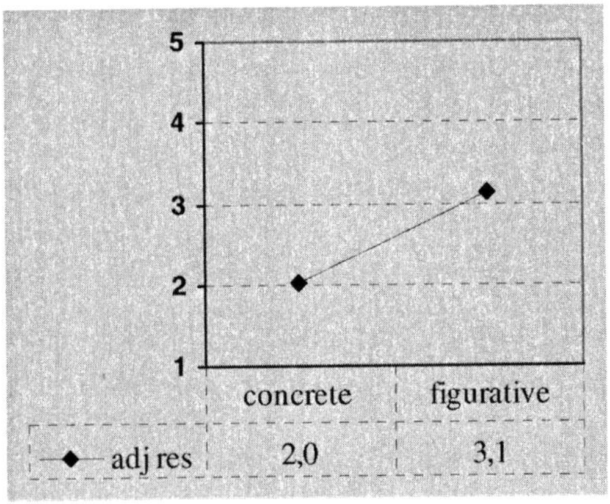

Figure 2. Mean ratings for the two experimental conditions (scale 5–1; 5 = good/natural, 1 = bad).

adjectival resultative formation only for one subset of unaccusative verbs, we wanted to test whether the verbs that received bad ratings in these experiments were really unable to form adjectival resultatives or whether they just needed additional contextual support for the formation of this construction type.

Our claim was that, given the right pragmatic support, basically all unaccusative verbs have the potential to form adjectival resultatives. Those adjectival resultative sentences with unaccusatives that are not acceptable without context should improve if either the extrasentential context or an alternative subject conveys a suitable resultative interpretation of the participle.

In Experiment 1, sentences which got bad ratings in a previous rating study were embedded in a neutral and a resultative context. We saw significantly better ratings for adjectival resultatives formed from those 'suboptimal' unaccusatives in the resultative contexts than in neutral ones.

In Experiment 2 we presented the sentences without context but manipulated the subjects. We tested concrete subjects as well as abstract ones supporting a figurative and thus resultative use of the participle. As expected, the results of Experiment 2 show much better ratings for adjectival resultatives with subjects triggering a figurative use of the participle than with concrete nouns.

Both kinds of pragmatic support – via an appropriate context or via a suitable subject – yield the same effect: The acceptability of adjectival resultative sentences increases significantly.

The results of our studies presented here are significant for a number of reasons. They provide empirical evidence for a new perspective on the admissibility of adjectival resultatives with different verb types. Adjectival resultative formation is less grammatically controlled than generally assumed in at least two respects. First, not only transitive verbs but also unaccusatives may build adjectival resultatives. And, secondly, whether or not adjectival resultative formation is possible is largely a matter of pragmatics.

Moreover, our results also demonstrate the benefit of combining data from different sources. Corpus evidence provided a first proof of existence for adjectival resultatives based on unaccusatives. Our first rating study corroborated the corpus findings. On this basis two further psycholinguistic studies demonstrated the important and so far widely underestimated role of pragmatics for the formation of adjectival resultatives. Our findings thus show that combining data from corpora, rating studies and introspection helps uncover linguistic structure.

Appendix

Appendix A – materials Experiment1

1 (resultative): Die gesamte Kunstwelt wartet schon lange darauf, dass der eigenwillige Bildhauer seine neue, langersehnte Skulptur fertig stellt, damit die groß angekündigte Ausstellung eröffnet werden kann. Der Galerist, der seit Monaten versucht, den Bildhauer zu erreichen, erwischt ihn endlich am Telefon und fragt sehr behutsam, wann man die Eröffnung der Ausstellung ankündigen dürfe. Der Bildhauer ist entsetzt, dass das noch nicht passiert ist und ruft empört:
(a)/(b) "Die Skulptur ist seit/vor Wochen entstanden."

1 (neutral): Der eigenwillige Bildhauer zeigt seinem Galeristen seine neue, vor einigen Wochen fertig gestellte Skulptur, um ihn davon zu überzeugen, eine neue Ausstellung für ihn zu organisieren. Tatsächlich ist der Galerist begeistert und fragt den Künstler, wann er dieses Meisterwerk denn kreiert habe. Der Bildhauer ist geschmeichelt und antwortet:
(a)/(b) "Die Skulptur ist seit/vor Wochen entstanden."

2 (resultative): Professor Strobel wird im Hotel sehnlichst erwartet, denn ohne ihn kann die Konferenz nicht beginnen, er hält schließlich die Eröffnungsrede. Zum wiederholten Male erkundigt sich der Konferenzmanager an der Rezeption, ob die Konferenz nun endlich beginnen kann. Endlich gibt ihm die Dame an der Rezeption grünes Licht. Sie sagt:
(a)/(b) "Der Gast ist seit/vor zehn Minuten erschienen."

2 (neutral): Professor Strobel soll auf der Konferenz im Hotel die Eröffnungsrede halten. Er ist in seinem Fach eine Größe, und der Konferenzmanager

behält es sich daher vor, ihn persönlich an der Rezeption zu begrüßen. Nach einer Weile nervösen Wartens bemerkt er einen Fleck auf seinem Anzug und eilt auf sein Zimmer, um sich umzuziehen. Als er nach einer Viertelstunde wieder ins Foyer kommt, sagt ihm die Dame an der Rezeption, dass er Professor Strobel verpasst hat. Der Konferenzmanager fragt, wann der Gast denn das Hotel betreten habe. Die Rezeptionistin antwortet:
(a)/(b) "Der Gast ist seit/vor zehn Minuten erschienen."

3 (resultative): Wenn Tante Hilde zu Besuch kommt, muss der 14-jährige Leo ihr immer sein Zimmer überlassen und im Keller schlafen. Er hasst das, und als die Tante mal wieder mit Sack und Pack vor der Tür steht und zwei Wochen bleiben will, weigert er sich, sein Zimmer zu verlassen und schließt die Tür ab. Seine Mutter versorgt die Tante mit Kaffee, klopft dann zaghaft an Leos Tür und bittet ihn, in den Keller umzuziehen. Als Leo fragt, warum er das tun solle, erinnert sie ihn an seine Gastgeberpflichten und fügt ermahnend hinzu:
(a)/(b) "Der Besuch ist seit/vor zwei Stunden gekommen."

3 (neutral): Leos Lieblingstante Hilde kommt zu Besuch, und Leo kann es kaum erwarten, dass die Schule zu Ende ist. Nach der Schule findet jedoch ein Fußballspiel statt, bei dem Leo den erkrankten Torwart vertreten muss. Als er abends nach Hause kommt, fragt er seine Mutter, ob Tante Hilde noch gar nicht da sei. Seine Mutter erklärt ihm, dass Hilde nur ganz kurz vorbeigeschaut habe und schon längst wieder weg ist. Als Leo dann noch wissen will, wann das denn war, antwortet sie:
(a)/(b) "Der Besuch ist seit/vor zwei Stunden gekommen."

4 (resultative): Aus dem Hochsicherheitstrakt des Gefängnisses ist ein Häftling geflohen. Der zuständige Polizeikommissar wartet nun schon seit Tagen auf die Auswertung der Videoaufzeichnungen. Doch noch immer sind seine Kollegen nicht soweit. Schließlich überkommt ihn die Angst, der Häftling habe sich auf Nimmerwiedersehen nach Südamerika abgesetzt, er treibt seine Kollegen zur Eile mit der Auswertung an und fügt hinzu:
(a)/(b) "Der Häftling ist seit/vor einer Woche geflohen."

4 (neutral): Ede sitzt im Hochsicherheitstrakt des Gefängnisses. Er hat mitbekommen, dass der geflohene Häftling aus der Zelle nebenan wieder gefasst wurde. Beim Hofgang unterhält er sich mit seinem Kumpel Heino über die spektakuläre Flucht. Heino fragt Ede, wie lange der Häftling denn die Freiheit genießen konnte. Ede antwortet:
(a)/(b) "Der Häftling ist seit/vor einer Woche geflohen."

5 (resultative): Die Tagung der Kommission zum Erhalt der deutschen Sprache beginnt, aber noch immer fehlen die Getränke auf den Tischen. Der Organisator läuft bestimmt zwei Stunden lang panisch herum und sucht seine Angestellten, die für die Verpflegung der hochrangigen Kommissionsmitglieder zuständig sind. Endlich findet er sie und brüllt sie an, sie sollen an die Arbeit gehen und die Getränke servieren, denn:
(a)/(b) "Die Kommission ist seit/vor einer Stunde zusammengetroffen."

5 (neutral): Die Tagung der Kommission zum Erhalt der deutschen Sprache hat nur eine Stunde gedauert, so schnell waren sich alle Mitglieder einig. Der Journalist der linguistischen Zeitschrift ist daher viel zu spät dran. Als er im Tagungshotel eintrifft, sind weit und breit keine Kommissionsmitglieder zu sehen. Er fragt an der Rezeption, ob die Kommission schon begonnen habe, worauf der Rezeptionist ihm mitteilt:
(a)/(b) "Die Kommission ist seit/vor einer Stunde zusammengetroffen."

6 (resultative): Normalerweise erreicht der Krankenwagen jeden Einsatzort in der Innenstadt innerhalb von höchstens sechs Minuten. Der kleine Florian liegt nun schon länger bewusstlos neben dem innerstädtischen Fußballfeld. Alle warten auf den Krankenwagen. Schließlich fragt der Trainer seinen Assistenten, ob der Krankenwagen denn tatsächlich gerufen sei. Der Assistent bejaht dies, bezweifelt aber, dass die richtige Adresse angegeben sei, sonst müsste der Krankenwagen doch schon längst da sein, denn:
(a)/(b) "Der Junge ist seit/vor zehn Minuten gefallen."

6 (neutral): Der kleine Florian ist beim Fußballtraining gestürzt und hat sich den Knöchel gebrochen. Sein Trainer hat auch gleich den Notarzt gerufen. Als der Krankenwagen eintrifft, humpelt Florian diesem mit zusammengebissenen Zähnen entgegen. Auf die Frage des Sanitäters, was denn passiert sei, antwortet der Trainer:
(a)/(b) "Der Junge ist seit/vor zehn Minuten gefallen."

7 (resultative): Für jeden Soldaten, der im Irakkrieg fällt, errichtet die amerikanische Regierung schnellstmöglich einen Grabstein auf dem Washingtoner Friedhof. Bei dem jungen Soldaten aus Kansas City jedoch geht etwas schief: Nach seinem Tod warten die Angehörigen vergeblich auf einen Grabstein. Sie beschweren sich bei der Regierung und fordern diese auf, endlich einen Grabstein aufzustellen, denn:
(a)/(b) "Der Soldat ist seit/vor zwei Monaten umgekommen."

7 (neutral): Alle Bürger von Kansas City sind in Trauer. Ein blutjunger Soldat aus ihrer Stadt ist im Irakkrieg gefallen. Mit großen Fotos des jungen

Mannes ziehen sie durch die Straßen der Innenstadt und demonstrieren gegen den Krieg. Ein Tourist sieht dies und fragt einen Demonstranten, was denn mit dem jungen Mann auf den Fotos passiert sei. Dieser antwortet:
(a)/(b) "Der Soldat ist seit/vor zwei Monaten umgekommen."

8 (resultative): Wie jeder weiß, wird das Bogenschützen-Festival stets durch das laute Platzen eines riesigen Luftballons eröffnet. Ein Besucher fragt den Mann an der Kasse: "Ist das Festival schon eröffnet?" Der Kartenverkäufer nickt und sagt:
(a)/(b) "Der Luftballon ist seit/vor zwei Minuten geplatzt."

8 (neutral): Wie jeder weiß, wird das Bogenschützen-Festival stets durch das laute Platzen eines riesigen Luftballons eröffnet. Dieses Jahr ist der Knall so laut, dass etliche Besucher danach über Ohrenschmerzen klagen. Jemand ruft deswegen sogar den Notarzt und der fragt bei seinem Eintreffen, was denn passiert sei. Ein verstörter Gast antwortet:
(a)/(b) "Der Luftballon ist seit/vor zwei Minuten geplatzt."

9 (resultative): Das Schillergymnasium verpflichtet Schüler, die sitzengeblieben sind, den Nachhilfeunterricht in den Pausen zu besuchen. Auch Thomas dreht gerade eine Extrarunde, hat aber keine Lust auf Nachhilfe und drückt sich davor. Als seine Leistungen immer schlechter werden, geht seine Mutter zum Klassenlehrer und erfährt erst dort, dass Thomas die Nachhilfe gar nicht besucht. Sie regt sich furchtbar darüber auf, dass niemand in der Schule darauf geachtet hat, dass Thomas den Nachhilfeunterricht auch tatsächlich besucht und ruft immerzu:
(a)/(b) "Der Junge ist seit/vor einem Jahr sitzengeblieben."

9 (neutral): In der Abschlussklasse des Schillergymnasium wird traditionell eine gemeinsame Klassenfahrt nach Paris unternommen. Thomas' Tante, die von diesem Brauch weiß, erkundigt sich bei dessen Mutter, warum denn Thomas nicht mit in Paris war. Die ist total genervt, schon wieder von Thomas' Schulversagen berichten zu müssen, und druckst zunächst etwas herum. Als die Tante nicht locker lässt, gibt sie aber schließlich doch zu:
(a)/(b) "Der Junge ist seit/vor einem Jahr sitzengeblieben."

10 (resultative): Das klackende Geräusch, dass der Toast macht, wenn er aus dem Toaster springt, ist für Jenny gewöhnlich das Signal zum Aufstehen und Frühstücken. Heute allerdings hat sie keinen Laut aus der Küche gehört und bleibt deshalb noch im Bett liegen. Irgendwann wird sie aber doch hungrig und fragt ihre Mutter durch die Tür, wann es denn endlich Frühstück gebe. Die Mutter antwortet:
(a)/(b) "Der Toast ist seit/vor einer Minute hochgesprungen."

10 (neutral): Jenny liegt morgens nach dem Aufwachen gerne noch eine Weile im Bett, döst vor sich hin und genießt die Stille. Als sie im Gästezimmer ihrer Freundin übernachtet, macht sie das genauso, wird aber durch ein lautes Klacken aus ihrem gemütlichen Dämmerzustand gerissen. Erschrocken springt sie auf und läuft in die Küche, wo ihre Freundin bereits beim Frühstück sitzt. Jenny fragt sie, was das gerade eben für ein Geräusch war, worauf die Freundin antwortet:
(a)/(b) "Der Toast ist seit/vor einer Minute hochgesprungen."

11 (resultative): Bevor der Archäologe mit seiner Arbeit beginnen kann, muss der Zugang zur antiken Grabkammer frei gesprengt werden. Der Archäologe ruft beim Bauleiter an und fragt: "Ist der Zugang schon frei?" Der Bauarbeiter bejaht und fügt hinzu:
(a)/(b) "Die Bombe ist seit/vor zwei Minuten explodiert."

11 (neutral): Bevor die Ausgrabungen beginnen können, muss der Zugang zur antiken Grabkammer frei gesprengt werden. Auf dem Weg zur Ausgrabungsstätte hört Peter einen lauten Knall und erschrickt sehr. An der Ausgrabungsstätte angekommen, erkundigt er sich deshalb beim Bauleiter, was denn gerade eben passiert sei. Dieser antwortet:
(a)/(b) "Die Bombe ist seit/vor zwei Minuten explodiert."

12 (resultative): Aus dem Stadtmuseum sind vor längerer Zeit mehrere wertvolle Gemälde von Monet gestohlen worden. Die Suche blieb bisher erfolglos. Seitdem sind die Besucherzahlen so stark zurückgegangen, dass die Schließung des Museums droht. In seiner Verzweiflung schnauzt der Museumsleiter den zuständigen Polizeikommissar an, endlich die Monet-Gemälde wiederzufinden und wirft ihm vor:
(a)/(b) "Das Verbrechen ist seit/vor zwei Jahren geschehen."

12 (neutral): Aus dem Stadtmuseum wurden mehrere wertvolle Gemälde von Monet gestohlen. Der Fall wurde schnell aufgeklärt, die Diebe gefasst und die Bilder wieder aufgehängt. Dennoch hat das Museum unter dem Verbrechen gelitten und seinen guten Ruf eingebüßt. Die Besucherzahlen gehen unaufhörlich zurück. Ein Journalist interviewt den Museumsleiter dazu und fragt ihn, wann der Diebstahl stattgefunden habe, worauf der Museumsleiter antwortet:
(a)/(b) "Das Verbrechen ist seit/vor zwei Jahren geschehen."

13 (resultative): Der als vermisst gemeldete Mann ist wieder zu Hause bei seiner Familie. Ihm ist nichts passiert, er wollte nur mal alleine Urlaub machen. Der Polizeibeamte, der für die Suchmeldungen zuständig ist, hört in

der Kantine von dieser Geschichte. Er fragt seine Kollegen, ob er denn dann die Suchmeldung aus der Datei löschen kann. Diese nicken und antworten: (a)/(b) "Der Vermisste ist seit/vor einer Woche aufgetaucht."

13 (neutral): Der als vermisst gemeldete Mann ist wieder zu Hause bei seiner Familie. Er war von einer gefährlichen Jugendbande festgehalten worden. Ihm ist aber glücklicherweise nichts passiert. Ein Reporter hört von dieser Geschichte und möchte eine große Story daraus machen, fragt sich aber, ob das Ganze überhaupt aktuell genug ist. Deshalb fragt er bei den Nachbarn des Entführten nach, wann der Mann zurückgekehrt sei. Diese antworten: (a)/(b) "Der Vermisste ist seit/vor einer Woche aufgetaucht."

14 (resultative): Flughafen Frankfurt. Die Maschine nach New York ist startbereit, aber es fehlt ein Passagier. Endlich kommt er angerannt und setzt sich keuchend auf seinen Platz. Jetzt könnte die Maschine eigentlich starten, aber nichts passiert. Alle warten. Schließlich geht eine Stewardess ins Cockpit und fragt, was los sei. Der Flugkapitän meint ahnungslos, dass man doch noch auf einen Passagier warte, woraufhin die Stewardess ihm verärgert mitteilt:
(a)/(b) "Der Passagier ist seit/vor zwanzig Minuten eingestiegen."

14 (neutral): Flughafen Frankfurt. Die Maschine nach New York ist startbereit, aber es kommt zu einem merkwürdigen Zwischenfall: Ein Passagier steigt ein, setzt sich auf seinen Platz, bekommt dann einen mysteriösen Anruf und rennt wieder aus dem Flugzeug hinaus, zurück ins Flughafengebäude. Da man Angst vor terroristischen Anschlägen hat, wird die Polizei eingeschaltet. Diese befragt kurz nach dem Vorfall die Stewardess an Bord nach dem genauen Ablauf des Geschehens. Die Stewardess beginnt ihren Bericht folgendermaßen:
(a)/(b) "Der Passagier ist seit/vor zwanzig Minuten eingestiegen."

15 (resultative): Nach mehreren Misserfolgen ist es Hardy, Tim und Rocky endlich gelungen, eine Bank auszurauben. Sie haben ausgemacht, das Geld gleich nach dem Coup brüderlich durch drei zu teilen, allerdings hält sich Hardy nicht an die Abmachung, sondern versteckt das Geld erst einmal – aus Sicherheitsgründen, wie er sagt. Nach ein paar Monaten weigert er sich immer noch, das Versteck den Freunden mitzuteilen – er meint, die Polizei könnte davon Wind bekommen. Da werden die beiden anderen wütend, sie wollen endlich ihr Geld, denn:
(a)/(b) "Der Coup ist seit/vor Monaten gelungen."

15 (neutral): Nach mehreren Misserfolgen ist es Hardy und Rocky endlich gelungen, eine Bank auszurauben. Ihr Freund Tim glaubt ihnen die Geschichte nicht, vor allem da sie das Geld aus Sicherheitsgründen auch Monate nach dem Überfall noch versteckt halten. Tim sagt abschätzig zu ihnen: "So einen großen Coup habt ihr doch noch nie gelandet und das werdet ihr bestimmt auch niemals hinkriegen!", woraufhin die beiden versuchen, ihn zu überzeugen. Sie beteuern:
(a)/(b) "Der Coup ist seit/vor Monaten gelungen."

16 (resultative): Das 5-Sterne-Hotel Gala begrüßt alle seine Gäste gleich beim Eintreffen im Hotel mit einer kleinen Tanzdarbietung und einem Cocktail. Als jedoch heute ein neuer Gast anreist, sind weit und breit keine Tänzer und Kellner zu sehen. Der Hotelmanager ist sauer und sucht sie überall, bis er sie Stunden später in der Bar findet. Er scheucht sie mit den Worten auf, dass sie endlich ihre Arbeit machen sollen, denn:
(a)/(b) "Der Feriengast ist seit/vor drei Stunden angereist."

16 (neutral): Das 5-Sterne-Hotel Gala begrüßt mittags alle seine neu eingetroffenen Gäste mit einem Cocktail. Anwesend ist dabei auch Herr Strowinsky, ein gut betuchter, adliger Gast. Nach dem Mittagessen kommt der Fotograf, der ein Begrüßungsfoto für die neuen Gäste machen möchte und sich schon auf sein – heute wohl besonders hohes – Trinkgeld freut. Auf seine Frage, ob der reiche Gast schon eingetroffen sei, antwortet der Hotelmanager:
(a)/(b) "Der Feriengast ist seit/vor drei Stunden angereist."

17 (resultative): Alle Kinder wissen, dass die Vorstellung im Zirkus Roncali mit dem Auftritt des Clowns beginnt. Ein Junge erkundigt sich beim Kartenverkauf, ob die Vorstellung schon angefangen habe. Der Kartenverkäufer nickt entschuldigend und antwortet:
(a)/(b) "Der Clown ist seit/vor zwanzig Minuten aufgetreten."

17 (neutral): Rolf kommt ein wenig zu spät zur Zirkusvorstellung und setzt sich neben seine Freunde. Die Vorstellung ist mittlerweile in vollem Gange, die Clowns, die Akrobaten und die Jongleure haben ihre Darbietungen schon beendet und in der Manege sind gerade zwei Elefanten zu sehen. Weil ihm die Clowns im Zirkus immer am besten gefallen, fragt Rolf seine Freunde, ob er den Clown denn schon verpasst habe. Diese bejahen bedauernd und fügen hinzu:
(a)/(b) "Der Clown ist seit/vor zwanzig Minuten aufgetreten."

18 (resultative): Wie jeder Arzt weiß, sind Wiederbelebungsmaßnahmen nur selten von Erfolg, wenn ein Herzstillstand länger als fünf Minuten anhält.

Bei der Ankunft eines Herzinfarktpatienten erkundigt sich der diensthabende Arzt beim Rettungssanitäter, ob denn noch Hoffnung bestehe. Der Sanitäter verneint und fügt hinzu:
(a)/(b) "Der Herzstillstand ist seit/vor zehn Minuten eingetreten."

18 (neutral): Schichtwechsel in der Kardiologie-Abteilung des Krankenhauses. Der Arzt, der gerade anfängt, erkundigt sich bei seinem offensichtlich aufgeregten Kollegen, was in der letzten Schicht mit dem Herzinfarkt-Patienten geschehen sei. Dieser antwortet:
(a)/(b) "Der Herzstillstand ist seit/vor zehn Minuten eingetreten."

19 (resultative): Robert Pfarr ist eindeutig als Mörder der einflussreichen Politikerin identifiziert worden, alles spricht gegen ihn, und die Staatsanwaltschaft hat bereits Haftbefehl erlassen. Das Problem ist nur, dass keiner den Täter finden kann. Er ist wie vom Erdboden verschluckt. Der Fahndungsleiter ist stinksauer und versteht nicht, wieso seine Leute den Mörder nicht finden können. Zwei Tage lang schaut er sich das an, dann beruft er eine Sitzung ein und brüllt seine Leute an, sich endlich mehr Mühe zu geben und den Kerl zu schnappen, denn:
(a)/(b) "Der Haftbefehl ist seit/vor zwei Tagen erfolgt."

19 (neutral): Robert Pfarr ist eindeutig als Mörder der einflussreichen Politikerin identifiziert worden, alles spricht gegen ihn, und die Staatsanwaltschaft hat bereits Haftbefehl erlassen. Robert gelingt es allerdings, sich nach Mallorca zu seiner Tante abzusetzen. Als er am zweiten Tag seiner Flucht ungewaschen und in zerrissenen Kleidern vor ihrer Tür auftaucht, fragt sie nur, ob er schon wieder gesucht werde, worauf er zugeben muss:
(a)/(b) "Der Haftbefehl ist seit/vor zwei Tagen erfolgt."

20 (resultative): Der Vater tritt mit dem Sohne vor Publikum auf. Die Show ist allseits beliebt und so bekannt, dass alle schon im Voraus wissen, wie sie ausgeht: Der Sohn rutscht mit lautem Getöse auf einer Bananenschale aus. Als die Zuschauer nach der Vorstellung aus dem Saal strömen, kommt ihnen ein Mann entgegengerannt, der die Show offensichtlich verpasst hat. Keuchend fragt er, ob die Vorstellung schon zu Ende sei. Eine Zuschauerin nickt und sagt:
(a)/(b) "Das Kind ist seit/vor fünfzehn Minuten ausgerutscht."

20 (neutral): Der Vater tritt mit dem Sohne vor Publikum auf. Die Show ist allseits beliebt und so bekannt, dass alle schon im Voraus wissen, wie sie ausgeht: Der Sohn rutscht mit lautem Getöse auf einer Bananenschale aus. Nur heute geht leider etwas schief: Das arme Kind rutscht wirklich aus

und bricht sich den Oberschenkel. Als der Notarzt kurze Zeit später ins Theater kommt, schreibt der Kleine schon wieder eifrig Autogramme. Der Arzt fragt, was passiert sei, woraufhin man ihm mitteilt:
(a)/(b) "Das Kind ist seit/vor fünfzehn Minuten ausgerutscht."

21 (resultative): Im Wahlkampf geht es hart zu. Als beim Minister ein Skandal um veruntreute Gelder aufgedeckt wird, bittet die Parteiführung ihn, so schnell wie möglich zurückzutreten, um den Wahlerfolg nicht weiter zu gefährden. Der Minister ignoriert diese Bitte allerdings. Zunächst lässt ihn die Kanzlerin gewähren, aber als die Umfragewerte in Folge des Skandals immer schlechter werden, greift sie doch ein und ermahnt ihn zum Rücktritt, denn:
(a)/(b) "Der Skandal ist seit/vor fünf Wochen bekanntgeworden."

21 (neutral): Im Wahlkampf geht es hart zu: Beim Kandidaten der linken Partei kommt ein schwerer Skandal um Steuerhinterziehung ans Tageslicht, sodass er die Kandidatur zurückziehen muss. Er gerät psychisch dadurch so unter Druck, dass er sich das Leben nimmt. Wochen später will eine engagierte junge Journalistin den Fall aufklären und fragt die Witwe des Politikers, wann genau die Steuerhinterziehung eigentlich aufgedeckt wurde. Die Witwe antwortet:
(a)/(b) "Der Skandal ist seit/vor fünf Wochen bekanntgeworden."

22 (resultative): Die Rentnerin, deren Sehvermögen schon lange schwach ist, weigert sich bisher, ihren Führerschein abzugeben. Ihrer Tochter hat sie versprochen, dies sofort zu tun, wenn sie einen – und sei es noch so kleinen – Unfall hat. Und das musste ja dann auch passieren: Sie fährt gegen ein parkendes Auto. Wirklich einsichtig ist die Frau immer noch nicht, doch ihre Tochter erinnert sie an ihr Versprechen und ermahnt sie:
(a)/(b) "Der Unfall ist seit/vor drei Tagen passiert."

22 (neutral): Die Rentnerin, deren Sehvermögen schon lange schwach ist, weigert sich bisher, ihren Führerschein abzugeben. Wie befürchtet baut sie auch einen kleinen Unfall: Sie fährt gegen ein parkendes Auto. Aus Panik begeht sie Fahrerflucht, wird aber nach drei Tagen von der Polizei aufgespürt und nach dem Unfallhergang befragt. Bei der Aufnahme des Protokolls im Polizeirevier wird sie nach dem Unfallzeitpunkt gefragt, woraufhin sie zu Protokoll gibt:
(a)/(b) "Der Unfall ist seit/vor drei Tagen passiert."

23 (resultative): Jörg hat versprochen, gleich bei Sonnenaufgang zu Manfred zu fahren, um diesem beim Umzug zu helfen. Als Manfred um neun Uhr

immer noch alleine Kisten schleppen muss, ruft er bei Jörg an und wirft ihm vor:
(a)/(b) "Die Sonne ist seit/vor zwei Stunden aufgegangen."

23 (neutral): Jörg arbeitet in einer Wetterstation. Seine Aufgabe dort ist es, den Zeitpunkt der Sonnenauf- und -untergänge zu protokollieren. Heute morgen hat Jörg allerdings verschlafen. Als er auf der Arbeit ankommt, fragt er seinen Kollegen, ob er weiß, wann die Sonne aufgegangen sei. Sein Kollege schaut auf die Uhr und antwortet:
(a)/(b) "Die Sonne ist seit/vor zwei Stunden aufgegangen."

24 (resultative): Die Regierung hat angekündigt, die Benzinsteuer sofort zu senken, wenn die Rohölpreise in diesem Jahr noch einmal steigen. Als es dann aber tatsächlich zu einem bedeutenden Preisanstieg an den Rohölmärkten kommt und die Regierung wochenlang nichts unternimmt, wirft die Opposition der Regierung Wortbruch vor, denn:
(a)/(b) "Die Preise sind seit/vor drei Wochen gestiegen."

24 (neutral): Anfang April steigen die Benzinpreise einmalig, aber sehr sprunghaft an, was – angeführt von der Autopartei – zu wochenlangen, massiven Protesten führt. Bei einer Pressekonferenz des Vorsitzenden der Autopartei fragt ein ausländischer Journalist diesen nach dem Zeitpunkt des Preisanstiegs. Der Vorsitzende antwortet:
(a)/(b) "Die Preise sind seit/vor drei Wochen gestiegen."

Appendix B – materials Experiment2

1	concrete	Der Gast ist seit zehn Minuten erschienen.
1	figurative	Das Buch ist seit März erschienen.
2	concrete	Das Paket ist seit einer Woche gekommen.
2	figurative	Die Sorge ist seit einigen Tagen gekommen.
3	concrete	Der Junge ist seit zehn Minuten gefallen.
3	figurative	Die Grenzen sind seit zwei Tagen gefallen.
4	concrete	Der Luftballon ist seit zwei Minuten geplatzt.
4	figurative	Die Aktienblase ist seit zwei Wochen geplatzt.
5	concrete	Der Toast ist seit einer Minute hochgesprungen.
5	figurative	Der Dollarkurs ist seit kurzem hochgesprungen.
6	concrete	Die Bombe ist seit zwanzig Minuten explodiert.
6	figurative	Die Arbeitslosigkeit ist seit drei Monaten explodiert.
7	concrete	Der Pinguin ist seit einer Minute aufgetaucht.
7	figurative	Der Verdacht ist seit einer Woche aufgetaucht.

8	concrete	Der Fahrgast ist seit zwei Stunden eingestiegen.
8	figurative	Der Finanzinvestor ist seit einem Jahr eingestiegen.
9	concrete	Die Suppe ist seit zehn Minuten gelungen.
9	figurative	Der große Durchbruch ist seit kurzem gelungen.
10	concrete	Der Freund ist seit fünf Minuten eingetreten.
10	figurative	Der Katastrophenfall ist seit fünfzehn Minuten eingetreten.
11	concrete	Der Reißverschluss ist seit Stunden aufgegangen.
11	figurative	Die Rechnung ist seit kurzem aufgegangen
12	concrete	Der Heißluftballon ist seit zwei Stunden gestiegen.
12	figurative	Ihre Chancen sind seit drei Wochen gestiegen.

Notes

1. This construction does not exist in English. To make it more transparent for the reader we will consistently translate it as "since … ago", although the resulting sentences are not grammatical in English.

References

Gese, Helga, Claudia Maienborn and Britta Stolterfoht
2008 On the formation of adjectival passives: the case of unaccusatives. Ms. Submitted.

Helbig, Gerhard
1983 Zustandspassiv, *sein*-Passiv oder Stativ? In: Gerhard Helbig (ed.), *Studien zur deutschen Syntax*, vol. 1, 47–57. Leipzig.
1987 Zur Klassifizierung der Konstruktion mit *sein*+PartizipII (Was ist ein Zustandspassiv?). In: CRLG (eds.), *Das Passiv im Deutschen. Akten des Colloquiums über das Passiv im Deutschen, Nizza 1986*, 215–233. Tübingen: Niemeyer.

Höhle, Tilman
1978 *Lexikalistische Syntax: Die Aktiv-Passiv-Relation und andere Infinitkonstruktionen im Deutschen*. Tübingen: Niemeyer.

Kratzer, Angelika
2000 Building statives. In: *Berkeley Linguistic Society* 26. [http://semanticsarchive.net/Archive/GI5MmI0M/kratzer.building.statives.pdf]

Lang, Ewald
1984 *The semantics of coordination*. Amsterdam: Benjamins.

Lenz, Barbara
1994 Probleme der Kategorisierung deutscher Partizipien. *Zeitschrift für Sprachwissenschaft* 12: 39–76.

Litvinov, Viktor P. and Vladimir P. Nedjalkov
1988 *Resultativkonstruktionen im Deutschen*. Tübingen: Narr.

Maienborn, Claudia
2007 Das Zustandspassiv: Grammatische Einordnung – Bildungsbeschränkung – Interpretationsspielraum. *Zeitschrift für Germanistische Linguistik* 35 (1): 83–114.

Nedjalkov, Vladimir P.
1988 The Typology of Resultative Constructions. In V. P. Nedjalkov und S. J. Jaxontov (eds.), *The Typology of Resultative Constructions*, 2–62. Amsterdam: John Benjamins.

Nogami, Sanami
2000 *Resultativkonstruktionen im Deutschen und Japanischen*. Frankfurt a. M. et al.: Lang.

Rapp, Irene
1997 *Partizipien und semantische Struktur. Zu passivischen Konstruktionen mit dem 3. Status*. Tübingen: Stauffenburg.
1998 Zustand? Passiv? – Überlegungen zum sogenannten "Zustandspassiv". *Zeitschrift für Sprachwissenschaft* 15: 231–265.

Stechow, Arnim von
1998 German participles II in distributed morphology. Ms. Univ. Tübingen.
2002 German *seit* 'since' and the ambiguity of the German perfect. In: B. Stiebels and I. Kaufmann (eds.), *More than Words: A Festschrift for Dieter Wunderlich*, 393–432. Berlin: Akademie-Verlag.

Stolterfoht, Britta, Helga Gese and Claudia Maienborn
2008 Word category conversion causes processing costs: evidence from adjectival passives. Ms. Submitted to *Psychonomic Bulletin & Review*.

Wunderlich, Dieter
1997 *Participle perfect and passive in German*. Arbeiten des SFB 282 "Theorie des Lexikons" Nr. 99: Universität Düsseldorf.

New data on an old issue: Subject/object asymmetries in long extractions in German*

Tanja Kiziak

1. Introduction – the old issue

Constituent displacement or movement is taken to be a fundamental property of natural language, and it has thus received much attention in linguistic theory-building. Long extraction is one much-discussed case in point. Essential questions concern *mobility* 'Which constituents can be extracted?' and *permeability* 'Out of which syntactic contexts?'.

With regard to mobility, the subject/object asymmetry found in long *wh*-movement out of English *that*-clauses has stirred much interest and debate.

(1) a. **Who do you think that likes John?*
    b. *Who do you think that John likes?*

Subject/object asymmetries arise in a similar fashion with long movement from *wh*-islands (2) and other extractions sites. Thus the question of mobility is interconnected with aspects of permeability.

(2) a. **Which student do you wonder how could solve the problem?*
    b. ??*Which problem do you wonder how John could solve?*

While the judgement of this data appears to be largely uncontroversial in English, the explanation of it is much less so. Over the years, a number of accounts have been proposed for subject/object asymmetries. In generative grammar, the Empty Category Principle has played a predominant explanatory role, relating the asymmetry to differences in government. With the abolition of government in Minimalism, new explanations are called for. Moreover, the exclusively formal accounts of mobility and permeability have been challenged by explanations in terms of processing (e.g. Fanselow and Frisch 2004, Kluender and Kutas 1993) and information structure (e.g. Bayer 2005).

Considering universal grammar as the ultimate goal, linguists have searched for equivalents of the English extraction asymmetries in other languages. The findings of their quest in the case of German are highly controversial. While some linguists claim that any perceived asymmetry is just a case of wishful thinking ("ECP-Wunschdenken", Müller and Sabel 1989: 24), others take them to be real, and even use them as arguments for establishing the position of the subject in German sentence structure. The controversy regarding asymmetries encompasses both extractions from dependent declarative clauses as well as extractions from *wh*-islands. The contradictory views of long extraction asymmetries in German as well as the lack of any systematic empirical investigation have repeatedly been commented on (e.g. Lutz 2004: 76, Haider 1993: 148). What is thus called for is a systematic elicitation of the German extraction data.

To meet this demand, we have carried out a series of judgement studies on German, in which we systematically consider three aspects of extraction structures: mobility, permeability and movement type. In German, long *wh*-movement and long topicalization (= extraction of a non-interrogative constituent) show the same surface structure, (3). The question is thus whether the two movement types behave in parallel as far as mobility and permeability are concerned.

(3) a. *Wen glaubt sie, dass der Anwalt angerufen hat?*
who thinks she that the lawyer called hat
'Who does she think that the lawyer has called?'

b. *Den Richter glaubt sie, dass der Anwalt angerufen hat.*
the judge thinks she that the lawyer called hat.
'The lawyer has called the judge, she thinks.'

In this article, we will report one of our experiments in depth. The findings can be summarized thus: The subject/object asymmetry does exist and it shows up with both movement types and in a range of different extraction contexts. Bearing the continuing controversies in German linguistic literature in mind, this conclusion appears to be too simplistic, and in fact it is. We shall see that the asymmetry is at times difficult to recognise because it interacts with a number of independent factors such as the semantic complexity of the complementizer and word order preferences. Moreover, the asymmetry is blurred by floor effects. Despite these confounds, the experiment shows that subjects are indeed harder to extract than objects in German. We conclude this article by hinting at some explanations for the subject/object asymmetry in German.

2. Our judgement study – the new data

Although experimental work on long extractions in German is rare, we are not the first to investigate the subject/object asymmetry using judgement studies.

While Featherston (2005a) focussed on extractions from *dass*-clauses (*that*-clauses), our study takes a broader range of embedded clauses into account; apart from *dass*-extractions, we also tested extractions from indirect questions, i.e. extractions from *ob*-clauses (*whether*-clauses) and from sentences introduced by a *wh*-element, the so-called *wh*-islands. There is another extraction type in German which at first glance looks interesting for our survey, namely extractions from dependent verb-second clauses. These have been regarded as the equivalent of extractions from complementizerless clauses in English, see (4).

(4) *Wen glaubt sie hat der Anwalt angerufen?*
who thinks she has the lawyer called
'Who does she think the lawyer has called?'

However, there is some evidence that they are not extraction constructions at all, but that they should rather be analysed as simple sentences with an integrated verb-first parenthetical (*glaubt sie* in (4)), see e.g. Reis (1996), Kiziak (2007). For this reason we will neglect the controversial extractions from verb-second clauses throughout this article and focus on clear cases of long extractions instead.[1]

2.1. Methodology

We use the thermometer judgement method for eliciting strictly controlled judgements. This method is a further development of magnitude estimation (Bard et al. 1996). With magnitude estimation, the participants have to rate all example sentences relative to a single reference item. They can assign any numerical value to this reference item, and they are asked to express the ratings for subsequent example sentences relative to the score of the reference item. Thus in magnitude estimation, there are no preset values, and different participants might end up with completely different scales. With thermometer judgements, the scale is predetermined to some extent. Participants are asked to rate the example sentences in comparison to two reference items – one quite good, one quite bad –, which are assigned the values 20 and 30. The scale is nevertheless relatively flexible as each informant can use all positive numbers including decimals, i.e. there is no preset division. In contrast to classical magnitude estimation, we elicit linear rather than magnitude data, i.e. we ask for ratings which symbolize distances from the two reference items rather than for proportional ratings relative to one reference item. See Featherston (this volume) for a discussion of the two methods.

Since the results are numerical and form an interval scale, standard statistical tests can be applied. We utilize the repeated measures analysis of variance and pairwise t-tests as our main statistical tests.[2]

The experiment was carried out on the web using the WebExp2 software package (Keller et al. 2009). The object of interest was specified as the spoken language, rather than the written form and participants were instructed to judge the sentences using the criterion whether they "sound natural". After filling in a personal details form, participants carried out two practice phases in order to familiarize themselves with the task. In the first exercise they had to assign numeric values to line lengths relative to two reference lines. In the second practice phase the technique was extended to judging sentence naturalness. Only after this stage did the elicitation of the judgements reported here begin. We recruited 32 participants from the university environment of Tübingen (12 male, 20 female, average age 24.25).

2.2. Design and Material

In our judgement study, we considered the factors mobility, permeability and movement type. Mobility and movement type each had two values (subject vs. object extraction; long topicalization vs. long *wh*-movement), and permeability was elicited for six different kinds of clauses. We thus tested long extractions in $2 \times 2 \times 6 = 24$ conditions.

Since we are interested in subject/object asymmetries, the extracted elements were nominative and accusative NPs. All of them were animate, case-unambiguous masculine nouns in the singular. For long *wh*-movement we tested discourse-linked phrases, i.e. *welcher/welchen* (*which*) X, for long topicalizations we tested definite NPs.[3] The matrix subject was *du* (*you*) for *wh*-movement and *ich* (*I*) for topicalization, as these are the most natural matrix subjects in each case.

We tested extractions from *dass*-clauses (*that*-clauses) and from five types of indirect questions. One of these was an embedded yes/no-question, i.e. an *ob*-clause (*whether*-clause), the other four were embedded *wh*-questions introduced by *wann* (*when*), *warum* (*why*), *wen/wer* (*who*) and *welcher X/welchen X* (*which X*). With extractions from *dass*-clauses, the matrix predicate was *denken* (*to think*), with indirect questions it was *nicht wissen* (*to not know*). In (5) we give the schematic structures for object extraction in long topicalizations to show what the tested clause types looked like. For actual example sentences we refer the reader to the appendix.

(5) a. Extraction from dass-clause:

Den X denke ich, dass der Y geVERBt hat.
the X know I that the Y VERBed has
'The Y has VERBed the X, I think.'

b. Extraction from ob/wann/warum-clause:

Den X weiß ich nicht, ob/wann/why der Y geVERBt hat.
the X know I not whether/when/why the Y VERBed has
'I don't know whether/when/why the Y has VERBed the X.'

c. Extraction from wer/welcherX-clause:

Den X weiß ich nicht, wer/welcher Y geVERBt hat.
the X know I not who/which Y VERBed has
'I don't know who/which Y VERBed X .'

We further tested 8 non-extraction conditions. Four of these were simple mono-clausals, which we included for comparison (interrogative vs. declarative; subject-initial vs. object-initial, i.e. $2 \times 2 = 4$). The schematic representation for the object-initial declarative clause is given in (6).

(6) *Den X hat der Y geVERBt.*
the X has the Y VERBed
'The Y has VERBed the X.'

The remaining four conditions were the controversial apparent extractions from verb-second clauses, the results of which we will not report in this article (see above and footnote 2). All in all, each participant thus saw 32 conditions during the experiment: the 24 extraction conditions + 4 mono-clausal conditions + 4 controversial extraction conditions.

We constructed 16 lexical variants of the experimental material, and assigned them to the 32 conditions, i.e. each variant appeared twice during the experiment. The lexis was controlled for length, lemma frequency and semantic plausibility. We furthermore inserted 15 filler sentences.

2.3. Results and Discussion

For graphical representation, we normalize the data from all subjects by conversion to z-scores. This unifies the different scales that individual informants used, allowing for visual inspection of the results. We will present the results step by step, explaining the various factors that influence the subject/object asymmetry as we go along.

2.3.1. Word order preferences

We start with long extractions from *dass*-clauses and compare them to monoclausals. Consider the two charts in figure 1. The ratings for *wh*-movement are given in the left-hand chart, those for topicalizations on the right. In each chart, the left-hand pair of conditions shows the judgements for the monoclausals, and the extractions from *dass*-clauses are given on the right.

The vertical scales represent perceived wellformedness, with higher scores indicating better judgements. The error bars show 95% confidence intervals for the mean values. If they do not overlap or overlap only a little, we can assume clearly distinct scores.

With the *dass*-extractions, we can see that object extraction is rated better than subject extraction for both movement types, i.e. there is a clear subject/object asymmetry in both cases.[4] However, the gap between subject and object extraction is bigger for *wh*-movement than it is for long topicalization. Featherston (2005a) made the same observations, but he tested the two movement types in separate experiments, and thus he could not relate them as directly as we

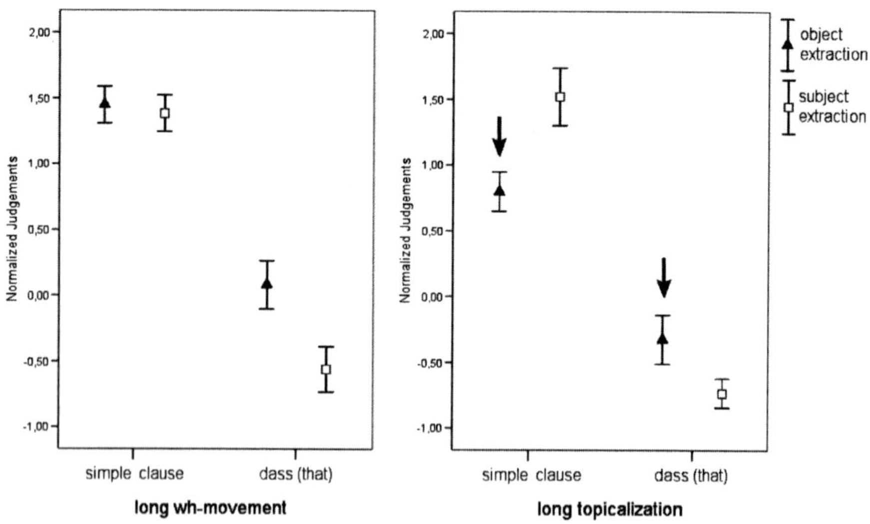

Figure 1. Monoclausals and dass-extractions for both movement types

can. Furthermore, Featherston did not include simple sentences in these studies. Comparing the long extractions to monoclausals is however helpful when trying to explain the difference in gap size for the two movement types. Consider the simple sentences on the left of each chart.

With monoclausal questions, subject – and object – initial sentences are rated equally good. Yet, with monoclausal declaratives, we see a clear dispreference for putting the object in sentence-initial position. It appears that this dispreference is reflected in the long extractions from *dass*-clauses; with long topicalizations, i.e. with the declarative version of long extraction, the object-initial sentences are dispreferred, too. We added arrows to the original graph to highlight this observation.

That our participants preferred subject-initial word order in monoclausal declaratives conforms to the standard assumptions about the German pre-field (cf. Fanselow 2002 for an overview): A nominative subject can appear in this position by default[5], whereas for the object to appear in clause-initial position, some kind of discourse motivation is needed. Without discourse motivation, i.e. without the right pragmatic context, German word order in declarative clauses appears to reflect an obliqueness hierarchy: the subject normally represents the thematic role agent, which is highest in the thematic hierarchy. In contrast to this, there are no such word order preferences for questions. Enquiries can concern any element of a sentence, with this element then automatically being in focus and appearing in clause-initial position.

So from a discourse-motivation point of view, subject-initial declarative clauses should always be better than their object-initial counterparts unless a special context is provided. That the ratings are nevertheless reversed in long topicalizations shows how heavily subject extraction is constrained. Although object extractions violate word order preferences for declarative clauses, they are still noticeably better than subject extractions.

2.3.2. The semantic heaviness of complementizers

We next compare extractions from *dass*-clauses to extractions from interrogative clauses in order to get an understanding of how the embedded clause type influences the subject/object asymmetry. Consider figure 2 which contains extractions from *dass*-clauses, *ob*-clauses and one of the *wh*-islands we tested, namely extraction from *wann*-clauses.

The object extractions are rated better than the subject extractions for each extraction pair. In the *dass*-extraction, the difference is large, but the error bars for subject and object extraction overlap with each other in *ob*-clauses and *wann*-clauses. Thus the contrast between subject and object extraction is not as large

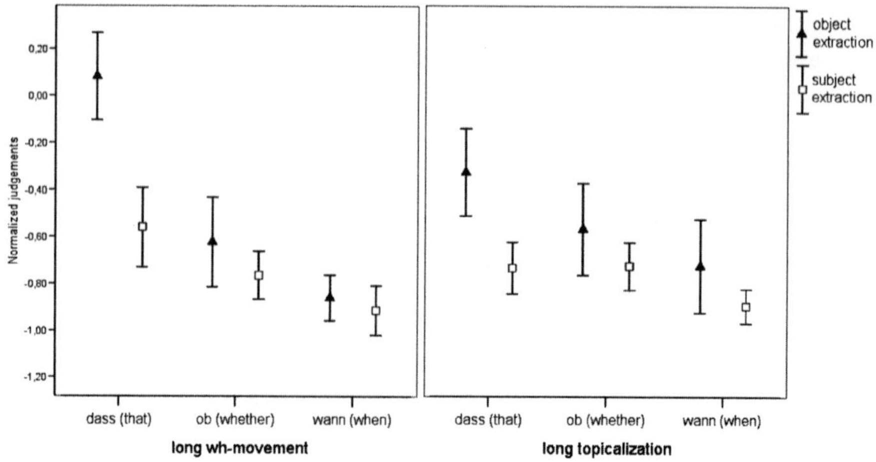

Figure 2. Subject/object asymmetries for extractions from dass-, ob- and wann-clauses with both movement types.

with the interrogative clauses as it is with the *dass*-clauses, but the asymmetry shows up as a clear trend. We will come back to the diminished contrast between subject and object extraction when we discuss floor effects in section 2.3.4. In this and the next section we will first focus on the complementizers' general effect on extraction.

Kluender (1992) claims that island constraints reflect principles of predication. The clause from which extraction takes place is part of a complex predicate, and the extracted element is its argument. For extractions to be possible, all heads and specifiers occurring in the complex predicate must be as non-specific in reference as possible. In short, the semantically lighter the complementizer/SpecCP-element of the embedded clause is, the more easily extraction across it can take place. Kluender and Kutas (1993) restate the same hypothesis, but they do not motivate it through predication structure, i.e. a semantic construct, but rather by the limitations of the human sentence processor. Maintaining the dependency between an extracted element and its gap across a clause-boundary causes syntactic processing effects. These effects combine and interact with the lexical processing effort induced by the complementizer of the embedded clause. Kluender and Kutas assume that different complementizers induce different degrees of processing effort. The complementizer *that* is semantically lightest as it merely signals that a proposition will follow, and consequently extraction from *that*-clauses should be easiest (disregarding extraction from complementizerless clauses for the moment). The complementizers *if* and *whether* are semantically more complex in that they 'index' possible states of affairs, so extraction from these clauses is expected to be worse than from *that*-clauses. Extraction from *wh*-islands is supposed to be hardest, especially with interrogative pronoun specifiers. For these, a mental representation of the referent has to be generated, thereby causing noticeable processing effort. *Wh*-islands with interrogative adverbials like *when* or *how* are assumed to be less demanding than pronominal *wh*-islands, but extractions from them should still be worse than extractions from *if*- and *that*-clauses.

Kluender and Kutas tested their hypothesis in judgements tasks and ERP studies. They did indeed find the hierarchy *that* < *if* < *wh*, i.e. extractions from *that*-clauses were rated best, whereas extractions from *wh*-islands with pronominal interrogatives were judged to be worst. The *if*-extraction was somewhere in the middle. Similarly, the processing effort (represented by an N400 effect) was smallest for extractions from *that*-clauses and largest for *wh*-islands.

We can see in figure 2 that the findings of Kluender and Kutas' judgement study on English *wh*-movement are reproduced in our own judgement study for German. With *wh*-movement in the left chart, we clearly see a general drop in acceptability as we move along the horizontal axis: Extractions from *dass*-clauses are rated better than extractions from *ob*-clauses and these in turn are rated better than extractions from *wh*-islands. The same hierarchy is visible for long topicalizations on the right, but it is not as pronounced as with *wh*-movement. In anticipation of the full array of topicalization data to be given in figure 4, we should add that *ob*-extractions do not perform better than all *wh*-islands tested – extraction from a *warum*-clause e.g. seems to be as good as extraction from an *ob*-clause. It might thus not be justified to adopt the ternary hierarchy of *that* < *if* < *wh* for long topicalization in German. We can however safely say that there is the hierarchy of *dass*-clause < interrogative clause for topicalization.

2.3.3. *How movement type interacts with complementizer type*

When we consider figure 2 carefully, we see that the drop in acceptability across the range of complementizers is sharper for *wh*-movement than it is for long topicalization. Figure 3 displays the interaction of movement type and complementizer type in greater clarity. In this graph we collapsed subject and object extraction.[6] On the left we see *wh*-movement versus topicalization for *dass*-extractions. On the right we contrast the movement types for all *wh*-islands we tested (i.e. the two error bars represent the joint ratings for the extractions from clauses introduced by *wann*, *warum*, *wer/wen* and *welcher/welchen X*). The results for *ob*-extraction in the middle are mainly added to complete the picture.

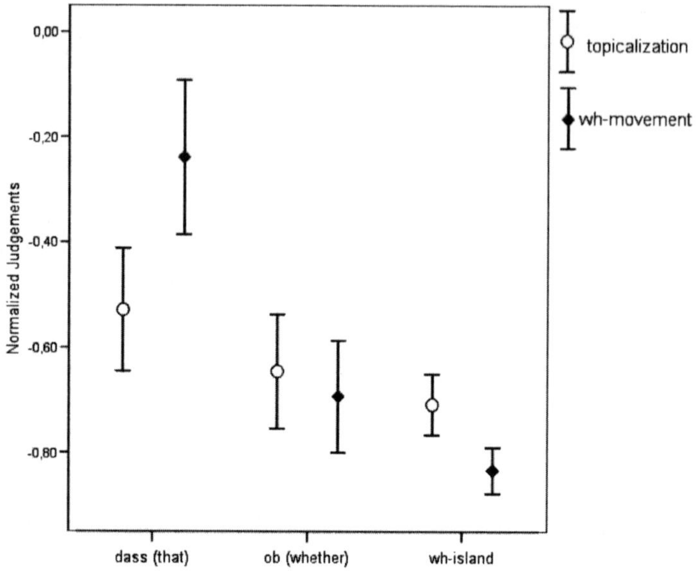

Figure 3. Comparing the two movement types for extractions from different clause-types

Let us first focus on the *dass*-extractions (left) and the *wh*-islands (right). The graph shows that *wh*-movement is rated better than topicalization with the declarative *dass*-clauses. In the *wh*-islands, the ratings are reversed for the two movement types. This attests that *wh*-movement is more severely affected if the complementizer is an interrogative element. The statistics confirms this as the interaction between movement type and clause type is highly significant by both subjects and items ($F_1(1,31) = 22.89$, $p_1 < 0.001$; $F_2(1,15) = 13.04$, $p_2 = 0.003$).[7]

It is hypothesized (e.g. Culicover 1999: 219) that intervening *wh*-elements are likely to interfere with the processing of fronted *wh*-items. Thus, with *wh*-movement from *wh*-islands, there are two interrogative elements interacting. This is evidently not the case for long topicalization from *wh*-islands, in which the *wh*-constituent at the embedded clause boundary is the only one. The rating pattern for the two movement types with *wh*-islands can thus be explained in terms of the processing difficulty of an additional interrogative element. Other, more formal accounts have been advanced, too, and it has been theorized that long topicalization targets a landing site different from *wh*-movement. Müller and Sternefeld (1993) postulate a Topic projection (TP) below CP, and long topicalization is assumed to proceed via and into SpecTP. In a more recent account, Sabel (2002: 306) keeps up the idea of different landing sites for the two movement types, although his overall account of extraction islands differs from Müller and Sternefeld (1993) due to the abolition of government in Minimalism.

The extractions from interrogative *ob*-clauses in the middle fit in with the overall finding of this section; compared to *dass*-extractions, the drop in acceptability is much sharper for *wh*-movement than for long topicalization. Even if *wh*-movement does not end up being worse than topicalization for *ob*-clauses (as was the case with *wh*-islands), we can still see that the interrogative nature of the embedded clause has a stronger effect on *wh*-movement than on topicalization.

Thus we find out two things: first, there is an 'interrogative island effect' for both movement types – with interrogative embedded clauses, both movement types are rated worse than with the declarative *dass*-clause. Second, the 'interrogative island effect' is much stronger for long *wh*-movement than for long topicalization.

To sum up our findings so far: The subject/object asymmetry is visible throughout the data. It is influenced by word-order preferences in declarative clauses, by the semantic heaviness of the complementizer, and furthermore, the movement type interacts with the utterance type of the embedded clause. There is one more issue we need to comment on: so-called floor effects.

2.3.4. Floor Effects

One thing that blurs the otherwise clear subject/object asymmetries are the floor effects we find with the subject extractions. 'Floor effect' is a descriptive term for the fact that at a certain level of 'badness', judgements do not get much worse, even if theoretically there should be a contrast in acceptability between two structures because one violates more constraints than the other – for the cumulative view of constraint violation we refer the reader to Keller (2000). Floor effects can be seen in figure 2, but it is worth looking ahead to figures 4 and 5 as they are much clearer cases. To stay in the metaphor: In these figures, it looks as if the judgements of the subject extractions have reached a floor, and therefore the subject/object asymmetry gets compressed with the clause types towards the right. Floor effects appear when various factors coincide to make a structure particularly bad. In the case at hand, floor effects are therefore not surprising; long extractions from finite clauses are unanimously considered as rather marginal data in German.

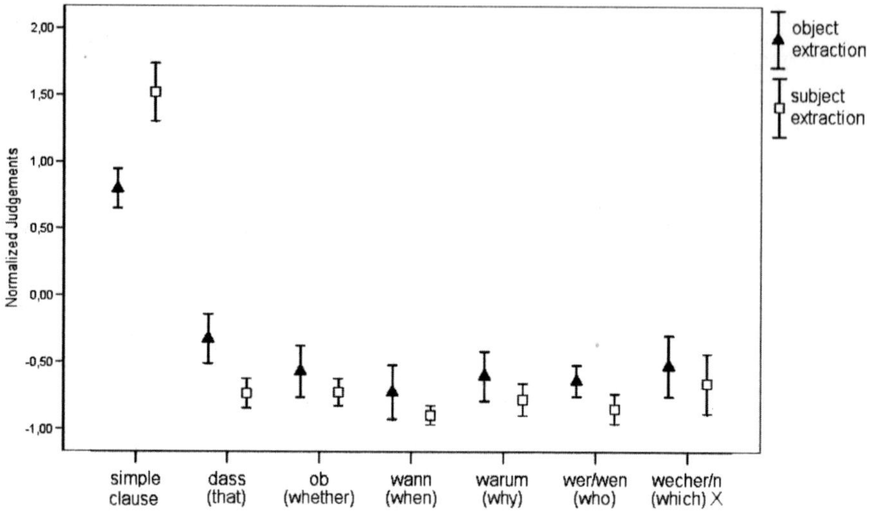

Figure 4. Long topicalization for all embedded clauses we tested.

2.3.5. The full picture

Let us now look at long topicalization with the full range of embedded clauses we tested. In figure 4, we see that object extraction is rated better than subject extraction for each of the six extraction pairs on the right. This is all the more noteworthy since there is a preference for subject-initial word order in declarative non-extraction contexts, as shown by the monoclausals on the very left.

The subject/object asymmetry is most evident for *dass*-extractions, as the error bars do not overlap. The diminished contrast between subject and object extractions for the other topicalizations can be attributed to floor effects. But in spite of the floor effects, the overall tendency is still clearly visible throughout: object extraction is again and again rated better than subject extraction. Thus the original question whether German exhibits subject/object asymmetries can be answered in the affirmative for long topicalizations. The statistics confirms this. The subject/object asymmetry is revealed in a highly significant main effect for Case in both the by subjects and by items analyses ($F_1(1{,}31) = 9.8$, $p_1 = 0.004$; $F_2(1{,}15) = 41{,}59$, $p_2 < 0.001$).[8]

The full picture for long *wh*-movement looks somewhat different (figure 5). While we see a profound contrast between subject and object extraction with the *dass*-clauses, and at least a clear trend for the *ob*-extractions, the other data from *wh*-islands does not readily lend support to the existence of subject/object asymmetries. One probable reason for this has been given in section 2.3.3:

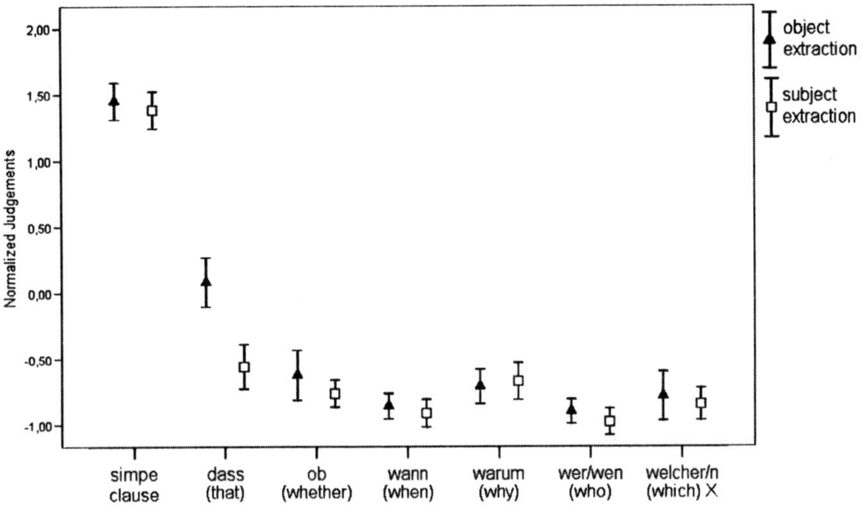

Figure 5. Long *wh*-movement for all embedded clauses we tested.

the *wh*-element at the embedded clause boundary interferes too strongly with long *wh*-movement, i.e. object extractions are rated so bad that they already reach the judgemental floor and can no longer be distinguished from subject extractions. This data is nevertheless compatible with the asymmetry: in all *wh*-islands except the *warum*-case, the means for object extractions are at least a touch higher. Statistically, however, we do not find any significant effects for the interrogative clause types due to the floor effects (all t_1/t_2 smaller than 1.7). In contrast to this, the subject/object asymmetry bears highly significant effects for *dass*-extractions ($t_1(31) = 6.165$; $p < 0.001$; $t_2(15) = 6.914$; $p < 0.001$).

Long *wh*-movement from *warum*-clauses stands out from the other *wh*-islands in two respects: first, the relation of subject and object extraction appears to be reversed – but due to the overlap of error bars, this hardly has any meaning –, and second, the *warum*-case is rated better than the other adverbial *wh*-island, the *wann*-clause. The reason for this is not entirely clear, but Ross (1968:17) already remarked that extractions across *why* appear better than extractions across other *wh*-islands. One might suspect that it is due to the semantics of *why*. While other *wh*-elements have the same semantics as indefinites, namely referring to individuals, places or times ('for which x, p(x)'), *warum/why* refers to propositions ('for which p, p causes q').

Let us lastly comment on extraction across *welcher/welchen X* at the very right. It is rated surprisingly good with *wh*-movement, and also with long topicalization in figure 4. Featherston (2005b) noticed in his superiority studies that ratings improve if either both *wh*-elements are discourse-linked or neither of them. He relates this to a preference for parallelity. The same might come into play in our study; all extracted elements are full DPs, and therefore having a full DP rather than an interrogative pronoun at the embedded clause-boundary might boost the ratings to some extent.

3. Conclusions and further studies in fast forward

Our judgement study shows (a) that word-order preferences which exist for simple declarative clauses also figure in long topicalizations, (b) that extraction is better from *dass*-clauses than from embedded interrogative clauses, (c) that movement type interacts with embedded clause-type, i.e. *wh*-movement is more strongly affected by the interrogative nature of an embedded clause than long topicalization, and (d) that contrasts get compressed due to floor effects in very bad examples. The combination of all of these factors obscures the picture for subject/object asymmetries in German, and we take this to be the reason why opinions on this topic have been contradictory in linguistic literature. By disentangling the factors involved, our study constitutes a major step towards settling the data dispute.

We conclude that the subject/object asymmetry is a property of long extractions in German, and that it exists for both movement types and with the full range of embedded clauses types we tested. However, since the subject/object asymmetry cumulates with other factors such as floor effects and complementizer type, it can become imperceptible as for example with *wh*-movement from *wh*-islands.

We have thus come a long way towards clarifying German extraction data. Yet there are many more questions to be addressed. In our study we were only concerned with extractions from complement clauses. Extractions from subject clauses and adverbial clauses provide an equally interesting domain for future investigations, and so we could easily expand our investigations with regard to permeability. As far as mobility is concerned, we have already carried out additional studies. Bearing the asymmetry between nominative subjects and accusative objects in mind, we wanted to see how dative objects fit into the picture. We found out that they are rated in the same way as accusative objects, i.e. we find a dative/accusative symmetry and a dative/nominative asymmetry of a very similar nature[9]. We also tested adverbial extraction to some extent.

Broadening the empirical database is a valuable goal for long extractions in German. Judgement studies can however also take on another goal: They can be used to get a better understanding of the reasons underlying the asymmetry. After all, a whole range of different explanations have been given in the literature.

For example, the most familiar generative account, the ECP-account, locates the problem for subject extraction with the trace, which is said to not be properly governed. For German, an entirely different line of reasoning makes sense too. In contrast to English, German NPs display morphological case-marking. Andersson/Kvam (1984: 58–62) make the case/agreement clash between an extracted nominative and the matrix verb responsible for the poor quality of subject extractions. Fanselow (2007), too, hypothesizes that overt case-marking in general, and nominative case in particular, might have an effect on judgements of extraction constructions in German.

We have embarked on further judgement studies which focus on the case-marking of the extracted element. One of our findings is that the extraction of a subject with nominative case-marking is quite good when it is base-generated in object position, e.g. in passive sentences. Thus we would conclude that case-marking as such is not an insurmountable obstacle for extraction, and in fact this is likely to be a processing factor which should not be modelled in the narrow syntax. We have also started to investigate more structural reasons for the subject/object asymmetry, e.g. we carried out an experiment on Pesetsky's Path Containment Condition (Pesetsky 1982), and the results appear to favour it. All of the mentioned studies are reported in Kiziak (in prep).

It is not within the scope of this article to provide a full account of the reasons underlying the subject/object asymmetry. This article deliberately focusses on the preliminary step: Before giving explanations for a much-debated data pattern, one should first put the data on a sound empirical basis. We hope to have shown in this article that the subject/object asymmetry in German extractions is not merely a case of 'wishful thinking' (to repeat the words of Müller and Sabel 1989), but quite to the contrary it is a consistent pattern which shows up throughout the extraction data we investigated.

Appendix

Materials: We present the long wh-movement structures each in one of our lexical variants. The long topicalization structures are virtually the same; you only have to change the determiner of the extracted phrase from *welcher/welchen* to *der/den*, replace the second person singular in the matrix clause by first person singular, and change the question mark to a full stop – as an illustration we included the topicalizations from *dass*-clause.

Extraction from *dass*-clause:

Welcher Häftling denkst du, dass den Wärter provoziert hat?
which prisoner think you that the guard provoked hat
'Which prisoner do you think that has provoked the guard?'

Welchen Cowboy denkst du, dass der Sheriff verhaftet hat?
which cowboy think you that the sheriff arrested has
'Which cowboy do you think that the sheriff has arrested?'

Der Häftling denke ich, dass den Wärter provoziert hat.
the prisoner think I that the guard provoked has
'The prisoner has provoked the guard, I think.'

Den Cowboy denke ich, dass der Sheriff verhaftet hat.
the cowboy think I that the sheriff arrested has
'The sheriff has arrested the cowboy, I think.'

Extraction from *ob*-clause:

Welcher General weißt du nicht, ob den Offizier beleidigt hat?
which general know you not, whether the officer insulted has
'Which general do you not know whether has insulted the officer?'

Welchen Herzog weißt du nicht, ob der Ritter getötet hat?
which duke know you not whether the knight killed has
'Which duke do you not know whether the knight has killed?'

Extraction from *wann*-clause:

Welcher Student weißt du nicht, wann den Professor verärgert hat?
which student know you not when the professor annoyed has
'Which student do you not know when has annoyed the professor?'

Welchen Täter weißt du nicht, wann der Redner verteidigt hat?
which offender know you not when the speaker defended has
'Which offender do you not know when the speaker has defended?'

Extraction from *warum*-clause:

Welcher Meister weißt du nicht, warum den Lehrling gelobt hat?
which master know you not why the apprentice praised has
'Which master do you not know why has praised the apprentice?'

Welchen Minister weißt du nicht, warum der Agent beobachtet hat?
which minister know you not why the spy observed has
'Which minister do you not know why the spy has observed?

Extraction from *wer/wen*-clause:

Welcher Richter weißt du nicht, wen gestern angerufen hat?
which judge know you not whom yesterday called has
'Which judge do you not know whom has called yesterday?'

Welchen Bewerber weißt du nicht, wer gestern abgelehnt hat?
which applicant know you not who yesterday rejected has
'Which applicant do you not know who has rejected yesterday?'

Extraction from *welcher/welchen X*-clause:

Welcher Sportler weißt du nicht, welchen Trainer gestern enttäuscht hat?
which athlete know you not which coach yesterday disappointed has
'Which athlete do you not know has disappointed which coach yesterday?'

Welchen Filmstar weißt du nicht, welcher Reporter gestern verfolgt hat?
which film star know you not which reporter yesterday pursued has
'Which film star do you not know which reporter pursued yesterday?'

Monoclausals (for comparison):

Welcher Lehrer hat den Schüler getadelt?
which teacher has the pupil told_off
Which teacher has told off the pupil?

Welchen Gärtner hat der Verwalter entlassen?
Which gardener has the administator dismissed
'Which gardener has the caretaker dismissed?'

Extraction from verb-second clause (not considered in this article):

Welcher Bischof denkst du hat den Priester ermahnt?
Which bishop think you has the priest warned
'Which bishop do you think has warned the priest?'

Welchen Sänger denkst du hat der Dirigent kritisiert?
Which singer think you has the conductor criticised
'Which singer do you think the conductor has criticised?'

Notes

* This work was supported by the Deutsche Forschungsgemeinschaft within the SFB 441 'Linguistische Datenstrukturen'. Thanks are due to my project leader Wolfgang Sternefeld, my colleagues Oliver Bott and Sam Featherston as well as many other members of the SFB for support and advice. All remaining errors are my own.

1. Although we do not report the results in this article, we elicited judgements on subject/object asymmetries in so-called extractions from verb second clauses. In our view, the findings constitute another piece of evidence in favour of the parenthetical analysis, see Kiziak (in prep). For both movement types, the construction is rated differently from clear cases of long extractions and in parallel to simple matrix clauses. The latter is expected if purported extractions from verb-second claues are in fact matrix clauses with a parenthetical insert. Our own data is confirmed by earlier findings of Featherston (2005a), who also shows that *dass*-extractions behave differently from the controversial construction with regard to subject/object asymmetries. Featherston, however, does not investigate simple matrix clauses, and he interprets his results differently from us. He takes the differences as evidence that German shows the classical *that*-trace effect found for English.
2. We always use the Huynh-Feldt correction procedure, but for reasons of simplicity we only report uncorrected degrees of freedom.
3. It has been claimed that long topicalizations from *wh*-islands are most acceptable for bare plurals (D'Avis 1996, Bayer 1990). As we wanted the extracted element to be case-unambiguous, we tested with definite NPs in the singular rather than with bare plurals. In the plural, most nouns are ambiguous between nominative and accusative case in German. In our experiment, case-ambiguity is undesirable due to potential garden-path effects. It has been shown that there is a 'subject before object' preference in German, i.e. clause-initial, case-ambiguous NPs are preferably parsed as subjects (for an overview see Bader and Bayer 2006: 87–104).
4. It has been said that the *that*-trace effect exists for standard and Northern varieties of German, but not for Southern varieties (e.g. Grewendorf 1995). Our results contradict this view since the majority of our participants are from the South (22 out of 32), and we can still see a subject/object asymmetry. The asymmetry is the same when we exclude the data of non-Southern speakers.
5. This is at least true for the verbs we tested (see appendix). Word-order preferences are different for non-canonical verbs, for example unaccusatives.
6. We could equally well have presented object extractions on their own rather than the combined results for object and subject extractions. With object extractions alone, judgements are in general a bit better, i.e. error bars appear higher on the scale, but the relationship between *wh*-movement and topicalization stays exactly the same. We can even see the same basic pattern when we regard subject extractions on their own, although the floor effects with *wh*-islands diminish the difference between *wh*-movement and topicalization (see section 2.3.4 on floor effects).

7. Note that with *wh*-islands, four clause types were aggregated over, whereas there is only one clause type in the *dass*-extration. This results in inhomogeneous variances across conditions. We can compensate for this by adopting a more conservative alpha-level. Our results are significant even with an alpha-level of 0.005.
8. The main effect for Case is also significant when we consider the five interrogative embedded clauses on their own ($F_1(1,31) = 6.401, p_1 = 0.017$; $F_2(1,15) = 21.15$, $p_2 < 0.000$). We furthermore carried out pairwise one-tailed t-tests:

	mean subject-object differences	by subjects $t_1(31) =$	by items $t_2(15) =$
dass	0.401	3.93; **p< 0.001**	4.718; **p < 0.001**
ob	0.156	1.258; p = 0.109	1.334; p = 0.101
wann	0.170	1.794; **p = 0.042**	2.363; **p = 0.016**
warum	0.175	1.615; p = 0.058	1.608; p = 0.065
wer/wen	0.208	2.669; **p = 0.006**	2.675; **p = 0.008**
welchX	0.130	0.972; p = 0.168	0.914; p = 0.187

We see that the subject/object asymmetry reaches significance for three of the six clause types. And although the results are not significant for all clause types, the value for the subject-object difference is always positive, i.e. the trend is the same for all clause types.
9. Some of the work on dative extraction was carried out jointly with Maria Melchiors. See Melchiors (2007: 123–138) for the first study on dative extraction.

References

Andersson, S.-G. and Kvam, S.
1984 *Satzverschränkung im heutigen Deutsch*. Tübingen: Narr.

Bard, E., Robertson, D. and Sorace, A.
1996 Magnitude estimation of linguistic acceptability. *Language 72* (1): 32–68.

Bader, M. and Bayer, J.
2006 *Case and Linking in Language Comprehension. Evidence from German*. Dordrecht: Springer.

Bayer, J.
1990 Notes on the ECP in English and German. *Groninger Arbeiten zur Linguistik (GAGL)* 30: 1–55.
2005 Was beschränkt die Extraktion? Subjekt – Objekt vs. Topic – Fokus. In: F.-J. D'Avis (ed.), *Deutsche Syntax: Empirie und Theorie*, 233–257. Göteborg: Acta Universitatis Gothoburgensis.

Culicover, P. W.
1999 *Syntactic Nuts. Hard Cases, Syntactic Theory and Language Acquisition.* Oxford: Oxford University Press.

D'Avis, F.-J.
1996 On *wh*-islands in German. In: U. Lutz and J Pafel. (eds.), *On Extraction and Extraposition in German*, 89–120. Amsterdam: Benjamins.

Fanselow, G.
2002 Quirky subjects and other specifiers. In: B. Kaufmann and B. Stiebels (eds.), *More than words*, 227–250. Berlin: Akademie Verlag.
2007 Carrots – perfect as vegetable, but please not as a main dish. *Theoretical Linguistics* 33: 353–367.

Fanselow, G. and Frisch, S.
2004 Effects of Processing Difficulty on Judgments of Acceptability. In: G. Fanselow, C. Féry, M. Schlesewsky, R.Vogel (eds.), *Gradience in Grammar*, 291–316. Oxford: Oxford University Press.

Featherston, S.
2005a *That*-trace in German. *Lingua* 115: 1277–1302.
2005b Universals and grammaticality: Wh-constraints in German and English. *Linguistics* 43 (4): 667–711.

Grewendorf, G.
1995 Syntaktische Skizzen. In: J. Jacobs, A.v. Stechow, W. Sternefeld and T. Vennemann (eds.), *Syntax. Ein internationales Handbuch zeitgenössischer Forschung.* 1288–1319. Berlin, New York: de Gruyter.

Haider, H.
1993 *Deutsche Syntax Generativ.* Tübingen: Gunter Narr.

Keller, F.
2000 Gradience in grammar. Experimental and Computational Aspects of Degrees of Grammaticality. PhD Thesis, University of Edinburgh.

Keller, F., Gunasekharan, S., Mayo, N. and Corley, M.
2009 Timing accuracy of web experiments: A case study using the WebExp software package. *Behaviour Research Methods* 41 (1): 1–12.

Kiziak, T.
2007 Long extraction or parenthetical insertion? Evidence from judgement studies. In: N. Dehé and Y. Kavalova (eds.), *Parentheticals*. 121–144. Amsterdam: Benjamins.
in prep Raising the subject of movement asymmetrics. Experimental evidence on German long extraction. Dissertation, University of Tübingen.

Kluender, R.
1992 Deriving island constraints from principles of predication. In: H. Goodluck and M. Rochemont (eds.), *Island Constraints: theory, acquisition and processing*, 223–258. Dordrecht: Kluwer.

Kluender, R. and Kutas, M.
1993 Subjacency as a Processing Phenomenon. *Language and cognitive processes* 8 (4): 573–633.

Lutz, U.
2004 Studien zu Extraktion und Projektion im Deutschen. Dissertation, University of Tübingen.

Melchiors, M.
2007 Die syntaktische Analyse des deutschen Dativs – ein komplizierter Fall. Dissertation, University of Tübingen.

Müller, G. and Sabel, J.
1989 Aufgebrochene Barrieren. *Frankfurter Linguistische Forschungen* 6: 20–40.

Müller, G. and Sternefeld, W.
1993 Improper Movement and Unambiguous Binding. *Linguistic Inquiry* 24 (3): 461–507.

Pesetsky, M.
1982 *Paths and Categories*. Cambridge, Massachusetts: MIT dissertation

Reis, M.
1996 Extractions from Verb-Second Clauses in German? In: U. Lutz and J Pafel (eds.), *On Extraction and Extraposition in German*, 45–88. Amsterdam: Benjamins.

Ross, J. R.
1968 *Constraints on Variables in Syntax*. Cambridge, Massachusetts: MIT dissertation

Sabel, J.
2002 A minimalist analysis of syntactic islands. *The Linguistic Review* 19 (3): 271–315.

Parallelism and information structure: Across-the-board extraction from coordinate ellipsis

Andreas Konietzko

1. Introduction

In this paper I discuss the grammar and information structure of parallel constructions in German. Under the notion parallel construction I subsume instances of ellipsis which cannot cross sentence boundaries, such as Bare Argument Ellipsis (BAE) and Gapping. These types of ellipsis are generally restricted to coordinate structures as illustrated in (1a–d) and share the property of being banned from subordination which distinguishes them clearly from other types of ellipsis such as sluicing or English VP-ellipsis (cf. 1e–f):

(1) a. *Sandy spielt Fußball aber Anna nicht.* *(BAE)*
Sandy plays soccer but Anna not.

b. **Sandy spielt Fußball, obwohl Anna nicht.*
Sandy plays soccer although Anna not.

c. *Sandy spielt Fußball und Anna Tennis.* *(Gapping)*
Sandy plays soccer and Anna tennis

d. **Sandy spielt Fußball während Anna Tennis.*
Sandy plays soccer while Anna tennis

e. *Sandy spielt Fußball aber ich weiß nicht wo.* *(Sluicing)*
Sandy plays soccer but I know not where

f. *Sandy plays soccer and Anna says that Kim does, too.* (*VP*-ellipsis)

Recent approaches to parallelism in grammar have sought to formulate parallelism conditions in terms of syntactic and semantic notions (e.g. Dalrymple et al. 1991, Fiengo and May 1994, Asher et al. 2001). What has been paid less attention to are the information structural requirements imposed on parallel constructions. Coordinate ellipsis offers an elegant way to study the impact of information structure on parallelism since ellipsis is sensitive to the information structure of the clause in a systematic way. First, deletion only targets given material and second, the remnants are often associated with specific information structural functions (cf. e.g. Winkler 2005). It is the latter property which will allow us to detect the interaction between parallelism and information structure.

Concentrating on BAE in German we will try to explicate the interaction of the two notions using 'Across-the-board' (ATB)-extraction (Williams 1978) from BAE. The main claim put forth in this paper is the following:

(i) Bare Argument Ellipsis obeys a *Parallelism Constraint* which requires that IS-functions be mapped onto syntactic structure in a parallel fashion in both conjuncts.

The assumption in (i) can be viewed as a well-formedness condition on coordinate ellipsis. Thus, violations of the Parallelism Constraint result in a global markedness of the structure. One way of conceptualizing markedness is to link it to processing difficulty. Under this view markedness can be the result of various sources such as structural complexity, semantic ambiguity, discourse incoherence, lack of an appropriate intonation, to mention just a few. To detect a specific source for markedness in a given context requires that other potential sources be controlled for, as it is normally the case in an experimental setting. Since the purpose of the present study is to investigate information structural mismatches in coordinate ellipsis the following hypothesis, which links information structural markedness and processing will be tested:

(ii) Processing of Coordinate Ellipsis Hypothesis: Processing of coordinate ellipsis is facilitated if the conjuncts exhibit a parallel Information Structure.

Although the hypothesis in (ii) might end up being too strong in its present form since non-parallel information structure might well be licensed by an appropriate context or intonation contour, let us assume for the moment that (ii) holds. What (ii) basically states is that IS-syntax mapping is relevant for the processing of coordinate ellipsis. Thus, (i) and (ii) together essentially predict that non-parallel syntax-IS mappings should be globally dispreferred, an effect that should be detectable in experimental rating studies.

The paper has three parts. In the first part I will introduce the phenomenon and discuss the syntax of BAE in German. The second part deals with syntactic parallelism conditions for BAE. The third part contains a discussion of the information structural notions of BAE and introduces novel experimental data on parallelism and information structure.

2. The syntax of BAE

In this section I will discuss the syntax of BAE in German. After describing the main syntactic properties of BAE, I will show that the syntax in these constructions generates strictly parallel structures and thus cannot be taken to be the source for certain asymmetries observed in BAE. I will draw evidence for the claim from word order diagnostics such as adverb placement, well-established syntactic constraints as such the coordinate structure contraints (CSC) as proposed by Ross (1967) and information structural diagnostics regarding the distribution of topical and focal material in German clauses.

Let us consider the following data:

(2) a. *Maria liest Zeitschriften aber Anna vermutlich *(nicht).*
Maria reads magazines but Anna probably not.

b. *Maria liest Zeitschriften und Anna ??(auch).*
Maria reads magazines and Anna too.

c. *MARIA liest keine Zeitschriften aber ANNA.*
Maria reads no magazines but Anna.

As originally observed by Hankamer and Sag (1976), BAE involves deletion of given material in the second conjunct of a coordinate structure except for one remnant constituent and some additional element such as negation (cf. 2a) or a focus particle (cf. 2b). The presence of such an element is strongly preferred if not obligatory. These elements serve the function of being the focus exponent in the second conjunct. Alternatively, the focus can also fall on the remnant phrase itself. This is demonstrated in (2c) where the absence of a focal element forces the remnant and the correlate to bear strong focal accents for the sentence to be grammatical. In certain cases the focus on the remnant can also be induced by the particle. The additive particle *auch* induces the phrase which is associated with it to bear focal stress if the phrase follows it (Reis and Rosengren 1997). This behaviour can also be observed in BAE (cf. 3a). Similarly, the remnant carries focal stress if it follows negation (cf. 3b):

(3) a. *Maria liest Zeitschriften und auch ANNA.*
Maria reads magazines and also Anna.

b. *Maria liest Zeitschriften aber nicht ANNA.*
Maria reads magazines but not Anna.

As already observed by Hankamer and Sag BAE may also contain certain types of modifiers. Generally, these modifiers are speech act operators such as sentential adverbs (cf. 2a) and modal particles as illustrated in the following example:

(4) *Maria liest Zeitschriften aber Anna eben nicht.*
Maria reads magazines but Anna prt. not.

The occurrence of modifiers already gives us certain hints as to the syntactic status of the reduced conjunct. For instance, modal particles may only occur in the middle field whereas sentential adverbs are usually associated with the IP/TP domain. These distributional restrictions imply that elliptical clauses presumably have a richer syntactic structure than what can be observed directly on the surface.[1]

There are basically two lines of research regarding the syntax of coordinate ellipsis. One line follows the idea that coordinate ellipsis involves the coordination of small conjuncts such as VPs. These approaches make use of ATB-movement to generate the surface word order (cf. Johnson 1996). The second line of research assumes that coordinate ellipsis involves clausal conjuncts with deletion of given material in the second conjunct. (cf. e.g. Wilder 1997, Hartmann 2000)

One problem concerning the syntax of coordinate ellipsis seems to be that a phenomenon such as Gapping which exhibits stable properties cross-linguistically receives different analyses in related languages such as English and German. Johnson (1996) among others has argued that Gapping in English involves coordination of vP conjuncts. This analysis suggests that the subject DP occupies distinct positions in the two conjuncts. While the subject of the first conjunct undergoes movement in an ATB fashion into the specifier of the higher IP node, the subject of the second conjunct remains in spec vP. This analysis has the advantage that no deletion process has to be assumed. Further, it seems to capture the syntactic parallelism found in Gapping in a straightforward fashion. A central problem of this analysis is that it seems to violate the CSC formulated by Ross (1967). This follows from the fact that the subject has been extracted out of the first conjunct only, as noted by Johnson (1996). The problem can be circumvented if one assumes that the CSC only holds for A'-movement. Since subject raising in English is an instance of A-movement the CSC violation does not arise. In fact, the CSC was motivated by Ross on A'-movement data. While this analysis works for English, it runs into problems for German. According to standard assumptions, movement into the German prefield, the position directly preceding the finite verb in root clauses, is an instance of A'-movement. This situation is illustrated in the following example in which the subject *Maria* occupies the prefield in the first conjunct:

(5) *Maria spielt Fußball und Anna Tennis.*
Maria plays soccer and Anna tennis.

The problem with the small conjunct analysis is illustrated in (6) below, this time using BAE. Here the structure must contain coordinated IPs since sentential adverbs such as *vermutlich* ('probably') are usually taken to be IP modifiers. According to standard assumptions, German root clauses are analysed as CPs. The subject *Maria* has to be extracted out of the first conjunct and raised to SpecCP to fill the prefield. However, the subject of the second conjunct remains in the second conjunct and is raised locally above the sentential adverb. This analysis is on a par with Johnson's analysis for Gapping in English. The resulting structure violates the CSC since an element has been extracted only out of one conjunct. Johnson's assumption that the CSC is not sensitive to A-movement, however, is not an option for German, since movement to the prefield indeed involves A'-movement (cf. e.g. Frey 2006).

(6)

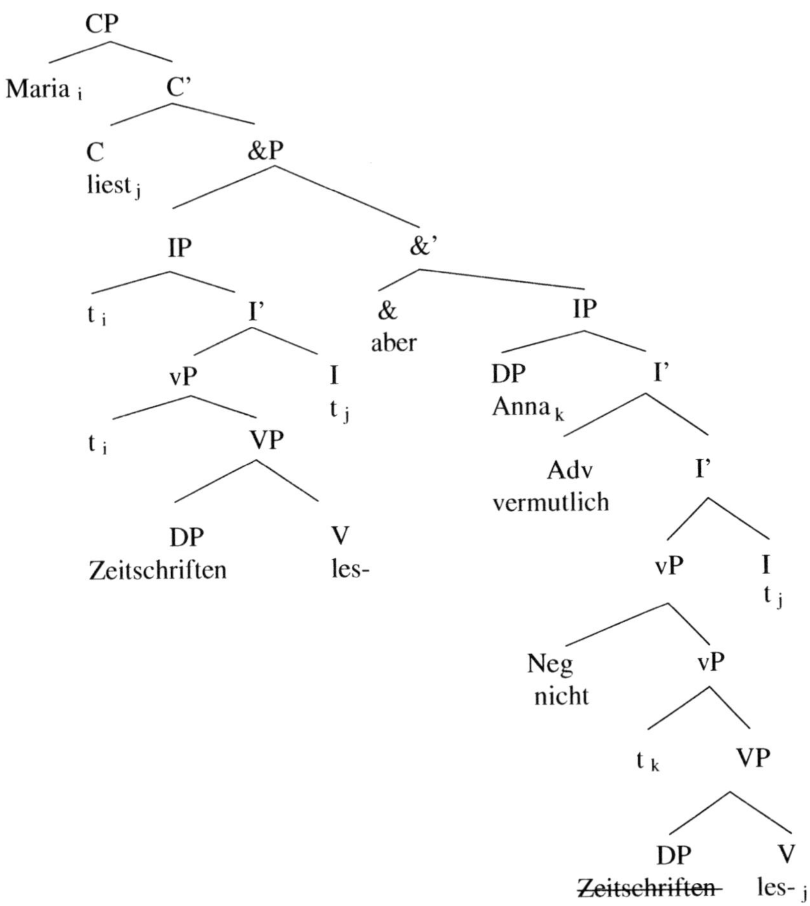

Thus, it seems that a large conjunct analysis is the most consistent approach at least for the German data. Therefore I will propose here that BAE in German indeed involves coordination of CPs as illustrated in (7) below:

(7)

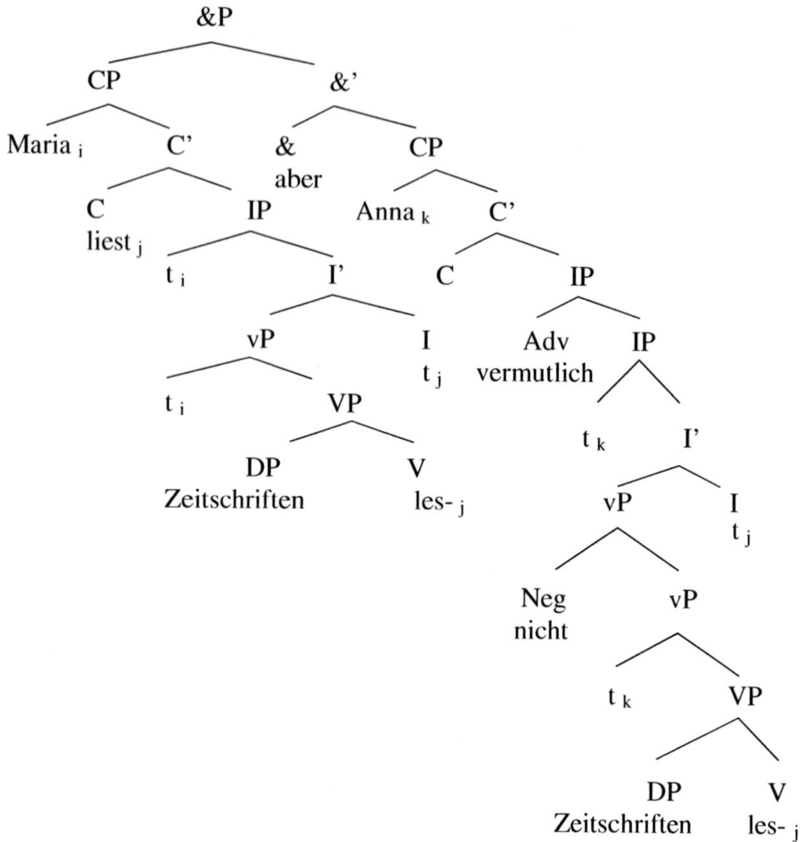

3. Bare Argument Ellipsis and ATB-extraction

Having established a parallel syntax for BAE, we are now in the position to take a closer look at ATB-extraction which will finally give us the data to test parallelism. ATB-movement refers to an operation in coordinated structures which extracts an element out of both conjunct. ATB-movement is thus an exception to the well-known coordinate structure constraint (CSC) formulated by Ross (1967), which rules out the extraction of elements contained within a conjunct:

(8) a. **Was hat Peter gekauft und ein Buch gelesen.*
What has Peter bought and a book read

b. **Was hat Peter einen Roman gekauft und gelesen.*
What has Peter a novel bought and read.

The phenomenon of ATB-movemnt is demonstrated in (9). Here the *wh*-phrase 'welcher Polizist' is subject of the embedded clause in the first conjunct as well as of the second conjunct.

(9) a. ?*Ich weiß nicht, welcher Polizist den Dieb*
I know not, $\text{which}_{\text{Nom}}$ policeman the_{Acc} thief
verfolgte und nicht den Mörder.
chased and not the_{Acc} murderer.

b. ??*Ich weiß nicht, welchen Dieb der Polizist*
I know not, $\text{which}_{\text{Acc}}$ thief the_{Nom} policeman
verfolgte aber der Kommissar nicht.
chased but the_{Nom} detective not

Recent research on coordination (cf. Reich 2007) has emphasized that ATB-extraction is a distinct property of symmetric coordination. More precisely, Reich (2007: 5) proposes that the option of ATB-extraction is a condition for symmetric sentential coordination. This assumption has far reaching consequences for a theory of Bare Argument Ellipsis. If ATB-extraction out of BAE is indeed possible we would have another argument in favour of a clausal analysis for BAE as presented in (7) above. Let us consider the following data which exhibit *wh*-extraction in an ATB fashion leaving behind an elliptical clause in the second conjunct.

Building on the analysis proposed in (7), the data in (9) might be analysed as illustrated in (10) below where the *wh*-element undergoes movement to SpecCP in both conjuncts before it is ATB-extracted and adjoined to &P (cf. also Reich 2007).

(10)

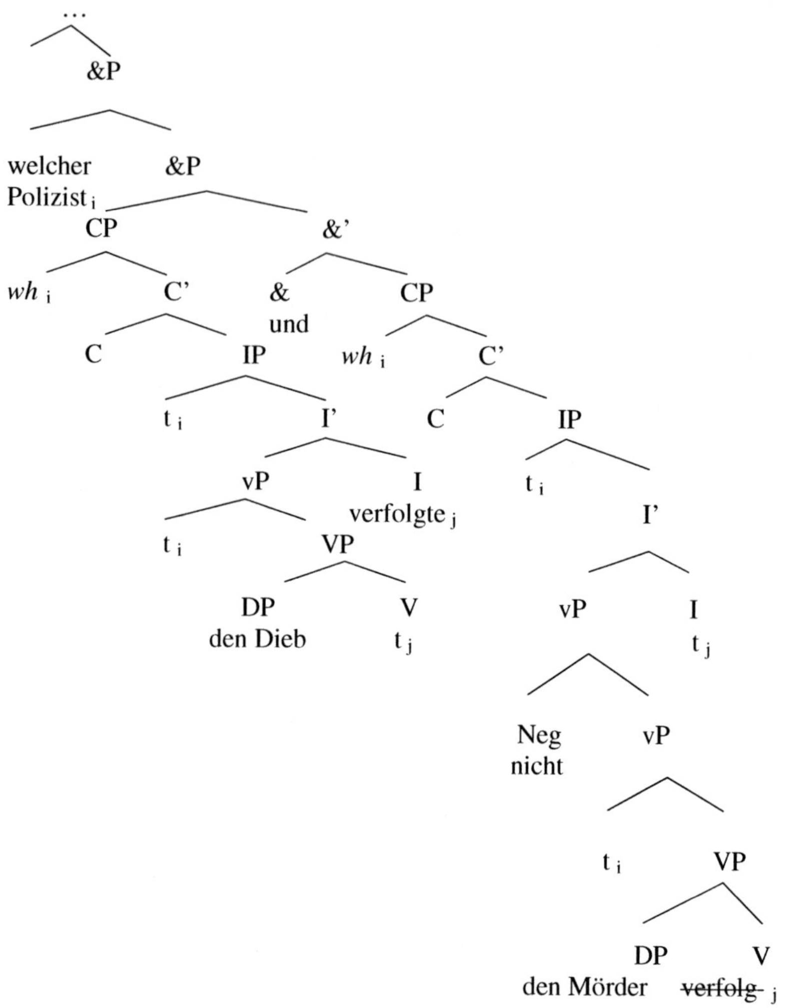

Although the data seem to be marked, they are not ungrammatical. Interestingly, there also seems to be some variation in acceptability depending on the choice of the conjunction and the type of BAE involved as the following examples show:

(11) a. ?*Ich weiß nicht, welcher Polizist den Dieb*
I know not, which$_{Nom}$ policeman the$_{Acc}$ thief
verfolgt hat aber nicht den Mörder.
chased has but not the$_{Acc}$ murderer

b. ??*Ich weiß nicht, welchen Dieb der Polizist*
I know not, $\text{which}_{\text{Acc}}$ thief the_{Nom} policemen
verfolgt hat aber der Kommissar nicht.
chased has but the_{Nom} detective not

Intuitively, (11a) is perceived as better than (11b). There are two possible syntactic reasons for the difference in grammaticality. One reason could be the grammatical function of the extracted element. The other could be the type of BAE involved. For instance, in (11a) the extracted element is the subject of the clause, in (11b) it is the object. Similarly, in (11a) the remnant of the elliptical clause follows negation, in (11b) we have the reversed word order. However, these syntactic differences are not likely to be the reason for the difference in grammaticality. First, German shows a preference for object extraction (cf. Kiziak this volume). Thus (11b) should be judged better than (11a). Second, BAE in German prefers the remnant to precede negation, whereas for the reverse word order to be fully grammatical a specific intonation seems to be required (cf. Konietzko and Winkler to appear). Again, this would also predict that (11b) should be better than (11a). This suggests that the explanation for the difference in (11) is not a syntactic one. What seems to be crucial in these examples is the specific information structure. It is well known that ellipsis displays specific information structural properties. Generally, the remnants are instances of new material associated with phonological prominence whereas elliptical material is discourse old and recoverable from the context. It has been argued (cf. Winkler 2005) that BAE in German is subject to information structural variation. Whereas in (11a) the remnant in the second conjunct is a contrastive focus, it is a contrastive topic in (11b). As already observed on the data in (9), the acceptability seems also to be dependent on the conjunction involved. This points towards an information structural difference. In the literature on connectives it is often suggested that *aber* ('but') ist associated with a contrastive interpretation (Sæbø 2003, Umbach 2005). One way to model this semantic requirement is in terms of information structure (cf. Umbach 2005). By contrast, the connective *und* ('and') is neutral in this respect, consequently it should be less restrictive with regard to the information structural status of the phrases in the conjuncts.

4. BAE and parallelism

In this section we present experimental evidence supporting the claim that parallelism and information structure interact. Experimental tudies on parallelism in Ellipsis (cf. e.g. Frazier and Clifton 1998, Carlson 2002, Stolterfoht 2005) have already proposed that elliptical constructions, in particular those occurring in coordination, are subject to certain parallelism constraints. These constraints have mainly been formulated on syntactic and phonological notions. For instance, Carlson (2002) argues that processing of elliptical constructions is facilitated if DPs that share certain syntactic, prosodic, and semantic features appear also in similar syntactic positions. More specifically, Carlson found that in related constructions such as Bare Argument Ellipsis (Stripping), Replacives and Comparatives participants interpreted the remnant as a subject more often in (12a) than they did in (12b) and (12c), with (12b) showing a greater proportion of subject interpretations than (12c).

(12) a. *Cecilia ran into a mailbox on Friday, not/but not Carol.*
Strong Subject Parallelism

b. *Maude called a policeman for help, not/but not Marjorie.*
Weak Subject Parallelism

c. *Maude called a policeman for help, not/but not a fireman.*
Object Parallelism

Carlson attributes this finding to the different strength of the subject parallelism in (12a–b) and the object parallelism in (12c). An auditory study with comparatives points to the same direction. The remnant was interpreted as subject more often in (13a) than in (13b). Capitals mark high pitch accents.

(13) a. *TASHA called Bella more often than SONYA.*

b. *Tasha called BELLA more often than SONYA.*

However, as the result was graded, Carlson concludes that accenting alone is not sufficient to force a specific interpretation.

Investigating the impact of focus on the processing of Replacives in German, Stolterfoht (2005) argues that the presence of a focus particle in the first conjunct facilitates processing of the elliptical second conjunct. She attributes this finding to a parallelism requirement on focus structure. Thus in (14b) processing of the second conjunct is facilitated since the presence of the focus particle in the first conjunct requires the associated object DP to have narrow focus. As the remnant also carries narrow focus the two conjuncts have a parallel focus structure.

(14) a. *Am Dienstag hat der Direktor den Schüler*
On Tuesday has the$_{\text{Nom}}$ principal the$_{\text{Acc}}$ pupil
getadelt, und nicht den Lehrer.
criticized, and not the$_{\text{Acc}}$ teacher.

b. *Am Dienstag hat der Direktor nur den Schüler*
On Tuesday has the$_{\text{Nom}}$ principal only the$_{\text{Acc}}$ pupil
getadelt, und nicht den Lehrer.
criticized, and not the$_{\text{Acc}}$ teacher.

By contrast, in (14a), which lacks a focus particle, the first conjunct initially receives a default wide focus interpretation. This construal has to be reanalysed when the second conjunct is encountered, which causes processing difficulty. These findings clearly show that focus plays a role in the processing of elliptical constructions.

4.1. Experimental Evidence

Testing the parallelism conditions for BAE in German, we have constructed two judgement studies. One tested the conjunction *und* ('and'), the other the conjunction *aber* ('but'). In each experiment we used the following 6 conditions:

(15) Conditions:

1. *Ich weiß nicht, welchen Dieb der Polizist*
I know not, which$_{\text{Acc}}$ thief the$_{\text{Nom}}$ policeman
verfolgt hat und/aber nicht der [KOMMISSAR$_{\text{Foc}}$].
chased has and/but not the$_{\text{Nom}}$ detective

2. ... *welcher Polizist den Dieb verfolgt hat*
... which$_{\text{Nom}}$ policeman the$_{\text{Acc}}$ thief chased has
und/aber nicht den [MÖRDER$_{\text{Foc}}$].
and/but not the$_{\text{Acc}}$ murderer

3. ... *welchen Dieb der Polizist verfolgt hat*
... which$_{\text{Acc}}$ thief the$_{\text{Nom}}$ policeman chased has
und/aber der [KOMMISSAR$_{\text{Top}}$] *nicht.*
and/but the$_{\text{Nom}}$ detective not

4. ... *welcher Polizist den Dieb verfolgt hat*
... which$_{\text{Nom}}$ policeman the$_{\text{Acc}}$ thief chased has
und/aber den [MÖRDER$_{\text{Top}}$] *nicht.*
and/but the$_{\text{Acc}}$ murderer not.

5. ... *welcher Polizist den Dieb verfolgt hat.*
... which$_{\text{Nom}}$ policeman the$_{\text{Acc}}$ thief chased has

6. ... *welchen Dieb der Polizist verfolgt hat.*
... which$_{\text{Acc}}$ thief the$_{\text{Nom}}$ policeman chased has

Condition 1 and 2 contained instances of contrastive focus as remnant, conditions 3 and 4 contrastive topic. Each remnant type was tested with object extraction and subject extraction. In addition, we added two conditions (5–6) containing uncoordinated instances of subject and object extraction to make sure that it does not influence the results.

4.2. Stimuli

24 experimental items were constructed according to the scheme in (15). The items were counterbalanced such that a subject only saw a given item in one condition. We also included 52 distractor sentences. 32 of them were experimental items from an unrelated study. The remaining 20 fillers were normed sentences representing 5 levels of grammaticality.

4.3. Procedure

We conducted two judgement studies using the thermometer judgements paradigm which has proven to be able to detect fine-grained differences in grammaticality (Featherston 2009). This method requires participants to judge the grammaticality of sentences according to a reference item of medial grammaticality. After assigning an arbitrary value to the reference item every experimental sentence is assigned a value relative to the reference item. Each grammaticality judgement was elicited after reading the whole sentence. The experiment was conducted on the WWW using the WebEx software (Keller et al. 1998). The sentences were presented in isolation. First participants read the written instructions. This was followed by a practice session to familiarize participants with the task. The first set of practice items consisted of lines which the subject had to rate with respect to a reference line. In a second step nine practice sentences were given which were rated with respect to a reference item. After the practice the 32 items and 52 distractors were presented in an individually randomized order.

4.4. Participants

24 native German speakers participated in each experiment for a payment. They were all students at the University of Tübingen and had been recruited by flyers with a financial incentive.

4.5. Results for Experiment 1 (*und*)

The results in Figure 1 show that ATB-extraction from BAE is generally marked but not ungrammatical. On a grammaticality scale represented by the fillers (category A–E), ATB-extractions are assigned an intermediate value. We found a significant main effect for ellipsis type. Sentences containing a contrastive focus ellipsis were judged significantly worse than those with contrastive topics ($F(1,23) = 6,74$; $p < .05$) Extraction type did not show any effect (($F(1,23) = 2,04$; $p = 0,17$) We also found a significant effect for condition 1, which was judged worse than conditions 2–4 ($t(23) = 2,69$; $p < .05$). The control conditions 5–6 do not show a difference between subject and object extraction.

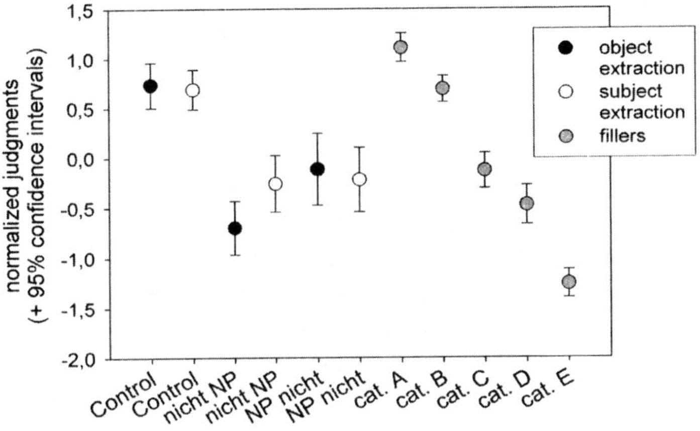

Figure 1. Judgements for the experimental items

4.6. Results for Experiment 2 (*aber*)

As figure 2 shows, we found a significant main effect for the factor 'extraction type' i.e. conditions 2 and 4 are judges better than conditions 1 and 3 (($F(1,23) = 13,19$; $p < .01$). Moreover, we also found a weak main effect for the factor ellipsis type ($F(1,23 = 4,12$; $p = .05$). Contrastive focus ellipsis was rated generally better than contrastive topic ellipsis. The control conditions 5–6 do not show a difference.

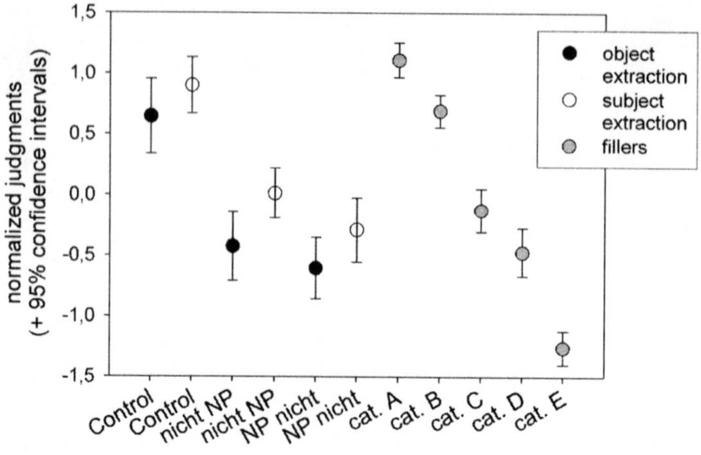

Figure 2. Judgements for the experimental items

4.7. Discussion

Our results support our hypothesis that information structure has influence on parallelism. The first experiment revealed that contrastive focus in the elliptical clause is generally dispreferred with the connective *und*. In particular, contrastive focus was judged worse if the remnant was a subject, i.e. in the case of object extraction. These findings suggest that the connective *und* is not an adequate licensor for contrastive focus, especially if the focus falls on the subject. In the case of *aber* which requires contrast to be realized, the conditions with contrastive focus were judged generally better than those with contrastive topics. In addition conditions in which the contrasted elements were subjects were rated lower than those with contrast realized on objects. This finding can be explained if we assume that there is a strong preference for subject DPs, especially if they are definite, as in our cases, to be deaccented in which case the contrast requirement of *aber* cannot be fulfilled.

5. Conclusion

We have argued that parallelism is a complex notion which is relevant not only in the syntactic component of grammar but also in the information structural component. Parallelism is thus best described as an interface phenomenon which maps information structural functions onto syntactic structure in coordinate ellipsis. Our results show that the two connectives *und* and *aber* realize parallelism in a different way. Under the assumption that these connectives are sensitive to discourse grammar, this is a welcome result. Finally, the experimental data also support the view that mismatches between syntax and information structure cause processing difficulty resulting in lower grammaticality ratings. This is supported by the fact that our experimental items exhibited the same degree of syntactic well-formedness.

Acknowledgments. This research was carried out in the Project *Ellipsis and Coordination* of the SFB 441 *Linguistic Data Structures* funded by the Deutsche Forschungsgemeinschaft. I would like to thank project leader Susanne Winkler as well as Oliver Bott, Sam Featherston, Jutta Hartmann, Tanja Kiziak and Janina Radó for many valuable comments and discussions. All errors are mine.

Notes

1. Further evidence for structure in the ellipsis site is reported in Fiengo and May (1992), Kennedy (2003), Merchant (2001, 2005), Frazier and Clifton (2005) and Frazier (this volume), among many others.

References

Asher, N., D. Hardt and J. Busquets
2001 Discourse parallelism, ellipsis, and ambiguity. *Journal of Semantics* 18 (1): 1–25.

Carlson, K.
2002 *Parallelism and Prosody in the Processing of Ellipsis Sentences*. London: Routledge.

Dalrymple, M., S. Shieber and F. Pereira
1991 Ellipsis and higher-order unification. *Lingutistics and Philosophy* 14 (4): 399–452.

Featherston, S.
2009 Thermometer judgements as linguistic evidence. In: Rothe A. (ed.), *Was ist linguistische Evidenz?*, 69–89. Herzogenrath: Shakerverlag.

Fiengo, R. and R. May
1992 The eliminative puzzles of ellipsis. In: S. Berman and A. Hestvik (eds.), *Sprachtheoretische Grundlagen fur die Computerlinguistik, Proceedings of the Stuttgart Ellipsis Workshop*. Stuttgart: University of Stuttgart.

1994 *Indices and Identity*. Cambridge: MIT Press

Frazier, L.
2009 Explorations in ellipsis: the grammar and processing of silence. This volume.

Frazier, L. and C. Clifton, Jr.
1998 Comprehension of Sluiced Sentences. *Language and Cognitive Processes* 13 (4): 499–520.

Frey, W.,
2006 Contrast and movement to the German prefield. In: Molnár, V., and S. Winkler (eds.), *The Architecture of Focus*, 235–264. Berlin/New York: de Gruyter.

Hankamer, J. and I. A. Sag.
1976 Deep and surface anaphora. *Linguistic Inquiry* 7: 391–426.

Hartmann, K.
2000 *Right Node Raising and Gapping: Interface Conditions on Prosodic Deletion*. Amsterdam: Benjamins.

Johnson, K.
1996 Gapping: In search of the middle field. Ms., University of Massachusetts, Amherst.

Keller F., M. Corley, S. Corley, L. Konieczny and A. Todirascu
1998 WebExp: A Java toolbox for web-based psychological experiments. Technical Report HCRC/TR-99, University of Edinburgh, Human Communication Research Centre.

Kennedy, C.
2003 Ellipsis and syntactic representation. In: K. Schwabe and S. Winkler (eds.) *The Interfaces: Deriving and Interpreting Omitted Structures,* 29–53. Amsterdam: Benjamins.

Kiziak, T.
2009 New data on an old issue: Subject/Object asymmetries in long extractions in German. This volume.

Konietzko, A. and S. Winkler
to appear Contrastive ellipsis: Mapping between syntax and information structure. To appear in *Lingua*.

Merchant, J.
2001 *The Syntax of Silence*. Oxford: Oxford University Press.
2005 Fragments and ellipsis. *Linguistics and Philosophy* 27: 661–738.

Reich, I.
2007 Asymmetrische Koordination im Deutschen. Habilitationsschrift, Universität Tübingen.

Reis, M. and I. Rosengren
1997 A modular approach to the grammar of additive particles: The case of German *auch*. *Journal of Semantics* 14: 237–309.

Ross, J. R.
1967 Constraints on Variables in Syntax. Ph. D. diss, MIT.

Sæbø, K. J.
2003 Presupposition and contrast: German *aber* as a topic particle. In: M. Weisgerber (ed.), *Proceedings of Sinn und Bedeutung 7*, 257–271. Konstanz: University of Konstanz.

Stolterfoht, B.
2005 *Processing Word Order Variations and Ellipses: The Interplay of Syntax and Information Structure during Sentence Comprehension.* Leipzig: MPI Series in Human Cognitive and Brain Sciences.

Umbach, C.
2005 Contrast and information structure: A focus-based analysis of *but. Linguistics* 43 (1): 207–232.

Wilder, C.
1997 Some properties of ellipsis in coordination. In: A. Alexiadou and T. Hall (eds.) *Studies in Universal Grammar and Typological Variation,* 59–107. Amsterdam: Benjamins.

Williams E.
1978 Across-the-Board rule application. *Linguistic Inquiry* 9: 31–43.

Winkler, S.
2005 *Ellipsis and Focus in Generative Grammar*. Berlin/New York: de Guyter.

An empirical perspective on positive polarity items in German

Mingya Liu and Jan-Philipp Soehn

1. Introduction

Polarity effects are pervasive in natural language and have drawn linguists' interest since Klima's (1964) work on negation. The lexical inventory consists for the most part of items which are not sensitive to polarity, i.e. those items that can occur in both negative and positive contexts. However, there are also polarity items (PIs), which can be further divided into negative polarity items (NPIs), i.e. those that tend to occur only in negative contexts, and positive polarity items (PPIs), i.e. those that tend to occur only in positive contexts. This classification is illustrated in Table 1.

Table 1. Polarity sensitivity in the lexicon

Non-PIs	PIs	
	NPIs	PPIs
besonders 'particularly'	*sonderlich* 'particularly'	*ziemlich* 'pretty'

(1) shows that the non-PI *besonders* can appear with or without negation, whereas the NPI *sonderlich* always appears with negation – the PPI *ziemlich* never does.

(1) a. *Finanziell sieht es für den Verlag (nicht)*
Financially looks it for the publishing house not
besonders *dunkel aus.*
particularly dark out
'For the publishing house, the financial prospects are (not) particularly dim.'

b. *Finanziell sieht es für den Verlag *(nicht)*
Financially looks it for the publishing house not
sonderlich *dunkel aus.*
particularly dark out
'For the publishing house, the financial prospects are (not) particularly dim.'

c. *Finanziell sieht es für den Verlag* (**nicht*)
Financially looks it for the publishing house not
ziemlich *dunkel aus.*
pretty dark out
'For the publishing house, the financial prospects are (not) pretty dim.'

Although most attention has been paid to NPIs, the study of PPIs also dates back as early as Baker (1970). However, many linguists, even when they do admit the existence of PPIs, take it as a marginal phenomenon, saying e.g. "their number, productivity, and strength are less impressive" (Horn 1989: 157). It is true that compared with NPIs, PPIs are difficult to track down, as in well-formed sentences with a PPI negation is absent and thus out of sight. However, we would like to put forward not only that PPIs exist but that they are a category as empirically robust as NPIs. Our current work aims at collecting and validating PPIs in German, given that the documentation of PPIs across languages is still very poor.

It is impossible to talk about PPIs without mentioning NPIs, because they are both part of the polarity phenomenon and also because the preceding literature is mostly about NPIs. Words such as *any*, *ever*, *yet*, *at all*, and *lift a finger* are labelled as NPIs since they demand negation; they must occur in the semantic scope of negation to be licensed. A sentence that contains an unlicensed NPI is not grammatical. The existing literature indicates that the possible NPI-licensing contexts include not only negation but also a variety of other semantic or pragmatic environments, but no single approach has been able to account for all of these contexts. Ladusaw (1980) marks NPI licensing contexts as downward entailing (DE), which covers *not,* n-words (*nobody*, *nothing*, *never*), *few, hardly, without*, conditionals, etc. This remains the most influential theory on polarity licensing but also continues to be a matter of debate. Giannakidou (1998) proposes nonveridicality as the necessary NPI licensing condition because NPIs also occur in non-DE contexts such as questions, modals, and disjunctions. However, neither of these definitions can capture the full range of licensing contexts and only these. Among the most notoriously problematic cases are the restrictor of universal quantifiers and superlatives, adversative predicates (*be surprised*), comparative *than*-clauses and *only*. Moreover, why do two virtually synonymous words such as *besonders* and *sonderlich* show different distributional behaviours in terms of negation? Because of these facts, van der Wouden (1997) treats the relation between the NPI-licensing contexts and the NPIs as a collocational phenomenon; in other words, NPIs have idiosyncratic restrictions on their contexts.

PPIs tend not to occur in NPI licensing contexts, that is, these contexts are potential anti-licensers of PPIs.[1] Consider the following examples:[2]

(2) a. *Hans war mit dem Ergebnis* ***durchaus*** *zufrieden.*
Hans was with the result definitely content
'Hans was completely satisfied with the result.'

b. **Niemand war mit dem Ergebnis* ***durchaus*** *zufrieden.*
nobody was with the result definitely content
'Nobody was completely satisfied with the result.'

c. *Niemand war mit dem* ***durchaus*** *brauchbaren Ergebnis zufrieden.*
nobody was with the definitely useful result content
'Nobody was satisfied with the definitely useful result.'

d. *Niemand* ***bekräftigte*** *nicht die Bedeutung des Klimaschutzes.*
nobody affirmed not the importance of climate protection
'Nobody didn't affirm the importance of climate protection.'

The PPI adverb *durchaus* 'absolutely' is licensed in (2a) but anti-licensed in (2b) due to the presence of negation. However, prepositional phrases, adjective phrases or relative clauses can shield PPIs from being anti-licensed, or in the case of double negation, they cancel each other out so that PPIs do not get affected, as shown in (2c) and (2d).

These facts affirm a general parallelism between NPIs and PPIs in that they show oppositional behaviours towards negativity: if we say NPIs are addicted to negation, PPIs are allergic to it. As Pearce (2001: 43) introduced the term *anti-collocations* for "those words which must **not** be used with the target word since they will lead to unnatural readings", we suggest that the relation between the above listed NPI-licensing contexts and PPIs is anti-collocational.

Just like NPIs, PPIs can be single- or multi-worded and occur in various parts-of-speech: verbs, for example, *munkeln* 'rumor', *bekräftigen* 'affirm', the indefinite article *ein* 'a', the indefinite pronoun *man* 'one', numerals '1, 2, 3, . . . ', and most often, adverbs such as *durchaus* 'absolutely', *sogar* 'even' or *geradezu* 'downright' and *ganz und gar* 'utterly'.

To get a better picture of the domain of PPIs, we are currently compiling a list of German PPIs, mainly from the literature, starting with Baker (1970). It is worth noting that a PI in one language is not necessarily one in another language: in English, we have such nice NPI/PPI pairs as *yet*/*already*, *still*/*anymore* and *either/too* (Levinson 2007) and in French *non plus/aussi* 'either/too', whereas German does not have an equivalent to *either/non plus*. In contrast, *auch* 'also' can be used for positive and negative contexts; in other words, it is not a PI. In addition, *noch* is used for both *yet* and *still*, e.g. *Tom ist noch nicht angekommen* 'Tom has not yet arrived' and *Tom ist noch hier* 'Tom is still here'.

Van Os (1989) suggests that most German intensifying adverbs such as *fast* 'almost' or *ziemlich* 'pretty' are PPIs. Ernst (2005) claims that speaker-oriented adverbs such as *vielleicht* 'maybe' or *tragischerweise* 'tragically' are also PPIs. Soehn (2006) indicates that idioms can be positive polar as well, e.g. *jdm. den Lebensfaden abschneiden* 'to kill sb.', *klar wie Kloßbrühe sein* 'to be crystal clear', or *jdm. ein Bein stellen* 'to trip sb. up'. Finally, our intuitions tell us that colloquial compound similies e.g. *ratten-scharf* 'rat hot – red-hot', *affengeil* 'ape cool – awesome' are also potential PPIs.

This list of PPI candidates is currently being validated. We first searched for their co-occurrence with the anti-licensing contexts using the corpora of the Institut für Deutsche Sprache (COSMAS II) and the internet via Google. We retained only those items that do not occur within the immediate semantic scope of negation or anti-additive (AA) expressions, which means that relative clauses, adjective phrases, and prepositional phrases were excluded. Furthermore, as for items such as *freilich* 'certainly', although they syntactically do co-occur with NPI licensers as in (3), they semantically always outscope negation or other NPI licensers, which is actually the case with many other PPI candidates.

(3) *Daß sein Führerschein eine Totalfälschung war, störte*
That his driver's license a complete forgery was disturbed
ihn weniger als ***freilich*** *die Grenzpolizei.*[3]
him less than certainly the border patrol.
'The fact that his driver's license was a complete forgery certainly bothered him less than it did the border control.'

In the following section, we will report on two experiments that we have done so far in order to psycholinguistically corroborate the PPI-hood of the items in our list.

2. Experiment 1: Thermometer Judgements

PPIs look very much like non-PIs due to the fact that they tend not to occur in anti-licensing contexts. As Horn (1989: 157) claims, "their trigger can be specified only negatively, in terms of the absence of a negative or affective element". Accordingly, PPIs can be differentiated from non-PIs only by the introduction of an anti-licenser. The prediction is that sentences with a PPI and an anti-licenser should get lower acceptability ratings than those with a non-PI and an anti-licenser. We used the method of thermometer judgements, which differs from magnitude estimation in that it abandons a magnitude scale and yields acceptability ratings relative to two reference points instead of one (Featherston 2007).

2.1. Method

Stimuli and design. We chose a two-factorial design with the factors PPI-hood (presumed PPI or non-PI) and Context (negative or positive), which, crossed with each other, yielded four conditions: PPI in negative context (anti-licensed), PPI in positive context (licensed), non-PI in negative context, and non-PI in positive context. A fifth independent control condition was NPIs in positive context (unlicensed). The hypothesis is that only PPIs are affected by negative contexts and that anti-licensed PPIs (Condition II in Table 2) are to be rated significantly worse than licensed PPIs (Condition I) and non-PIs in both contexts (Conditions III and IV).

Table 2. Factors and conditions

	PPI	Non-PI
positive context	I. licensed PPI	III. 'licensed' non-PPI
negative context	II. anti-licensed PPI	IV. 'anti-licensed' non-PPI

For each PPI candidate, e.g. *durchaus* 'absolutely', we used a non-PI counterpart of the same syntactic category and with a meaning as close as possible, *sehr* 'very' in this case, and then embedded them into anti-additive[4] (AA) contexts such as *nicht* 'not', *kein (N)* 'no (N)', *keinesfalls* 'by no means'. This resulted in four conditions, exemplified in (4). As fillers, we took sentences with unlicensed NPIs, e.g. *jemals* 'ever' in (5).

(4) a. *Sozialhilfebedürftigkeit ist heutzutage* ***durchaus*** *problematisch.*
social welfare need is nowadays absolutely problematic
'The need for social welfare is nowadays absolutely problematic.'

b. **Sozialhilfebedürftigkeit ist heutzutage nicht* ***durchaus*** *problematisch.*
social welfare need is nowadays not absolutely problematic
'The need for social welfare is nowadays not absolutely problematic.'

c. *Sozialhilfebedürftigkeit ist heutzutage* ***sehr*** *problematisch.*
social welfare need is nowadays very problematic
'The need for social welfare is nowadays very problematic.'

d. *Sozialhilfebedürftigkeit ist heutzutage nicht* ***sehr*** *problematisch*
social welfare need is nowadays not very problematic
'The need for social welfare is nowadays not very problematic.'

(5) **Hans war* ***jemals*** *am Plattensee*
Hans was ever at the Balaton lake
'Hans was ever at the Lake Balaton.'

We used a total of 56[5] PPI candidates in the experiment which we divided into two sub-experiments in order to obtain a reasonable number of test items per subject.

Subjects. In each sub-experiment, 48 German native speakers were asked to give acceptability judgements on the stimuli, which were split up into four counterbalanced sets. In the first one, each subject saw in total 60 sentences and in the second one, each subject saw altogether 30 sentences.

Procedure. Both experiments were conducted online using the WebExp2 software[6]. Subjects could participate in the experiment when- and wherever desired. A practice stage introduced the method, giving informants a multi-point scale on which to locate their intuitions of acceptability. At the same time they learned that they were entitled to use numerical values between, above, and below the two reference values. During the experimental stage, the two reference sentences remained visible.

Data Analysis. As Table 3 shows, in the second sub-experiment, we tested 24 items, including 8 new ones and 16 old ones that had already been tested in the first experiment but had not been judged as expected. We compared the two ratings for these 16 items respectively and, based on the test sentences, we

Table 3. Division of the experiment

	PPI candidates	Materials
1	48	4 versions with 48 sentences plus 12 fillers for each
2	24	4 versions with 24 sentences plus 6 fillers for each

chose one of the ratings for the final analysis. 45 (approximately 1%) invalid answers out of 3552 were excluded. We computed the z-score means per condition per subject as well as per condition per item. We performed variance analyses (ANOVAs) by subjects and by items separately with two factors, namely PPI-hood and Context, each with two levels, that is, PPI or Non-PI and with or without negation.

2.2. Results

Z-score means in the thermometer judgement experiment are displayed in the error bar chart below:

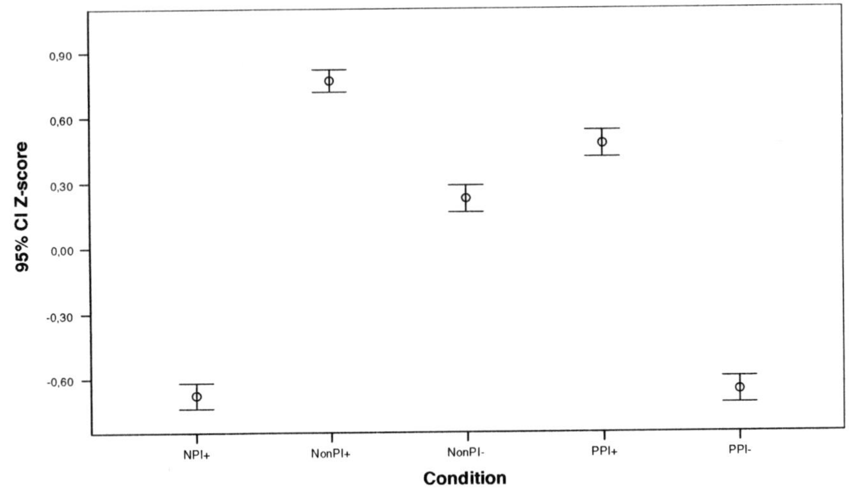

Figure 1. The x-axis marks the four critical conditions and the one independent condition, i.e. of the fillers. The minus symbol – is for negative sentences and + for positive ones. The scale y-axis indicates the normalised judgements of each condition with the 95% confidence interval.

The results are as follows: first, we got a similarly low rating for both NPIs in positive contexts and PPIs in negative contexts compared to the other conditions, which affirms the parallelism between NPIs and PPIs. Second, there is a main effect that negated sentences were rated worse than non-negated ones. Third and crucially, PPIs in negative contexts (anti-licensed PPIs) were judged considerably lower in comparison to the other three conditions, which is in line with our hypothesis.

In both the ANOVAs by subjects and by items, the main effect of Context (F_1 (1,95) = 356.722, $p < 0.001$; F_2 (1,55) = 257.693, $p < 0.001$) and the interaction of the two factors PPI-hood × Context (F_1 (1,95) = 133.861, $p < 0.001$; F_2 (1,55) = 44.495, $p < 0.001$) were highly significant.

2.3. Discussion

The results of the relative acceptability judgement experiment show that subjects rejected PPIs in negative contexts as expected. This supports our categorization of the candidates as PPIs and simultaneously provides evidence for the assumption that AA contexts and PPIs are in an anti-licensing relation. For the main effect that negated sentences were rated worse than non-negated ones among the group of non-PIs, the explanation lies in the fact that negated sentences were presented without context and therefore the conveyed content was not informative enough per se. It is often claimed that negated sentences are marked and parasitic on their positive counterparts while negation is more complex to process. This issue will be discussed in more detail later in the paper.

We have shown how the PPI candidates behaved as a whole. It is clear that the 56 items did not all react the same way to AA contexts, as they are simply different in terms of their parts-of-speech, and more importantly, of their semantics and pragmatics. Thus, we calculated the distance for all of them between positive (licensing) and negative (anti-licensing) contexts in terms of their respective z-score means.

The 'best' PPI was supposed to have a high mean in positive context and a low one in negative context and thus exhibit a big difference between the two, which therefore makes those at the right end better candidates than those at the left-hand end, at least in AA contexts. Interestingly, we find many adverbs at the right-hand end and many idioms at the left-hand end: the former include for example *ziemlich* 'pretty', *durchaus* 'absolutely', *lieber* 'rather', *nahezu* 'almost', *geradezu* 'downright'. These actually correspond to the examples of PPIs usually found in the literature. The reason why idioms were not rated as we had expected is, in our opinion, because the subjects were not equally familiar with all of them and thus made disparate judgements.

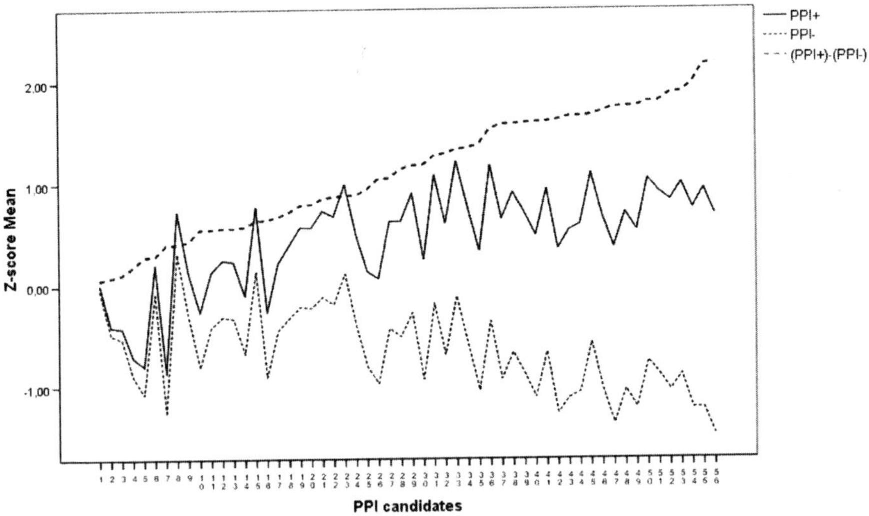

Figure 2. The *x*-axis indicates the 56 PPI candidates and the scale y-axis the normalised judgements. The middle line in the figure marks the mean judgments for PPIs in positive contexts, the bottom line the mean judgements for PPIs in negative contexts and the top line for the difference between the two means.

3. Speeded acceptability judgements

In the thermometer judgement experiment, the subjects had as much time as they needed, which we think made it possible for them to come up with larger contexts so that the 'bad' sentences became better. Therefore, we wanted to test the same items again but with a limited reaction time and thus used the method of speeded acceptability judgements. E-prime was used as the software.

3.1. Rapid Serial visual presentation

Rapid serial visual presentation (RSVP) is a widely applied technique, not only in psycholinguistics. The sentences are presented to the subjects word by word in the centre of the computer screen at a speeded rate. To obtain an optimal presentation rate, we let several German native speakers pre-test the experiment at different rates and then set the final rate at (224 ms + 14 ms/letter) per word; this rate is also used in Bader (2007). For very rare cases of extremely long words such as *Sozialhilfebedürftigkeit*, we set slightly longer time slots as pre-test participants complained that they did not have enough time to read the words through. After the last word of each sentence, the subjects would see a new window with the question: "Does it sound natural?" They had to give a yes/no-answer within a maximal interval of 2.5 seconds, or else they would get a message saying "Reaction too slow!"

3.2. Method

We tested the same list of 56 PPI candidates in four conditions as in the last experiment, counterbalanced in four subsets. This time, we used more fillers, namely 14 sentences with unlicensed NPIs, 14 with the same NPIs licensed, 12 pragmatically odd sentences, and 24 plain grammatical sentences without negation. This means that each subject saw 56 PPI test sentences, 14 NPI sentences, all 12 pragmatically odd and all 24 plain sentences, adding up to 106 sentences in total. In each subset, the sentences were divided into four blocks appearing randomly with small pauses in-between. The sentences in each block were also randomized. 24 German native speakers from University of Tübingen took part in the experiment. The instruction for their task (English translation) was as follows:

> 'In this experiment you will be shown sentences on the screen. The sentences are presented word by word at a relatively high rate. Your task is to decide for each of these sentences whether the sentence sounds natural and the expressed meaning makes sense. Note that you should answer as fast as possible as you only have few seconds' time.
>
> A sentence that sounds natural is e.g. "Philipp did not have the foggiest idea about how the new microwave works", whereas "Philipp had the foggiest idea about how the new microwave works" is to be rated as unnatural.
>
> You will start with the practice stage of 10 sentences. After that, the real experiment with 106 sentences follows.'

For the analysis, we again excluded invalid answers. The answers were absolute judgements, i.e. either 1 (acceptable) or 0 (unacceptable) and we computed the means per condition per subject and per condition per item. We performed two separate ANOVAs by subjects and items in the same way as in the last experiment.

3.3. Results

The results show a similar picture to the first experiment. First, leaving the fillers aside and just considering PPIs and non-PIs, we got a main effect that negated sentences were rated worse than non-negated ones and also that anti-licensed PPIs were rated considerably worse than all the other three conditions.

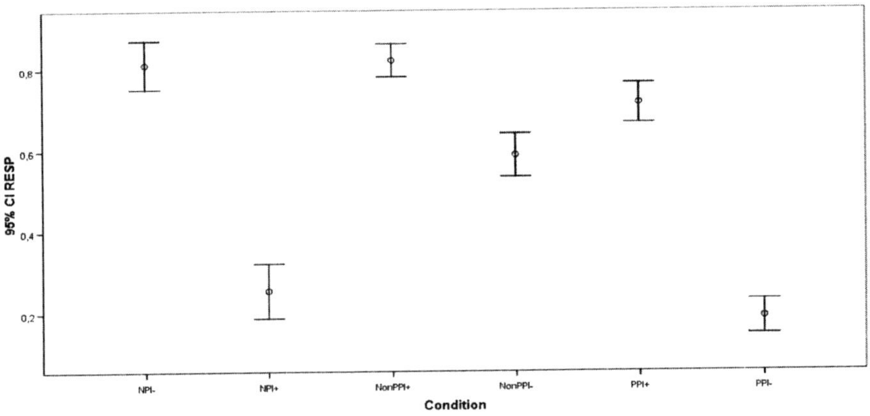

Figure 3. The *x*-axis marks the four critical conditions and the two independent conditions, namely NPI in negative context (NPI-) and NPI in positive context (NPI+). The scale *y*-axis indicates the mean judgements of each condition with the 95% confidence interval (RESP for response).

Comparing NPIs and PPIs, subjects reacted as expected: unlicensed NPIs and anti-licensed PPIs were both rated as very bad while licensed NPIs and PPIs were rated as good. This again proves the parallelism between NPIs and PPIs towards negation.

The statistical analysis confirms that the main effect between negated and non-negated sentences (F_1 (1,23) = 142.345, $p < 0.001$; F_2 (1,55) = 134.050, $p < 0.001$) and the interaction between the two factors PPI-hood and negation (F_1 (1,23) = 58.863, $p < 0.001$; F_2 (1,55) = 20.686, $p < 0.001$) were both highly significant.

4. Discussion

4.1. Negation is more marked and costly

In both the experiments, we obtained a main effect that negated sentences were rated worse than non-negated ones. This is in line with the observations that cross-linguistically, negation is structurally more complex than affirmation, and that negated sentences are less frequent than affirmative ones. Givón (1978) and Horn (1989) inter alia claim that negative sentences are more marked than their affirmative counterparts. However, simply stating that negation is more marked is not very satisfying, because the notion of markedness describes a (dis-)preference but offers no insightful explanations for why it is so. Consider the following examples: (6a) and (6b) were test sentences with the non-PI *sehr* 'very'. The numbers in brackets are the mean ratings we got for them in the speeded acceptability judgement experiment, which means that the subjects all accepted (6a) and rejected (6b).

(6) a. *Der deutsche Aktienmarkt war sehr schwach.* (1.0)
'The German stock market was very weak.'
b. *Der deutsche Aktienmarkt war nicht sehr schwach.* (0.0)
'The German stock market was not very weak.'
c. *Der deutsche Aktienmarkt war stark.*
'The German stock market was strong.'
d. *Der deutsche Aktienmarkt war nicht stark.*
'The German stock market was not strong.'

We assume two possible reasons why (6b) was completely rejected. First, Horn, along with Givón, recognizes negation as "contributing less information to the discourse than the corresponding unmarked affirmative (*My hat is not red* vs. *My hat is red*)" (Horn 1989: 157). (6b) is less informative than (6a) and, more importantly, than (6c) as well. Saying *My hat is red* or *My hat is green* conveys more information than saying *My hat is not red.* Analogously, when presented with (6b) and (6c), the speaker/hearer prefers the affirmative choice, namely (6c).

The second explanation also serves as an indirect reply to the question why (6d) is more acceptable than (6b), although both are negated. Givón (1978) claims that "from a strictly logical point of view, while the speaker asserts $\sim p$ he presupposes p" (p.70) and thus the felicity condition for use of the negative is the presence of the corresponding affirmative in discourse or in the psychological state of someone relevant in context. It follows that (6b) is not exactly bad per se, but simply lacks an appropriate context like one in which the sentence is uttered to deny (6a). In general, of such "polar antonyms" (Cruse 1986) as *strong/weak, tall/short, old/young*, the former members are unmarked and only these, as Cruse notes, can appear in *how*-questions and renders impartial meaning (cf. *How tall/old/strong is he?* but ?*How short/young/weak is he?*). This also holds with sentences with explicit degree arguments (cf. *Peter is 1.55cm tall* but ?*Peter is 1.55cm short*) and with negation: therefore, *Der deutsche Aktienmarkt war nicht stark* 'The German stock market was not strong' sounds better than *Der deutsche Aktienmarkt war nicht schwach* 'The German stock market was not weak', if both are uttered out of the blue.

These theoretical insights are evidently supported by Wason's (1961; 1965) earlier works on negation. In his (1961) paper, Wason reports on longer response latencies to negative statements than to affirmative ones, both in the absence of context. Wason (1965) considers the effect of pragmatic factors on the response time to negative statements. His experimental results suggest that the plausibility of denial depends on "the formal characteristics of the contrast class of which the property is, explicitly or implicitly, predicated" (Wason 1965: 10). The greater this contrast class is, the more appropriate it is to negate its property.

To sum up, negation is more costly to process. A negative utterance often presupposes the existence of an affirmative one and thus its interpretation often needs go beyond narrow context and involve intonation, discourse contrast, etc. When no appropriate context is available, a negative sentence tends to sound odd.

4.2. Classification of PPIs and un-anti-licensed PPIs

As discussed earlier, PPI candidates vary in their sensitivity towards anti-additivity, i.e. they don't share the same degree of PPI-hood. This was illustrated in Figure 2.

Van der Wouden (1997) distinguished three types of negative contexts according to their logical properties and put them into a hierarchy as shown in Table 4. Anti-morphic contexts have the strongest negativity, e.g. *nicht* 'not', *ohne* 'without' and thus take the highest place in the hierarchy, while the DE ones occupy the lowest. Giannakidou (1998) adds yet another, more general, context type. She proposes that nonveridical contexts constitute a natural class for polarity item licensing which is a proper superset of the downward-entailing contexts.

Table 4. Classification of negative Contexts

classic	regular	minimal	other Lic.
not	*nothing*	*at most*	questions
without	*nobody*	*seldom*	modals
not believe, that	*never*	*few*	*before*
anti-morphic	anti-additive	downward entailing	nonveridical
$f(x \cap y) = f(x) \cup f(y)$ $f(x \cup y) = f(x) \cap f(y)$	$f(x \cup y) = f(x) \cap f(y)$	$(x \subseteq y) \rightarrow (f(y) \subseteq f(x))$	$f(x) \nrightarrow x$

In terms of the combinational possibilities, PPIs that can co-occur with anti-additive and weaker negative contexts are labelled as weak PPIs whereas strong PPIs should never occur in any DE context, as shown in Table 5.

Table 5. Classification of PPIs per strength

PPI	Negation classic	regular	minimal	Non-veridical other Lic.
strong medium weak	–	–	–	?
	–	–	+	+
	–	+	+	+

The next experiment on our schedule will investigate the German PPIs in our updated list by combining them with contexts of the different degrees of negativity shown in Table 4 in order to classify them according to their strength.

However, the logical properties of negative contexts do not bring the story to an end, for at least two reasons: first of all, just like the notion of markedness, the classification of PPIs according to their combinational restrictions with negative contexts exhibits distributional facts about them but does not provide any theoretical explanation. Second, the relation between a PPI of a certain strength and the corresponding contexts of certain logical properties is not coherent, i.e. a PPI is sometimes bad in one negative context but good in another of the same logical property, for example, *Kein Politiker bekräftigte die Notwendigkeit des Klimaschutzes* 'no politician affirmed the importance of the climate protection' is better than *Niemand bekräftigte die Notwendigkeit des Klimaschutzes* 'nobody affirmed the importance of the climate protection', although *kein Politiker* and *niemand* are both AA operators. We assume that the clash between negation and PPIs is due to the lexical pragmatics of PPIs that presupposes the existence of e.g. an event or a property, which then should not be denied at the same time. But such a clash is not categorical, because an enriched context could perform a pragmatic rescuing even when a PPI is in the semantic scope of negation. There are many ways to achieve this.

In the speeded acceptability judgement experiment, we got for example the following results for the PPIs *munkeln* 'rumor' and *bekräftigen* 'affirm'.

(7) a. *Man* ***munkelt****, dass die Frau des Präsidenten fremdgeht.* (1.0)
'It is rumoured that the First Lady is having an affair.'

b. *Niemand* ***munkelt****, dass die Frau des Präsidenten fremdgeht.* (0.5)
'Nobody is spreading rumours that the First Lady is having an affair.'

(8) a. *Politiker* ***bekräftigten*** *auf der Pressekonferenz die Notwendigkeit des Klimaschutzes.* (1.0)
'Politicians affirmed the necessity of climate protection at the press conference.'

b. *Kein Politiker* ***bekräftigte*** *auf der Pressekonferenz die Notwendigkeit des Klimaschutzes.* (0.67)
'No politician affirmed the necessity of climate protection at the press conference.'

The contrast between (7a) and (7b) and that between (8a) and (8b) would not be high enough to label the two verbs as PPIs. We still did so because *munkeln* and *bekräftigen* not only tend to occur in positive contexts but also presuppose something of a positive nature in their meaning, namely, the existence of the indicated events. Similarly, the PPI adverb *durchaus* 'absolutely' presupposes the existence of a property that it modifies as *mit dem Ergebnis zufrieden* 'happy with the result' in (2a), otherwise the sentence turns out sounding odd, as illustrated by (2b).

In brief, there is a difference between unlicensed NPIs and anti-licensed PPIs: NPIs in affirmatives render a sentence ungrammatical while PPIs in negatives make sentences pragmatically odd. Saddy, Drenhaus and Frisch (2004) report that their experiments show that in comparison to licensed NPIs and PPIs, unlicensed NPIs and anti-licensed PPIs both exhibited an N400, which according to them, reflected "the cost of semantic or thematic integration", but only anti-licensed PPIs showed a P600 that is "associated with syntactic reanalysis and repair" and "found in enhanced syntactic complexity [...] including ambiguity" (Saddy, Drenhaus and Frisch 2004: 496). We assume that we got the relatively good ratings for (7b) and (8b) possibly because some, but not all, subjects succeeded in reanalysis, either structurally, namely, interpreting the PPIs out of the scope of negation, or in this case, rather pragmatically, that is, interpreting the negation as contrastive denial. We show with (9) below that pragmatic rescuing of PPIs in the semantic scope of negation works better with enriched contexts: e.g. in (9a), the sentence with *niemand... mehr* 'nobody ... anymore' implies that *it was rumoured before ...* and in (9b) the presupposition of contrastive, i.e. positive nature is explicitly there.

(9) a. *Niemand* ***munkelt*** *mehr, dass die Frau des Präsidenten fremdgeht.*
'Nobody is spreading rumours anymore that the First Lady is having an affair.'

b. *Kein Politiker* ***bekräftigte*** *auf der Pressekonferenz die Notwendigkeit des Klimaschutzes, einige Wissenschaftler allerdings schon*
'No politicians affirmed the necessity of climate protection at the press conference, but some scientists did.'

5. Conclusion

In this paper, we have identified a distinctive pattern for PPIs in both experiments that we have carried out. This means that it is not a marginal category but one that is at least as empirically robust as NPIs. Accordingly, a grammatical theory should certainly take it into account. The related discussion also reveals the theoretic significance of PPIs for a better understanding of negation. Due to the complex interplay of the logical strength of licensers and their syntactic position with respect to a polarity item, it is important to look at a sufficient quantity of data in order to capture the distribution of PPIs as well as NPIs. Our research aims to improve the data base for German by providing a validated list of PPIs. The updated list with 53 validated PPIs can be found in Appendix A. This list of PPIs and their respective occurrences found in corpora will be made available online in the Collection of Idiosyncratic Items at http://www.sfb441.uni-tuebingen.de/a5/codii/ We are constantly enlarging the list of PPIs. We thus hope that our collection will serve as a resource for linguists working on polarity phenomena.

Acknowledgements. Our research project was supported by the "Landesstiftung Baden-Württemberg" and associated with the Sonderforschungsbereich 441 "Linguistic Data Structures" at the University of Tübingen. We are indebted above all to our colleagues Oliver Bott, Sam Featherston and Janina Radó for helping with the experiments and the statistic analyses. We also want to thank Manfred Sailer for his very helpful advice on the earlier version of this paper. Last but not least, many thanks to our student assistant Johannes Fiegenbaum for the corpus search work, to Helga Gese and Britta Stolterfoht for their useful comments, and to Lucas Ogden for the proofreading. Any remaining mistakes are of course our own.

Appendix: List of PPI candidates tested in the experiments

Candidates whose PPI-status could not be confirmed in the experiments are crossed out.

Intensifying adverbials:

ausgesprochen 'markedly' / ~~beträchtlich~~ 'considerable' / buchstäblich 'literally – without exaggeration' / definitiv 'definitively' / durchaus 'absolutely' / geradezu 'downright' / leidlich 'middling' / nahezu 'almost' / total 'totally' / überaus 'extremely' / regelrecht 'downright'

Colloquials:

abgefahren 'wacky' / affengeil 'awesome' / geil 'cool' / rattenscharf 'red-hot' / stocksauer 'pissed off' / volle Kanne 'full pitcher – full throttle'

Speaker-oriented adverbs:

erstaunlicherweise 'astonishingly' / geheimnisvollerweise 'mysteriously' / glücklicherweise 'fortunately' / möglicherweise 'possibly' / ~~notwendigerweise~~ 'necessarily' / tragischerweise 'tragically' / unglaublicherweise 'unbelievably' / unglücklicherweise 'unfortunately' / zweckmäßigerweise 'expediently'

Others:

bekräftigen 'to affirm' / erstmals 'for the first time' / munkeln 'to rumour' / ungeachtet 'notwithstanding' / unvermindert 'undiminished' / ~~verdient~~ 'merited' / grassieren 'to rage' / lieber 'rather' / sowieso 'in any case' / ziemlich 'pretty'

Positive polar idioms:

Augenschondienst haben 'to be on eye-saving-duty – to sleep' / jdm. ein Bein stellen 'sb. a leg put – to trip sb. up' / jmd. den Buckel runter rutschen 'sb. can slide down one's back – sb. can take a slow boat to China' / jdm. gestohlen bleiben 'sb. can remain stolen for sb. – sb. can go to hell' / jdm. über die Hutschnur gehen 'over the hat string go – to go too far' / etwas an den Hut stecken 'to pin sth. on the hat – to stick sth. where the sun don't shine' / jdm. den Lebensfaden abschneiden 'sb. the life-thread cut off – to kill sb.' / Mattscheibe haben 'glass plane have – to have a mental blank' / sich mausig machen 'to make oneself mousy – to be as cheeky as a monkey' / eine Meise haben 'to have a tomtit – to have a screw loose' / einen in der Krone haben 'to have one in the crown – to be drunk' / klar wie Klossbrühe 'clear as dumpling-broth – to be crystal clear' / die Ohren steif halten 'the ears stiff hold – to keep one's chin up' / jdm. die Pest an den Hals wünschen 'sb. the pest at the throat wish – to wish sb. would drop dead' / auf jdn. einen Pik haben 'on sb. a pike have – to dislike sb.' / Ruhe in die Sache bringen 'peace in the affair bring – to calm sth. down' / sattsam bekannt sein 'widely known be – to be notorious' / immer auf dem Sprung sein 'always on the jump be – to be always on the go' / einen Teufel tun 'a devil do – to do anything but that' / jdm. zum Teufel wünschen 'sb. to the devil wish – wish that sb. go to hell'

Notes

1. However, not all of them are anti-licensers, as we have noticed, e.g. both NPIs and PPIs can occur in the restriction of universal quantifiers as in *All students who have ever/already read the book came to the lecture*. PPIs seem to be fine in modals, conditionals and questions as well e.g. *Peter would have lifted a finger/Peter would have liked it a whole lot*, *If Peter has any/some of these books, . . .*, Does Peter like it anymore / Does Peter still like it?
2. It is to note that (2d) is clearly marked in comparison to (2a) and (2c). However, we want to stress the contrast between those and (2b) where the PPI is anti-licensed.
3. Source: *Tiroler Tageszeitung, 10.12.1997, Ressort: Regional Unterinntal; Grenzpolizei kontrolliert schon das Hinterland.*
4. Following Szabolcsi (2004), we assume that it is not DE but the AA that PPIs detest. For example, *few*, *seldom*, being DE, can often co-occur with PPIs as in *Few people said something*.
5. While we tested 56 PPI candidates, our list is constantly being expanded. As of April 2008 it comprises 70 PPI candidates.
6. Cf. http://www.hcrc.ed.ac.uk/web_exp/
7. We re-tested some of the items in the second experiment, compared their ratings with those in the first experiment and chose the more plausible ones.
8. "Veridicality is a property of sentence embedding function: such a function F is veridical of F_p entails or presupposes the truth of p. If inference to the truth under F is not possible, F is nonveridical; nonveridicality thus captures a state of unknown (or as yet undefined) truth value. Veridicality and nonveridicality thus replace the traditional characterizations of REALIS (veridical) and IRREALIS (non-veridical). Within the class of the nonveridical expressions, negation is identified as ANTI-VERIDICAL in that *NOT p* entails that p is false" (Giannakidou, to appear).

References

Bader, Markus
2007 Auxiliarinversion im Deutschen [Auxiliary inversion in German]. Handout of a talk given at SFB 441, University of Tübingen.

Baker, Carl Lee
1970 Double negatives. *Linguistic Inquiry* 1: 169–186.

Cruse, D. Alan
1986 *Lexical Semantics*. Cambridge University Press.

Drenhaus, Heiner, Stefan Frisch and Douglas Saddy
2005 Processing Negative Polarity Items: When Negation Comes through the Backdoor. In: Stephan Kepser and Marga Reis (eds.), *Linguistic Evidence: Empirical, Theoretical, and Computational Perspectives*, 145–163. Berlin/New York: Mouton de Gruyter.

Ernst, Thomas
2005 On Speaker-oriented Adverbs as Positive Polarity Items. In *Polarity from Different Perspectives*, poster at the Workshop held at New York University. 11.–13. March 2005.

Featherston, Sam
2007 Thermometer Judgements as Linguistic Evidence. In: Claudia Maria Riehl and Astrid Rothe (eds.), *Was ist linguistische Evidenz?* Aachen: Shaker Verlag.

Giannakidou, Anastasia
1998 *Polarity Sensitivity as (Non)veridical Dependency*. Amsterdam: Benjamins.
to appear Negative and Positive Polarity Items: Variation, Licensing, and Compositionality. Prepared for: Claudia Maienborn, Klaus von Heusinger and Paul Portner (eds.), *Semantics: An International Handbook of Natural Language Meaning*. Berlin: Mouton de Gruyter.

Givón, Talmy
1978 Negation in Language: Pragmatics, Function, Ontology. In: Peter Cole (ed.), *Syntax and Semantics Vol. 9. Pragmatics*, 69–112. New York: Academic Press.

Klima, Edward
1964 Negation in English. In: Jerry Fodor and Jerrold Katz (eds.), *The Structure of Language*, 246–323. New Jersey: Prentice Hall.

Levinson, Dmitry
2007 Licensing of Negative Polarity Particles in English. Presented at the Workshop on Negation and Polarity at the University of Tübingen, March 2007.

Ladusaw, William
1980 *Polarity Sensitivity as Inherent Scope Relations*. New York: Garland Press.

Van Os, Charles
1989 *Aspekte der Intensivierung im Deutschen* [Aspects of the intensification in German]. Tübingen: Gunter Narr Verlag.

Pearce, Darren
2001 Synonymy in Collocation Extraction. In: *WordNet and Other Lexical Resources: Applications, Extensions and Customizations* (NAACL 2001 Workshop), 41–46. Carnegie Mellon University, Pittsburgh.

Saddy, Douglas, Heiner Drenhaus and Stefan Frisch
2004 Processing Polarity Items: Contrastive Licensing Costs. *Brain and Language Vol. 90*, Issues 1-3, July-September 2004: 495–502.

Soehn, Jan-Philipp
2006 Über *Bärendienste* und *erstaunte Bauklötze* – Idiome ohne freie Lesart in der HPSG [On *Bärendienste* and *erstaunte Bauklötze* – idioms without free reading in HPSG]. Phil. Dissertation at Friedrich-Schiller-Universität Jena. Frankfurt/M: Peter Lang Publishing Group.

Szabolcsi, Anna
2004 Positive Polarity - Negative Polarity. *Natural Language and Linguistic Theory* 22(2): 409–452.

Wason, Peter Cathcart
1961 Response to Affirmative and Negative Binary Statements. *British Journal of Psychology* 52: 133–142.
1965 The Contexts of Plausible Denial. *Journal of Verbal Meaning and Verbal Behavior* 4: 7–11.

Van der Wouden, Ton
1997 *Negative Contexts. Collocation, Polarity and Multiple Negation*. London/New York: Routledge.

Zwarts, Frans
1995 Nonveridical Contexts. *Linguistic Analysis* 25: 286–312.

First-mention definites: More than exceptional cases

Marta Recasens, M. Antònia Martí and Mariona Taulé

1. Introduction

Coreference resolution is a challenging task for Natural Language Processing (NLP), one of the major obstacles being the great amount and variety of knowledge involved in it. Existing systems have relied greatly on traditional linguistic accounts which assume the definite article to be a mark of anaphoricity. First-mention uses are thus treated as exceptions deserving no special attention. This widely-held view, however, is strongly based on English and tends to be limited to evidence from constructed examples. When natural data is taken into account and from languages other than English, classical treatments of definites collapse and the need for a language-specific approach becomes apparent.

Acknowledging the considerable number of definite NPs that are used as first mentions, some works in the field of NLP (Bean and Riloff 1999; Ng and Cardie 2002; Uryupina 2003; Vieira and Poesio 2000) have added an automatic classifier able to distinguish those definite NPs that have no antecedent in order to stop the coreference resolution system from looking erroneously for a previous mention and wasting time. However, only few non-anaphoric detectors have been proposed to date, and none exists either for Catalan or Spanish.

This paper arises from the idea that the role played by the definite article in (1a) and (1b) differs in that, whereas the definite noun phrase (NP) *la premsa* 'the press' can introduce a new entity into the text for the first time, the definite NP *l'actor* 'the actor' relies on a previous mention for its interpretation.

(1) Catalan

a. *L' enfrontament ha ressorgit a les pàgines de* ***la***
The confrontation has reappeared in the pages of the
premsa.
press.
'The confrontation has reappeared in the pages of **the press**.'

b. ***L' actor*** *va ser incinerat, tal com era el seu desig.*
The actor was cremated, just as was the his wish.
'**The actor** was cremated, just as it was his wish.'

We begin by reviewing four different accounts, each of which takes a different perspective, yet we bring together some of their claims so as to understand the difference between the definites in (1a) and (1b), both for Catalan and Spanish. In a nutshell, definites of the first type have a head noun which is functional (Löbner 1985, Fraurud 1990) and a grammaticized definite article (Lyons 1999, Bybee 1998), while definites of the second type have a head noun which is sortal (Löbner 1985) and the definite article retains its semantic meaning (Lyons 1999).

We hold that certain nouns (functional nouns) combine more systematically with the definite article (a grammaticized article), constituting a "unit of usage" in Bybee and Hopper's (2001: 8) terms: "recurring units in the continuous stream of speech." In addition, units of usage like *la premsa* 'the press' (vs. *l'actor* 'the actor') are likely candidates to be *chain starting*, namely the first mention in a coreference chain. Our goal is delimiting such units of usage for Catalan and Spanish, since this can help a coreference resolution system distinguish first from coreferential mentions. The approach we take focuses on strings of words and their frequency occurrence, without considering their psycholinguistic basis or logical meaning (Chierchia 1998, Zamparelli 2005). A usage-based account in terms of frequency can reveal useful features to build a chain-starting detector of definite NPs for Catalan and Spanish.

The "units of usage" claim has prompted two empirical studies based on the AnCora corpora (Annotated Corpora for Catalan and Spanish). The first study seeks evidence for the grammaticization of the definite article; the second measures to what extent certain nouns show a tendency to co-occur with the definite article, with a view to determining units of usage. This study keeps non-modified definite NPs (simple) separate from modified definite NPs (complex). Complex definites like those in (2a) and (2b) are analysed in a second step so as to explore the intersection between units of usage and nominal modifiers.

(2) Catalan

a.

La	***premsa***	***local***	*va començar*	*ahir*	*la*	*seva*
The	press	local	began	yesterday	the	its

campanya.
campaign.
'**The local press** began its campaign yesterday.'

b.

Demà,	*a partir de*	*les*	*dotze,*	***l'***	***actor***	***Lionel***
Tomorrow,	from	the	twelve,	the	actor	Lionel

Valdés *[...]*
Valdés [...]
'Tomorrow, from twelve o'clock, **the actor Lionel Valdés** [...]'

After outlining the theoretical foundations underlying our claim and pointing out their connections (Section 2), the empirical approach is presented in Section 3, where results and discussions are presented for corpus studies I and II. Finally, Section 4 features our main conclusions and outlines for future work.

2. Theoretical perspective

In everyday language many uses of the definite article do not fall within the scope of traditional accounts of definiteness (Heim 1983). Many uses differ from the *a book/the book* pattern[1] (3).

(3) *John read* ***a book****. It was Mary who had given him* ***the book****.*

In the last twenty years, the awareness of the mismatch between deep-seated theories and real data has led more recent approaches, both from a theoretical and from an NLP point of view, to abandon traditional hypotheses. The increase in size and domains of electronic corpora has been very influential in this shift. The availability of large amounts of data that can be digitally stored and processed has opened a wide range of possibilities for a new analysis of language, one that does not build a theory and then construct suitable examples but which moves from the observation of real data to the subsequent description of the underlying theory. These more recent accounts question the assumption that definite phrases are typically anaphoric whereas non-anaphoric uses are exceptions of little importance.

Traditional theories suffer from two main weaknesses: (i) their restriction to fabricated examples, overlooking complexities that are inherent in everyday language, and (ii) their limitation to the English language. As a result, such classical accounts turn out to be of little use for NLP applications, which need to deal with raw input coming from the natural languages of a multilingual world. Thus, before modelling a chain-starting detector, our theoretical and empirical approaches are an attempt to overcome these weaknesses. This section provides the theoretical background and raises the issues which have prompted and guided the two empirical studies that follow in Section 3. The discussion is confined to those ideas suggested in previous works that are relevant in the present context.

2.1. Functional nouns

The starting point of the approaches by Löbner (1985) and Fraurud (1990) is the semantics of head nouns in definites, the latter study building on the former towards a computational model. Löbner's analysis of definiteness moves beyond the traditional approach in terms of uniqueness, advocating a new classification of nouns – or, more precisely, *concepts* – with a view to grounding his functional theory of definiteness, which argues that it is the semantics of the noun that makes the definite article (un)necessary in any given discourse. According to Löbner (1985: 292), "there are semantic subclasses of nouns that differ in the range of determiners with which they combine in certain contexts." He distinguishes between sortal (SC) and relational concepts (RC). The former, e.g. *woman*, classify objects according to the properties they exhibit; while the latter, e.g. *moon*, describe objects as standing in a certain relation to others. RCs are further subcategorized into one-to-one (functional concepts, FC), like *moon*, and one-to-many relational concepts, like *friend*.

On the basis of this noun categorization, Löbner (1985: 293) develops his functional theory of definiteness, arguing that just as "functions relate objects unambiguously (or one-to-one) to others," the role of the definite article is indicating that the following noun is to be taken as a FC. Given that definite NPs point unambiguously to terms ("individual expressions"), they can be regarded as FCs. The dividing line, however, between some definites and others lies in how the arguments for unambiguous reference are provided: by the lexical meaning of the head noun, as in the case of semantic definites, or by the discourse context (textual or physical), which is the case of pragmatic definites. More specifically, the textual discourse context can be split into the NP modifiers and the rest of the text.

The head of semantic definites is an FC – being already definite, the appearance of the definite article becomes redundant. Typical semantic definites are proper nouns and similar expressions (e.g. *the opera Rigoletto*; *the rumour that Reagan is going to resign*; *the Wall* in Berlin), and NPs which depend on a situational argument common to all temporal and spatial locations (e.g. *the moon*), or are unique in the "abstract" situation invoked by the discourse (e.g. *the post office*, being the one specifically inferred in context). Löbner also includes in this group definites with a non-FC head involving more than one argument which, however, according to him, become functional because of a modifier, be it explicit or implicit (e.g. *the closest shop*, *the meaning of the definite article*, *the Prime Minister*, etc.).[2]

In contrast, pragmatic definites always have an SC or one-to-many RC as head, but its reference is unambiguous, thanks to the immediate situation. The article in this case has a semantic content, indicating that the head noun is to be taken as an FC. Löbner includes anaphoric definites in this group, since they get their functional link from the text, as well as definites containing a restrictive relative clause or a prepositional or adverbial phrase, since the textual modifiers provide the required arguments. Complex NPs are divided into semantic and pragmatic definites. In a nutshell, semantic definites are candidates to be first mentions, while pragmatic definites are likely to be coreferential mentions when simple, and first mentions when complex.

On the basis of Löbner's distinction between semantic and pragmatic definites, a line can be drawn between NPs which are definite *per se* (in a certain language) and NPs whose definiteness depends on the immediate discourse. Like any linguistic classification, however, rather than being clear-cut, we believe that FC and SC concepts constitute the extremes of a continuum (see Section 3.3, below) in which intermediate cases remain an object of discussion among linguists. These in-between definite NPs, for which the source of the necessary arguments is not clear, fall under the umbrella class of "bridging definites" (Clark 1977) or "associative anaphoric uses" (Hawkins 1977). The information needed to resolve the function is provided partly by the textual context and partly by world knowledge. Given this complexity, no wonder that the computational interpretation of these definite NPs still poses many difficulties.

Löbner's notions of FC, RC and SC are the basis on which Fraurud (1990) builds her model of definite NP processing. Exploiting the notion of "relationality" at large, she is able to make sense of the results obtained from her empirical study on a 10,455-word Swedish corpus, in which only one third of all occurrences of definite NPs turn out to be coreferential mentions. This finding has also been empirically corroborated for English (Poesio and Vieira 1998). Fraurud stresses the idea that most definites appearing as first mentions in a discourse are relational in that they are interpreted by establishing different relations with certain arguments in the sense of Löbner. These arguments, called "anchors" by Fraurud, might be provided either within the discourse (referents previously mentioned in the text) or outside the discourse (background referents, i.e. extra-linguistic entities that we are all aware of because of world knowledge). According to Fraurud, the interpretation of first-mention definites can thus be equated to a process of *anchoring*. The amount of anchoring that a certain noun occurrence requires for its interpretation results both from its "inherent relationality" (the lexico-encyclopaedic knowledge) and from its "contextual relationality" (its interpretation in a specific context).

Fraurud's main claim is that in addition to the definiteness of an NP, the relationality of a definite NP might influence the way it is interpreted. More precisely – definite NPs whose head noun has a relational definition are more likely to be first-mention definites, while definite NPs with a head noun which has a sortal definition will tend to be anaphoric definites. This two-way classification maps well onto Löbner's semantic vs. pragmatic distinction. Fraurud's algorithm of NP interpretation only begins by applying an anaphoric pattern for sortal nouns (i.e. pragmatic definites), whereas relational nouns (i.e. semantic definites) are first processed as non-anaphoric.

2.2. Grammaticization of the definite article

The division between semantic and pragmatic definites makes one wonder why the definite article appears in both cases; what is then the specific role of the definite article? What is it that we call *definiteness*? Trying to answer these questions, Lyons (1999) conducts an in-depth analysis of definiteness across languages. After showing how much it varies not only in form, but also in function, Lyons concludes that no approach in terms of either uniqueness or identifiability can successfully account for all its uses. The failure to find a semantic or pragmatic notion that characterizes definiteness in all its uses leads Lyons to a turning point: definiteness is not a semantic but a grammatical category associated with a particular structural position within the Definiteness Phrase (DP). In the case of English, Catalan and Spanish, it occupies the specifier position of the DP. It is thus possible for the definite article to be a meaningless filler with the sole role of occupying the specifier position in the absence of any other meaningful item (such as a demonstrative), indicating that the DP is projected.

Definiteness originated as a category of meaning ("identifiability," according to Lyons), but it has grammaticized over time in a way comparable to other categories such as tense, mood, gender, etc. Consequently, given that "when a concept comes to be represented grammatically it takes on a new life" (Lyons 1999: 276), we cannot expect to find at present a one-to-one correspondence between the grammatical category and the category of meaning it is based on. Lyons claims that two kinds of definiteness can be distinguished nowadays: (i) "semantic or pragmatic definiteness", i.e. definite uses which retain the original meaning of definiteness, and (ii) "grammatical definiteness", i.e. definite uses that are the result of the grammaticization of the article and so represent an extension or abstraction of the prototypical meaning.

The analysis of the article as having undergone a historical process of grammaticization brings Lyons close to typologists such as Bybee (1998), who assumes that the only linguistic universals we can talk of are those of language change. From this point of view, the evolution of language results partly from universal tendencies of language change that cause all languages to move along the same paths. Grammaticization is the development from lexical to grammatical forms and from grammatical to even more grammatical forms (Heine and Kuteva 2002), which is often triggered by the repetition and recurrence of certain constructions. The more frequent these common constructions are, the more generalized and abstract their meaning becomes. The parameters of grammaticization or definitional criteria according to Bybee (1998) and Heine and Kuteva (2002) are:

1. Phonetic reduction: loss in phonetic substance.
2. Semantic bleaching: loss in meaning content.
3. Increase in frequency of use, i.e. context generalization.
4. Gradual process with full variation in both form and function.

Parameters 2 and 3 are closely interrelated and they are the concern of corpus study I (Section 3.2).

2.3. The meeting point

Given the range of concepts introduced in the previous sections, let us review them before proceeding. Table 1 shows the overlaps between Löbner (1985), Fraurud (1990) and Lyons (1999). Although the correspondence is not absolute, since obscure cases may fall into different categories, such a mapping succeeds in highlighting the major connections between the accounts revised above, thus linking both perspectives: the noun and the definite article.

Löbner's *semantic definites* and Fraurud's *definites with a relational definition* fit in Lyons' *grammatical definiteness*: the former focusing on the functionality of the noun semantics, the latter stressing the grammatical status (semantically redundant) of the definite article. The last row corresponds to the anaphoric use of the article, which is responsible for turning an SC or one-to-many RC into an FC. This second group of definite uses is the one that has been considered as paradigmatic according to traditional accounts. Consequently, little attention has been devoted to the first group, namely definite NPs that do not rely on a previous antecedent.[3] Our present study focuses precisely on this group, arguing for their being regarded as "units of usage."

Table 1. Mapping between Löbner, Fraurud and Lyons' categories

	Löbner (1985)	**Fraurud (1990)**	**Lyons (1999)**
	Noun		Definite Article
redundant article + FC	semantic definites	relational definition	grammatical definiteness
meaningful article + SC/one-to-many RC	pragmatic definites	sortal definition	semantic/pragmatic definiteness

Finally, let us briefly sum up the key points from each author that form the theoretical core of our study:

- Löbner (1985)
  1. FCs are semantically distinct from SCs and one-to-many RCs.
  2. The definite article is pleonastic when combined with an FC (i.e. semantic definites), as the noun on its own already implies a one-to-one reading.
- Fraurud (1990)
  1. Definites are not a homogenous group – more than fifty per cent of definite NPs in Swedish are used non-anaphorically.
  2. First-mention definites are interpreted by a process of anchoring, i.e. in relation to one or more anchors provided either by the local or global context.
- Lyons (1999)
  1. The definite article as a grammatical category (with a DP projection) does not correspond one-to-one with the original category of meaning.
  2. Across languages, the definite article can occupy different positions in the DP and serve different functions, so that languages vary with respect to the grammatical use of the article.
- Bybee (1998)
  1. Grammaticization is a diachronic process – semantic weakening occurred alongside the transformation of an early demonstrative into the definite article.
  2. Languages find themselves at different stages in the grammaticization continuum.

3. Empirical perspective

This section reports on two different corpus studies that we carried out for the purpose of securing linguistic evidence for our claim that in Catalan and Spanish we find article+noun units of usage when a functional noun in Löbner's (1985) terms is accompanied by the grammaticized definite article (Lyons 1999). We aim to obtain evidence from Catalan and Spanish for:

- The grammaticization of the definite article (Corpus study I).
- The existence of article+noun pairs with a strong bond between definite article and noun (Corpus study II).

The aim of the two following corpus studies is to pinpoint trends and probabilities (corpus-driven generalizations) with a view to translating them into relevant features in a coreference resolution system, since they can successfully guide a chain-starting detector. Our main concern in this paper is definite NPs, so we have focused strictly on this group and left the rest of NPs (indefinite, bare, demonstrative, etc.) for future work.

3.1. The corpus

The empirical data used in our experiments come from the AnCora corpora – Annotated Corpora for Catalan and Spanish (Taulé, Martí and Recasens 2008): AnCora-Ca (Catalan) and AnCora-Es (Spanish).[4] They consist of written texts, mainly newspaper and newswire texts, annotated from the morphological to the semantic level: part-of-speech tags, constituents and functions, argument structures and thematic roles, strong and weak named entities, and nominal WordNet synsets. We use the AnCora-Ca dataset of 400,000 words, which has 144,000 NPs, and the AnCora-Es dataset of 320,000 words, with 93,000 NPs. The rich syntactic annotation of the two corpora makes it possible not only to obtain the NP constituents, but also to distinguish between simple and complex NPs.

To begin with, all full NPs were extracted. By *full* NPs we mean NPs with a nominal head, omitting pronouns, NPs with an elliptical head, and coordinated NPs. Out of all NPs in the corpus, AnCora-Ca contains 119,893 full NPs and AnCora-Es 72,624. Table 2 (AnCora-Ca) and Table 3 (AnCora-Es) show the counts of definite and non-definite NPs (in any syntactic position) sorted into simple and complex. As *definite* we only include NPs introduced by the Catalan definite article *el, la/l', els, les*, and Spanish *el, la, los, las*.

Table 2. Overall distribution of full NPs in AnCora-Ca

	Definite	¬ Definite	Total
Simple	27,196	33,503	60,699 (51%)
Complex	34,133	25,061	59,194 (49%)
Total	61,329 (51%)	58,564 (49%)	119,893 (100%)

Table 3. Overall distribution of full NPs in AnCora-Es

	Definite	¬ Definite	Total
Simple	12,739	21,825	34,564 (48%)
Complex	20,447	17,613	38,060 (52%)
Total	33,186 (46%)	39,438 (54%)	72,624 (100%)

3.2. Corpus study I

The first experiment attempts to obtain evidence for the grammaticization of the definite article in Catalan and Spanish. We use the four parameters of grammaticization (Section 2.2) as a test. Concerning the first one, phonetic reduction, historical descriptions (Cano 1988, Badia 1984) indicate that the Catalan and Spanish articles come from the Latin demonstrative ILLE, ILLA, ILLUD: the Latin forms dropped one syllable to yield the Catalan and Spanish articles. Besides, the Catalan forms show a reduced vowel (schwa).

Cano's (1988: 144–145) words support the second and third parameters, semantic bleaching and increase in frequency of use:

> El notable incremento de uso de los demostrativos, en especial de ILLE, ante sustantivo hizo que en muchos casos su función señaladora quedara reducida a la simple determinación (...) el valor del artículo (...) va a indicar el carácter *real, existente* de lo referido por el nombre. [The considerable increase in the use of demonstratives, especially ILLE, before a noun meant that in many cases their signalling function became reduced to simple determination (...) the meaning of the article (...) is going to indicate the *real*, *existing* nature of the referent of the noun.]

Finally, the gradual process with full variation in both form and function (the fourth parameter) is documented in detail by Kabatek (2005), who comments on the grammaticization path followed by the definite article across Romance languages. Although grammaticization paths are universal, the speed and extent to which they occur often vary cross-linguistically. We believe that the definite article in Catalan and Spanish has grammaticized to a larger extent than in other European languages. On the basis of the third parameter (increase in frequency of use), we hypothesize that:

(4) The article is used more frequently in languages where it is grammaticized (e.g. Catalan, Spanish) than in languages where it is less or not grammaticized (e.g. English).

This first corpus study aims to demonstrate the high grammaticization of the definite article in Catalan and Spanish by quantitatively comparing its frequency of use in relation to other languages. In order to make such a comparison, we defined the *definiteness ratio*, a statistical parameter that captures the extent to which the definite article is used in a given language. The definiteness ratio is the ratio of definite NPs to the total number of full NPs.

3.2.1. *Results*

Based on the material at our disposal, the languages we chose for comparison were Swedish (Fraurud 1990) and English (BNC[5]). The values obtained by the definiteness ratio in the four languages are presented in Table 4.

Table 4. The definiteness ratio

	Catalan	Spanish	Swedish	English
Full NPs	119,893	72,624	2,434	18,034,875
Definite full NPs	61,329	33,186	745	4,821,093
Definiteness ratio	0.51	0.46	0.31	0.27

3.2.2. *Discussion*

According to the definiteness ratio, we can place each language on a scale from less to more frequent use of the definite article:

English < Swedish < Spanish < Catalan

This scale finds a parallel in Lyons' (1999) ranking of languages according to their progression in respect of definite article use:

- English: simple definites[6]
- French, Spanish: simple definites, generics
- Italian: simple definites, generics, possessives
- Greek, Catalan: simple definites, generics, possessives, personal names

The results of this first corpus study favour hypothesis (4), and we thus conclude that the definite article in Catalan and Spanish is highly grammaticized. The increase of use can be explained by the generalization of contexts in which the definite article appears (Table 5). Context generalization is directly connected

Table 5. Variation in the use of the definite article across languages

	Generic	Fixed expressions	Possessives	Personal names
English	*apples*	*go to school*	*his jacket*	*Sarah*
Spanish	*las manzanas*	*ir a la escuela*	*su chaqueta*	*Sara*
Italian	*le mele*	*andare a scuola*	*la sua giacca*	*Sara*
Catalan	*les pomes*	*anar a l'escola*	*la seva jaqueta*	*la Sara*

with semantic bleaching, since an extension of contexts must come at the cost of a loss in semantic meaning.

Definiteness is still semantically informative in English, where the article appears only with simple definites, but it has spread into a wider distribution in Romance languages. Like English, Spanish does not use the article before possessives and personal names, but it does with generics; Italian uses it with possessives too; and Catalan in all three contexts. Definites within fixed expressions are also more frequent in Catalan and Spanish. The article has tended to appear in more and more contexts: generics, before body parts, nominalized adjectives, relative clauses, etc. In present-day Spanish – even more in Catalan – bare NPs have become rare.

Generic phrases[7] mainly account for the definiteness ratios of the two Romance languages being twice as much that of English. Natural language is not only about specific individuals, but it is also full of references to kinds. Both singular (5a) and plural (5b) generics pervade journalistic texts, as they are useful labels for entire classes, even if their exact composition is often underspecified.

(5) a. Spanish

El mercado internacional ***del café***.
The market international of the coffee.
'The international **coffee** market.'

b. Catalan

Un pioner que utilitza codis atípics en el
A pioneer who uses codes atypical in the
llenguatge de ***les*** *imatges.*
language of the **images**.
'A pioneer who uses atypical codes in the language of **images**.'

Although fixed phrases are another area where the use of the article in Catalan and Spanish (6) often differs from other languages, they are not as numerically important as generics.

(6) Spanish

Villalobos dio ***las gracias*** *a los militantes.*
Villalobos gave the thanks to the militants.
'Villalobos thanked the militants.'

Definite NPs within these units have fossilized to the extent that they do not require any functional interpretation, as they do not point to any entity in the discourse – when we give thanks to somebody, we are not giving anything.

There is no point in regarding a subsequent mention of *las gracias* 'the thanks' as coreferential with the previous one. When building a coreference chain, this type of definites should be recognized and ruled out by the system in order to avoid any noise they could bring about. Finally, the uses of the article specific to Catalan account for the 0.05-point difference in frequency of occurrence (see Table 4) with regard to Spanish. More precisely, such a difference stems from the compulsory appearance of the article before possessive determiners since, in the case of personal names, these are not used colloquially (when they are preceded by the definite article) in newspaper articles.

The definiteness ratio, as an indicator of the degree of grammaticization of the article, makes a convincing case for the need to take the language into account when building a chain-starting detector, as there is no one-to-one correspondence between the uses of definites in English and those in Catalan and Spanish. On the other hand, the wide range of contexts where the article appears in the two languages under analysis prompts us to question the relevance of definiteness alone for a chain-starting detector.

3.3. Corpus study II

The goal of the second experiment is to find evidence in support of (7).

(7) Certain simple definite NPs show such a strong bond between definite article and noun that the article+noun pair they form can be considered as a unit of usage in the sense of Bybee and Hopper (2001).

We regard article+noun units of usage not as fixed idioms in the speaker's mind but as strings of words that are very likely to co-occur together in real language use. We hold that the definite article has become highly grammaticized in these units and is redundant because, since the head noun is functional in Löbner's (1985) terms, its reference is already unambiguous. This study of article+noun pairs was originally inspired by the one reported in (Nissim 2000), although she does not keep simple NPs distinct from complex ones and she only interprets the results in relation to bridging anaphora.

3.3.1. Results

There are 2,266 noun types in the AnCora-Ca corpus and 1,519 in AnCora-Es. Singular and plural nouns both masculine and feminine were kept as distinct types, and only nouns that occur a minimum of ten times were included in this study. In order to measure the bond between definite article and noun type,

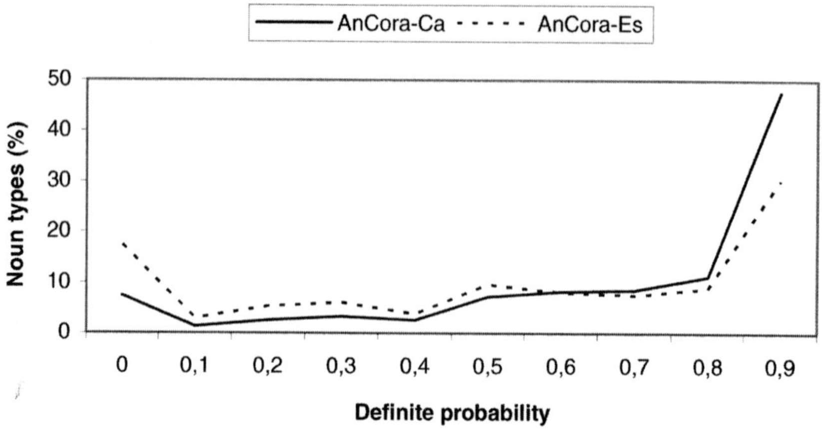

Figure 1. Distribution of nouns according to definite probability

a *definite probability*[8] was computed for each type, which we define as the number of times that a noun N occurs non-modified and preceded by the definite article, divided by the number of occurrences of N non-modified and preceded by any determiner. Nouns that never appeared preceded by the definite article were excluded. Figure 1 presents the distribution of nouns according to definite probability in the two corpora (in relative frequencies).

By way of an example, we provide twenty nouns ordered decreasingly by their definite probability (in brackets):

- AnCora-Ca: *premsa* 'press' (1.00), *història* 'history' (0.96), *ciutadania* 'citizens' (0.89), *conferència* 'conference' (0.71), *artista* 'artist' (0.67), *llibres* 'books' (0.55), *crisi* 'crisis' (0.43), *diumenge* 'Sunday' (0.33), *baralla* 'fight' (0.20), *edició* 'edition' (0.08).
- AnCora-Es: *Unión Europea* 'European Union' (1.00), *población* 'population' (0.92), *educación* 'education' (0.89), *región* 'region' (0.74), *niños* 'children' (0.53), *ideas* 'ideas' (0.40), *apertura* 'opening' (0.33), *bandera* 'flag' (0.25), *carta* 'letter' (0.17), *deseo* 'wish' (0.00).

The definite probability is an approximation of the real picture. However, given that only about 12% of all noun types occur more than fifty times, following a Zipfian distribution, the use of the definite probability alone to extract specific instances of article+noun units of usage can be biased when the corpus does not contain enough data. Consequently, we considered that confidence intervals (henceforth CI) needed to be computed as well, since the narrowness of the CI depends on the number of observed examples, thus showing how *reliable* the estimate is: the narrower the CI, the more accurate it becomes. The Minitab statistical package was used to compute a 95 percent CI for each noun type. For instance, the noun *Gobierno* 'Government', which was observed in the corpus 217 times preceded by a determiner, and 202 times as *el Gobierno* 'the Government', has a definite probability of 0.93, and its CI ranges from 0.89 to 0.96.

A noun with a probability whose lower confidence limit (henceforth LCL) is high implicitly tends to co-occur with the definite article (unit of usage), whereas a noun with a probability whose LCL is low is shown to occur with determiners other than the definite article. Our focus of interest was LCLs, given that we wanted to delimit the group of nouns that show a preference for the definite article, that is, those nouns whose LCL was closer to 1. We set 0.70 LCL as a threshold to guarantee that above this value the article+noun units are units of usage. Such delimitation results in a total of 353 units from AnCora-Ca and 120 units from AnCora-Es (the considerable difference in the size of the two sets is due to the smaller size of the AnCora-Es dataset). There was a big overlap between the units of usage obtained for Catalan and those for Spanish. The following provides a sample of units (their LCL in brackets):

- AnCora-Ca: *l'Ajuntament* 'the City Council' (0.99), *la Generalitat* 'the Catalan Government' (0.99), *el mercat* 'the market' (0.98), *el carrer* 'the street' (0.89), *la policia* 'the police' (0.87), *la pau* 'the peace' (0.85), *la premsa* 'the press' (0.83), *la història* 'the history' (0.82), *el futur* 'the future' (0.78), *els Pirineus* 'the Pyrenees' (0.74).
- AnCora-Es: *el euro* 'the euro' (0.92), *el Gobierno* 'the Government' (0.89), *la oposición* 'the opposition' (0.88), *la Unión Europea* 'the European Union' (0.87), *la OTAN* 'the NATO' (0.83), *los consumidores* 'the consumers' (0.83), *los sindicatos* 'the trade unions' (0.79), *la población* 'the population' (0.74), *la televisión* 'the television' (0.72), *las autoridades* 'the authorities' (0.70).

Up to this point we have only dealt with simple definite NPs. Like definiteness, modification is also language-specific (8). While postmodification is the rule in Catalan and Spanish, English makes use of both pre- and postmodification, but with a marked penchant for the former. We will use the general term "modifiers" to mean "postmodifiers."

(8) Spanish
El mercado internacional ***del café***.
The market international of the coffee.
'The international **coffee** market.'

Table 6. Absolute and relative (in brackets) frequencies of the intersection between units of usage and modifiers.

	Unit of usage		¬ Unit of usage	
	AnCora-Ca	AnCora-Es	AnCora-Ca	AnCora-Es
¬Modifier	9,044 (63)	2,448 (64)	8,835 (30)	4,973 (29)
Modifier	5,278 (37)	1,405 (36)	20,217 (70)	12,323 (71)
PP	2,650 (19)	558 (14)	10,915 (38)	6,347 (37)
AP	1,543 (11)	579 (15)	4,946 (17)	3,482 (20)
RC	456 (3)	114 (3)	2,537 (9)	1,269 (7)
NP	498 (3)	101 (3)	1,096 (4)	589 (3)
Other	131 (1)	53 (1)	723 (2)	636 (4)

After extracting the set of article+noun units of usage, we wondered to what extent they can take modifiers, and if so whether they show any preference for a certain syntactic type in comparison with nouns which do not appear in units of usage. Four main syntactic types are distinguished: prepositional phrase (PP), adjective phrase (AP), relative clause (RC, whether restrictive or non-restrictive), and NP. The intersection between units of usage and nominal modifiers is illustrated in Table 6. When a noun is followed by more than one modifier, only the syntactic type of the first modifier was taken into account.

3.3.2. *Discussion*

The results of corpus study II demonstrate that certain nouns tend to co-occur with the definite article (Figure 1) and that the use of CIs is a reliable way of delimiting the group of article+noun units of usage. Notice that setting a threshold at 0.70 LCL is a guarantee for obtaining "reliable" units of usage. If we had used the definite probability instead, the set of units of usage would have been much bigger but would have contained many dubious candidates. A closer look at the heads of the units confirms our expectations that they fit in Löbner's (1985) functional category: *euro* is a prototypical example of a functional noun, as it points unambiguously to one single referent. It might be argued that other nouns such as *Ajuntament* 'City Council' and *mercat* 'market' do not express a one-to-one relation, but they do refer to one single institution/location which is unambiguously identified by all citizens of the place where it is uttered (this corresponds to Löbner's implicit situational argument).

The head of article+noun units of usage is often a proper noun or the like, including generics.[9] The appearance of the definite article in these cases is redundant, as it does not add any meaning. Its presence can be accounted for by its high degree of grammaticization, which has meant a context generalization with a loss in semantic meaning. Thus, we find that the article has spread into generic phrases, giving rise to units of usage like *los consumidores* 'the consumers'.

Although Löbner talks of SC and FC as two distinct categories, the distribution shown in Figure 1 suggests that the boundary is rather fuzzy. We propose that nouns lie on a continuum between SC and FC, which can be equally read as a continuum ranging from common to proper nouns. This point is made very clearly by the coexistence of two spelling forms for nouns such as *el ayuntamiento* 'the city council' vs. *el Ayuntamiento* 'the City Council'. Borderline cases are those in which it is not clear whether the head is an FC with an implicit argument or whether it is an SC with an argument that needs to be recovered from the text ("FC2 semantic definites with implicit arguments"). From this perspective, the inherent functionality of a noun weakens as its definite probability (over a certain LCL threshold) decreases, so that the interpretation of the noun is more dependent on the specific situation. Definites like *las negociaciones* 'the negotiations' (0.69 LCL) or *el árbitro* 'the referee' (0.61 LCL) can all introduce an entity for the first time in a text provided that their scope of reference has been somehow delimited, either by a direct previous mention or by the general discourse setting.

Let us consider complex definites. Table 6 shows that units of usage display a tendency not to be modified (63% in Catalan, 64% in Spanish) whereas the converse is true for strings that are not units of usage (30% in Catalan, 29% in Spanish). This is further evidence for considering that article+noun units of usage constitute a single unit, which is referentially autonomous thanks to the functionality of the noun (making any modification redundant). As for the small group of units of usage that appear modified, what is observed for both languages is that PPs as modifiers are much more dominant in non-units of usage than in units of usage. It remains for further work to account for the different preferences of syntactic types, but the functionality of the head noun might offer a possible explanation.

4. Conclusion: towards a computational perspective

With a view to finding linguistic cues that can help detect those NPs that are candidates to start a coreference chain, this study has focused on definite NPs, which introduce an entity into the text for the first time over 50% of the time. Definiteness, however, is not universally fixed, but coded differently across languages, and this study has emphasized the need for a language-specific approach to Catalan and Spanish.

We have laid the theoretical basis for our study by merging different ideas of Löbner (1985), Fraurud (1990), Lyons (1999) and Bybee (1998). The first two argue that functional nouns differ from the rest in that they are inherently definite and so have a pleonastic definite article. The last two argue that definiteness has become a grammatical category. We have made explicit the link between functional nouns and a grammaticized definite article by correlating Löbner's (1985) distinction between semantic and pragmatic definites with that of Lyons' (1999) between grammatical definiteness and semantic/pragmatic definiteness. The terms used by each depend on whether attention is paid to the noun or to the definite article.

The meeting point between the four authors prompted two corpus studies designed to collate theoretical ideas with corpus data and yield linguistic evidence for our main claim – that functional nouns preceded by the (grammaticized) definite article constitute "units of usage" in Bybee and Hopper's (2001) terms. Firstly, we have provided evidence for the grammaticization of the definite article by computing the definiteness ratio for four different languages. According to this ratio, Swedish, English, Spanish and Catalan find themselves in different stages of the grammaticization process, the two Romance languages being those where the article is more frequently used. Languages with a higher ratio have a higher number of chain-starting definite NPs, as the article has extended its range of contexts. Within units of usage, it is simply redundant.

The second corpus study has provided support for the functional class of nouns and gone one step further by suggesting a functionality continuum. The combined use of definite probabilities and confidence intervals has made it possible to detect specific instances of article+noun units of usage. As for complex definites, the interrelation between units of usage and modification confirms the peculiar character of such units, since the figures clearly show that they obviate modification, whereas non-units of usage are much more likely to combine with modifiers.

The theoretical and empirical approaches reveal useful linguistic cues to building an automatic chain-starting classifier. The first corpus study has emphasised the need to take the language into account when developing such a classifier, so that definite NPs are given more or less emphasis, depending on the extent to which the definite article has grammaticized. From the second corpus study we have delimited article+noun units of usage for Catalan and Spanish. These lists can be incorporated into the classifier so that the units are given more prominent weight as chain starters, since they are likely candidates provided that no mention has previously appeared with the same head,[10] while the rest are not so likely to be first mentions.

Being able to detect those definite NPs that are not coreferential is a first step to lighten the daunting task of coreference resolution, which is well known for its complexity. Given that many sources of knowledge come into play, coreference resolution is still challenging. We believe that providing both theoretical and empirical accounts is the way to guarantee the development of linguistically well-founded heuristics, and by extension to guarantee the success of resulting computational algorithms.

Acknowledgements. For useful input on the work presented herein I would like to thank the participants in the 3rd International Conference on Linguistic Evidence, and the editors of this volume.

This work was supported by the FPU (AP2006-00994) grant from the Spanish Ministry of Education and Science, and Lang2World (TIN2006-15265-C06-06) – subproject of Textmess – and Praxem (HUM2006-27378-E) projects.

Notes

1. Birner and Ward (1994: 93) provide many counterexamples from English to traditional accounts in terms of familiarity and uniqueness, arguing that "neither approach alone can account for all felicitous uses of the definite article."
2. Löbner (1985) considers that all FCs have, at least, one obligatory argument, namely the situational argument, which is often implicit. In addition, they can take other object arguments. Depending on the number of arguments, FCs are then subdivided into FC1, FC2, etc.
3. Non-anaphoric NPs can, however, be coreferential with a previous mention in the discourse, but their interpretation does not depend on it.
4. Available from http://clic.ub.edu/ancora.
5. We made use of the numbers provided by Allan Ramsay based on the 100-million-word British National Corpus (Personal communication, Oct 2007). Unfortunately it was not possible to discard pronominal demonstrative and possessive phrases from the full NPs count, since they share the same tag with determiners. The figures for English are to be taken for a rough comparison.
6. Lyons (1999: 47) uses the term *simple definites* for those "NPs which correspond in terms of what they express, if approximately, to English NPs in which definiteness is signalled by, at most, the article *the*."
7. Generic phrases are not specifically annotated in the corpus, so they are candidates to participate in coreferential relations with other generic mentions.
8. Bean and Riloff (1999) and Uryupina (2003) employ a definite probability measure in a similar way, although the way the ratio is computed is slightly different, and excludes checking with confidence intervals.
9. Interestingly enough, this result is in accordance with Lyons' (1999) proposal of treating proper nouns as a kind of generic in the sense that they both denote kinds, although in the case of proper nouns the "ensembles" consist of one single entity. Inversely, Carlson (1977) treats bare plurals as proper nouns of "kinds."

10. Previous works (Ng and Cardie 2002) agree that the inclusion of a chain-starting classifier involves a substantial gain in precision – although accompanied by a loss in recall – provided that it runs after having ruled out those definites that match an earlier noun in the text.

References

Badia, Antoni
1984 *Gramàtica històrica catalana*. València: Edicions Tres i quatre.

Bean, David L. and Ellen Riloff
1999 Corpus-based identification of non-anaphoric noun phrases. *Proceedings of the 37th Annual Meeting of the Association for Computational Linguistics (ACL 1999)*, 373–380.

Birner Betty and Gregory Ward
1994 Uniqueness, familiarity, and the definite article in English. *Proceedings of the 20th Annual Meeting of the Berkeley Linguistics Society*, 93–102.

Bybee, Joan
1998 A functionalist approach to grammar and its evolution. *Evolution of Communication* 2: 249–278.

Bybee, Joan and Paul Hopper
2001 Introduction to frequency and the emergence of linguistic structure. In: Joan Bybee and Paul Hopper (eds.), *Frequency and the Emergence of Linguistic Structure*, 1–24. Amsterdam: John Benjamins.

Cano, Rafael
1988 *El español a través de los tiempos*. Madrid: Arco/Libros.

Carlson, Gregory
1977 A unified analysis of the English bare plural. *Linguistics and Philosophy* 1 (3): 413–456.

Chierchia, Gennaro
1998 Reference to kinds across languages. *Natural language semantics* 6, 339-405.

Clark, Herbert H.
1977 Bridging. In: Philip N. Johnson-Laird and Peter C. Wason (eds.), *Thinking: Readings in Cognitive Science*, 411–420. Cambridge: Cambridge University Press.

Fraurud, Kari
1990 Definiteness and the processing of NPs in natural discourse. *Journal of Semantics* 7: 395–433.

Hawkins, John A.
1977 *Definiteness and Indefiniteness*. London: Croom Helm.

Heim, Irene
1983 File change semantics and the familiarity theory of definiteness. In: Rainer Bäuerle, Christoph Schwarze, and Arnim von Stechow (eds.), *Meaning, Use, and Interpretation of Language*, 164–189. Berlin/New York: Mouton de Gruyter.

Heine, Bernd and Tania Kuteva
2002 *World Lexicon of Grammaticalization*. Cambridge: Cambridge University Press.

Kabatek, Johannes
2005 Existe-t-il un cycle de grammaticalisation de l'article dans les langues romanes? In: Rika van Deyck, Rosanna Sornicola, and Johannes Kabatek (eds.), *La variabilité en langue. II. Les quatre variations*, 139–172. Gand, Communication & Cognition.

Löbner, Sebastian
1985 Definites. *Journal of Semantics* 4: 279–326.

Lyons, Christopher
1999 *Definiteness*. Cambridge: Cambridge University Press.

Ng, Vincent and Claire Cardie
2002 Identifying anaphoric and non-anaphoric noun phrases to improve coreference resolution. In: *Proceedings of the 19th International Conference on Computational Linguistics (COLING 2002)*, 1–7.

Nissim, Malvina
2002 Bridging definites and possessives: Distribution of determiners in anaphoric noun phrases. Ph. D. diss., Department of Linguistics, University of Pavia.

Poesio, Massimo and Renata Vieira
1998 A corpus-based investigation of definite description use. *Computational Linguistics* 24 (2): 183–216.

Taulé, Mariona, M. Antònia Martí and Marta Recasens
2008 AnCora: Multilevel Annotated Corpora for Catalan and Spanish. *Proceedings of the 6th International Conference on Language Resources and Evaluation (LREC 2008).*

Uryupina, Olga
2003 High-precision identification of discourse-new and unique noun phrases. *Proceedings of the ACL 2003 Student Workshop*, 80–86.

Vieira, Renata and Massimo Poesio
2000 An empirically-based system for processing definite descriptions. *Computational Linguistics* 26 (4): 539–593.

Zamparelli, Roberto (ed.)
2005 The structure of (in)definiteness: issues in the form and interpretation of noun phrases. *Lingua* 115 (6).

Partial agreement in German: A processing issue?

Ilona Steiner

1. Introduction

While agreement between a plural subject and a verb is straightforward, resulting in a plural verb, the situation with conjoined subjects is less clear. When the subject consists of two conjoined DPs, agreement with only one DP is sometimes possible. (1) is an example in German.

(1) a. *Dort* *stehen*$_{PL}$ / *steht*$_{SG}$ [*ein Mann*]$_{SG}$ *und* [*eine Frau*]$_{SG}$.
There stand$_{PL}$ / stands$_{SG}$ [a man]$_{SG}$ and [a woman]$_{SG}$.

b. [*Ein Mann*]$_{SG}$ *und* [*eine Frau*]$_{SG}$ *stehen*$_{PL}$ / **steht*$_{SG}$ *dort.*
[A man]$_{SG}$ and [a woman]$_{SG}$ stand$_{PL}$ / *stands$_{SG}$ there.

Interestingly, agreement with one conjunct (partial agreement) is only possible if the subject is preceded by the verb as in (1a). Moreover, partial agreement in V-S word order is optional in German. This pattern also arises in many other languages, as reported, e.g., for Moroccan and Lebanese Arabic (Aoun et al. 1994), Russian (Babyonyshev 1997), Swahili (Marten 2005) and Polish (Citko 2004).

Partial agreement is generally explained by syntactic accounts (see Lorimor 2007 for an overview). Munn (2000), for example, takes partial agreement as evidence for an adjunction analysis where the first conjunct is the head of the coordinate phrase. Aoun et al. (1994) argue that partial agreement in Arabic provides evidence for a clausal analysis of coordination (*There stands a man and ~~there stands~~ a woman*). Syntactic accounts of single conjunct agreement however have the problem that different mechanisms have to be postulated depending on the position of the subject. The optionality of partial agreement is an additional difficulty for syntactic accounts.

Alternatively, partial agreement can also be explained by a processing account proposing that the word order asymmetry results from incremental language processing from left to right. The relevant factor is the information available when the finite verb is processed. If the subject is in preverbal position, the plurality of the subject is already computed when the verb is processed (resulting in full agreement). In V-S word order, information about the subject is not yet available at the verb. We assume that in language production, agreement with postverbal subjects depends on whether both conjuncts are already planned when the finite verb is processed. During comprehension the processing of agreement depends on how easy it is to retrieve verb information when the postverbal subject is processed, which can be influenced, for instance, by the distance between verb and subject.[1]

The preference for partial or full agreement in V-S constructions should therefore be strongly influenced by processing load (along the lines of Gibson 2000). The higher the processing load, the more locally the language system operates, so partial agreement should occur more frequently. Partial agreement should also be more acceptable in data sources that directly reflect processing mechanisms, as, for example, in spoken language or in reading times (online data), than in written texts or judgements (offline data). We derive the following hypotheses.

Hypothesis 1: Partial agreement should occur more frequently (or be processed more easily) when the subject is in postverbal position.
Hypothesis 2: Partial agreement should occur more frequently (or be processed more easily) when the distance between the verb and a postverbal subject is increased (higher processing load).
Hypothesis 3: Partial agreement should occur more frequently (or be processed more easily) in online data sources than in offline data.

In order to test these hypotheses, we compare four different types of linguistic evidence: spoken and written corpus data in German (language production), as well as an incremental grammaticality judgement task and a self-paced reading experiment (comprehension). Spoken corpora and self-paced reading experiments are online data sources, while written corpora and grammaticality judgements can be regarded as offline data. Online and offline data types certainly cannot be strictly separated into two classes, they rather constitute a continuum. We therefore conduct local comparisons between the more online and the more offline data with respect to Hypothesis 3. We compare spoken corpora with written corpus data and we contrast self-paced reading data with grammaticality judgements. Especially the comparison of more online and more offline data provides an important piece of evidence.

2. Corpus studies

We present corpus data from German newspaper texts (TÜBA-D/Z) and from spoken dialogues (TÜBA-D/S). The treebank TÜBA-D/Z (Telljohann et al. 2006) comprises 27,124 sentences taken from the newspaper *die tageszeitung* (taz). The treebank TÜBA-D/S (Hinrichs et al. 2000) consists of spoken dialogues in the domain of business appointments and comprises 38,196 sentences. Both treebanks have been annotated manually at the levels of morphosyntax (parts-of-speech categories), syntactic phrase structure and function-argument structure.

We searched a large part of the written TÜBA-D/Z treebank (14,940 sentences) and the complete spoken TÜBA-D/S treebank (38,196 sentences) for subjects consisting of singular DPs that are conjoined with *und* ('and'). The search was performed with the *TIGERSearch* query tool (Lezius 2002). We only selected those cases where the agreement with one conjunct results in a singular verb form and the agreement with both conjuncts in a plural verb form. Sometimes sentences allow only the singular or only the plural verb form for semantic reasons. This is the case, for example, when one of the conjuncts contains negation (resulting in a singular verb form)[2] or when the semantics of the verb requires a plural subject (resulting in a plural verb form). These occurrences were excluded from the study.

We first focus on the data from the written treebank. Some examples of partial agreement from TÜBA-D/Z are illustrated in (2). The sentences in (2a, b) contain subjects in postverbal position. (2c) is an example with a preverbal subject (see also Zinsmeister 2006 for further corpus examples of partial agreement from the TÜBA-D/Z).

(2) a. *In jeder Pilotenweste* ***ist***$_{SG}$ *[ein Kompass]*$_{SG}$ *und [ein*
In each pilot... jacket **is** [a compass] and [a
kleiner Sender zur Bestimmung des
small transmitter for... the location of... the
Abschussorts]$_{SG}$ *integriert.*
shooting... down] integrated.

b. *Bei heiteren bis wolkigen Abschnitten um die 18 Grad*
At sunny to cloudy stages around 18 degrees
kann$_{SG}$ *[Gemüse]*$_{SG}$ *und [Obst]*$_{SG}$ *auch in unseren*
can [vegetables] and [fruits] also in our
Breiten so richtig gedeihen.
zone really thrive.

c. *[Ein Abbruch des Daches]*$_{SG}$ *und [eine*
[A demolition of... the roof] and [a
Neuerrichtung mit leicht veränderter Konstruktion]$_{SG}$
reconstruction with slightly modified design]
würde$_{SG}$ *knapp 2,7 Millionen Mark kosten.*
would almost 2.7 million Marks cost.

Table 1. Partial agreement in TÜBA-D/Z (written)

Position of subject	**Agreement**	**V2 + VFinal** (unfiltered)	**V2 + VFinal** (filtered)
Preverbal	full	132 (98.51%)	111 (100%)
Preverbal	partial	2 (1.49%)	0 (0%)
Conjoined subjects (sg./sg.)		134	111
Postverbal	full	62 (84.93%)	53 (93.0%)
Postverbal	partial	11 (15.07%)	4 (7.0%)
Conjoined subjects (sg./sg.)		73	57

The corpus results of the written treebank TÜBA-D/Z are presented in Table 1 in the column marked "unfiltered" (the filtered data in the last column will be discussed below). The majority of the preverbal constructions (98.5%) exhibit full agreement, but only 1.5% partial agreement. In the postverbal constructions 84.9% of the cases exhibit full agreement, whereas 15.1% of the cases show partial agreement. The difference between the agreement with preverbal and postverbal subjects is significant ($\chi^2(1) = 9.7$; $p < 0.01$). Partial agreement thus occurs significantly more frequently with postverbal subjects than with preverbal ones. Nevertheless, there is a preference for full agreement with preverbal and postverbal subjects.

A corresponding search for conjoined singular subjects in the spoken treebank TÜBA-D/S reveals that subjects are coordinated much less frequently in spoken language than in written texts. In the written TÜBA-D/Z we found 207 relevant instances in a database of 14,940 sentences (= 1.4%). In the spoken TÜBA-D/S only 40 out of 38,196 sentences (= 0.1%) are relevant constructions.

Some examples of partial agreement from the spoken treebank TÜBA-D/S are illustrated in (3). The sentences in (3a, b) contain subjects in postverbal position. (3c) is an example with a preverbal subject.

(3) a. *Dann* ***ist***$_{\text{SG}}$ *dort* [*ein Hallenbad*]$_{\text{SG}}$ *und* [*ein Fitnessraum*]$_{\text{SG}}$.
Then **is** there [a swimming...pool] and [a fitness...room].

b. *Also* ***bleibt***$_{\text{SG}}$ *eigentlich nur noch* [*der Juni*]$_{\text{SG}}$ *und* [*der Juli*]$_{\text{SG}}$.
Thus **remains** actually only [the June] and [the July].

Table 2. Partial agreement in TÜBA-D/S (spoken)

Position of subject	**Agreement**	**V2 + VFinal** (unfiltered)	**V2 + VFinal** (filtered)
Preverbal	full	10 (41.67%)	7 (70%)
Preverbal	partial	14 (58.33%)	3 (30%)
Conjoined subjects (sg./sg.)		24	10
Postverbal	full	1 (6.25%)	1 (10%)
Postverbal	partial	15 (93.75%)	9 (90%)
Conjoined subjects (sg./sg.)		16	10

c. [*Dienstag*]$_{\mathrm{SG}}$ *und* [*Mittwoch*]$_{\mathrm{SG}}$ ***passt***$_{\mathrm{SG}}$ *ausgezeichnet.*
[Tuesday] and [Wednesday] **suits** perfectly.

The corpus results of the spoken TÜBA-D/S treebank are shown in Table 2 in the column marked "unfiltered" (the filtered data in the last column will be discussed below). In preverbal constructions there is no clear preference for partial or full agreement: 41.7% of the sentences show full agreement compared to 58.3% of partial agreement. In the postverbal constructions we found a strong preference for partial agreement: 93.75% of the cases exhibit partial agreement compared to 6.25% full agreement. The difference between the agreement with preverbal and postverbal subjects is significant ($\chi^2(1) = 6.04$; $p = 0.014$). Here again, partial agreement occurs significantly more frequently with postverbal subjects than with preverbal ones.

Overall, 6.3% of the occurrences in the written texts show partial agreement, as opposed to 72.5% in the spoken data. This difference is significant ($\chi^2(1) = 85.6$; $p < 0.01$). Partial agreement occurs significantly more frequently in spoken data than in written texts.

An objection that can be raised at this point is that there is an additional influence on agreement that can be attributed to the semantic type of the subject DP. Conjoined subjects that consist of abstract DPs may show singular agreement, because the conjuncts can easily form one abstract entity (see Lorimor 2007).[3] In our corpora this concerns, for example, mass nouns as in (2b), DPs that refer to events (2c) and other abstract DPs (3c). In these cases the subject DP can be replaced by the German singular pronoun *das* ('this'), hence singular agreement is favoured. In principle, the plural verb form is also possible, but the abstract-like type of these subject DPs facilitates singular agreement. In order to reduce the semantic influence as far as possible, we filtered the written and spoken corpus data. Sentences with a subject DP that can be replaced by the pronoun *das* ('this') were eliminated. The results of the filtered corpus data can be found in the last column of Table 1 and 2 marked "filtered".

As the results of the filtered data show, the agreement preferences are the same as in the unfiltered data except for the preverbal constructions in the spoken corpus. In the spoken data full agreement is now preferred in preverbal constructions, whereas partial agreement is preferred in postverbal constructions. In the written corpus there is still a preference for full agreement with preverbal and postverbal subjects. The *Fisher exact probability test* reveals that also in the filtered data partial agreement occurs significantly more frequently with postverbal subjects than with preverbal ones in written ($p = 0.012$) and in spoken corpora ($p < 0.01$).

Overall the filtered data exhibit 2.4% partial agreement in the written texts as opposed to 60.0% in the spoken dialogues. According to the *Fisher exact probability test*, this difference is significant ($p < 0.01$). The filtered data thus replicates that partial agreement occurs significantly more frequently in spoken data than in written texts.

To sum up the corpus results, partial agreement occurs significantly more frequently with postverbal subjects than with preverbal ones in written and in spoken data. This holds for the filtered as well as for the unfiltered data and provides evidence for Hypothesis 1. It was not possible to test whether an increased distance between the verb and a postverbal subject influences agreement preferences (Hypothesis 2) on the basis of the corpus counts, because the postverbal data were too sparse for further differentiation between different types of postverbal subjects. The results furthermore revealed that partial agreement occurs significantly more frequently in spoken data (online data) than in written texts (offline data). This is the case for the filtered and unfiltered data and provides evidence for Hypothesis 3. We were able to systematically test all three hypotheses using two experimental studies that will be described in the next section.

3. Experimental studies

The processing of partial agreement was investigated using an incremental grammaticality judgement task (offline data source) and a self-paced reading experiment (online data). There are several advantages of an experimental setup compared to the corpus studies. First, the interaction with semantics can be reduced. The sentences we used in the experiments contained subjects that are of semantic type "+ human". These subjects cannot be replaced by the singular pronoun *das* ('this'). Another advantage is that the processing load can be varied systematically, for example, by adding an increased distance between verb and subject.

In addition, we chose a design that allowed us to exclude the possibility that participants build up an elliptic structure for our test sentences according to Aoun et al. (1994). The experimental sentences were constructed in such a way that participants were forced to build up a phrasal structure for the subject DP.[4] Theoretically, it is conceivable that the phrasal structure is reanalysed into a clausal structure at the end of the sentence, but this should be detectable in the reading times. We will discuss this point in the *General Discussion*. In both experiments we used the same test material; we describe it below.

The test sentences consisted of verb second statements with three different word orders: a. subject in preverbal position (4a, b), b. subject postverbal (4c, d), c. subject postverbal with increased distance between verb and subject (4e, f). The subjects consisted of two singular DPs that are conjoined with *und* ('and'). The factor "word order" was crossed with two agreement types: singular and plural agreement. The resulting six conditions are illustrated in the following.

(4) a. [*Eine gutmütige Lehrerin*]$_{SG}$ / *und* / [*eine*
[A good-natured teacher]$_{SG}$ / and / [an
unerfahrene Referendarin]$_{SG}$ / ***gehen***$_{PL}$ / *nach dem*
inexperienced student...teacher]$_{SG}$ / **go**$_{PL}$ / after the
Unterricht / *frustriert* / *aus dem Klassenzimmer* /
class / frustrated / out...of the classroom /
einer elften Klasse.
of...an eleventh grade.

b. [*Eine gutmütige Lehrerin*]$_{SG}$ / *und* / [*eine*
[A good-natured teacher]$_{SG}$ / and / [an
unerfahrene Referendarin]$_{SG}$ / ***geht***$_{SG}$ / *nach dem*
inexperienced student...teacher]$_{SG}$ / **goes**$_{SG}$ / after the
Unterricht / *frustriert* / *aus dem Klassenzimmer* /
class / frustrated / out...of the classroom /
einer elften Klasse.
of...an eleventh grade.

c. *Frustriert* / ***gehen***$_{PL}$ / [*eine gutmütige Lehrerin*]$_{SG}$ /
Frustrated / **go**$_{PL}$ / [a good-natured teacher]$_{SG}$ /
und / [*eine unerfahrene Referendarin*]$_{SG}$ / *nach dem*
and / [an inexperienced student...teacher]$_{SG}$ / after the
Unterricht / *aus dem Klassenzimmer* / *einer*
class / out...of the classroom / of...an
elften Klasse.
eleventh grade.

d. *Frustriert* / ***geht***$_{SG}$ / [*eine gutmütige Lehrerin*]$_{SG}$ /
Frustrated / **goes**$_{SG}$ / [a good-natured teacher]$_{SG}$ /
und / [*eine unerfahrene Referendarin*]$_{SG}$ / *nach dem*
and / [an inexperienced student... teacher]$_{SG}$ / after the
Unterricht / *aus dem Klassenzimmer* / *einer*
class / out... of the classroom / of... an
elften Klasse.
eleventh grade.

e. *Frustriert* / ***gehen***$_{PL}$ / *nach dem Unterricht* / [*eine*
Frustrated / **go**$_{PL}$ / after the class / [a
gutmütige Lehrerin]$_{SG}$ / *und* / [*eine unerfahrene*
good-natured teacher]$_{SG}$ / and / [an inexperienced
Referendarin]$_{SG}$ / *aus dem Klassenzimmer* /
student... teacher]$_{SG}$ / out... of the classroom /
einer elften Klasse.
of... an eleventh grade.

f. *Frustriert* / ***geht***$_{SG}$ / *nach dem Unterricht* / [*eine*
Frustrated / **goes**$_{SG}$ / after the class / [a
gutmütige Lehrerin]$_{SG}$ / *und* / [*eine unerfahrene*
good-natured teacher]$_{SG}$ / and / [an inexperienced
Referendarin]$_{SG}$ / *aus dem Klassenzimmer* /
student... teacher]$_{SG}$ / out... of the classroom /
einer elften Klasse.
of... an eleventh grade.

In both experiments the test sentences were presented in eight regions. The segmentation is indicated in (4) by slashes. Some of these regions (*critical segments*) are of particular interest for the present study. Going through the sentences incrementally, the critical segment is the first region that allows us to identify clearly if the sentence is ungrammatical with respect to subject-verb agreement or not. For this purpose, both the subject and the verb had to be processed. In preverbal constructions the critical segment is the verb (Region 4). In postverbal constructions the critical segments depend on whether the parser considers both conjuncts to be relevant for the agreement process (operating globally) or whether it considers only the first conjunct (operating locally). When the parser operates *globally*, the critical segment in postverbal constructions is the second conjunct (Region 5 in (4c, d) and Region 6 in (4e, f)). When the parser operates *locally*, the critical segment is the first conjunct (Region 3 in (4c, d) and Region 4 in (4e, f)).

We constructed thirty-six test sentences in six versions each (4a–f), 20 control items in four versions each (5a,b) and 40 filler sentences. The control items contained non-conjoined plural subjects in two different word orders: a. subject in preverbal position (5a), b. subject in postverbal position (5b). The factor "word order" was crossed with two agreement types: singular and plural agreement. The sentences with singular agreement, that is 50% of the control items, were ungrammatical with regard to subject-verb agreement. The control items were designed to see whether the processing of conjoined subjects consisting of two singular DPs differs from the processing of non-conjoined plural subjects with respect to agreement.

(5) a. [*Drei motivierte Fußballspieler*]$_{PL}$ ***verlassen***$_{PL}$ / ***verlässt***$_{SG}$ *nach dem Training erschöpft das Stadion.*
[Three motivated football...players]$_{PL}$ **leave**$_{PL}$ / **leaves**$_{SG}$ after the training exhausted the stadium.

b. *Erschöpft* ***verlassen***$_{PL}$ / ***verlässt***$_{SG}$ [*drei motivierte Fußballspieler*]$_{PL}$ *nach dem Training das Stadion.*
Exhausted **leave**$_{PL}$ / **leaves**$_{SG}$ [three motivated football...players]$_{PL}$ after the training the stadium.

The filler sentences contained: a. conjoined subjects with *oder* ('or'), b. conjoined objects or adverbials with *oder* ('or'), c. conjoined objects with *und* ('and'), d. non-conjoined plural objects. Ten out of 40 filler sentences contained agreement violations that concern the marking of number, gender or case within a determiner phrase.

The overall materials consisted of 216 test sentences, 80 control items and 40 filler sentences. All items were compiled into 12 lists according to a Latin square design. Each list contained each test item and each control item in only one version resulting in 36 test sentences and 20 control items. The 40 filler sentences were added to each list. Each participant was presented with one list consisting of 96 sentences in randomised order. For 50% of the sentences we constructed yes/no comprehension questions which were evenly distributed across all conditions and filler types.

3.1. Experiment 1: Incremental grammaticality judgements

3.1.1. Subjects

Forty-eight students of the University of Tübingen were tested individually. All were native speakers of German and naive to the purpose of the study. The experiment took about 30 minutes, the subjects were paid for their participation.

3.1.2. Procedure

The participants performed a self-paced grammaticality judgement task using a non-cumulative moving window technique. A trial began with a series of dashes masking the characters in the sentence. To reveal the subsequent segment of the sentence participants had to press a button of a response box. At each segment participants had to make a decision. If the sentence was grammatical, they should proceed by pressing the rightmost button of the response box. If the sentence was ungrammatical they should abort the trial by pressing the leftmost button of the response box. Comprehension questions appeared after the final segment of the sentence and had to be answered with *Ja* ('Yes') or *Nein* ('No').

Before the main experiment started, a short list of nine practice items each followed by a question were presented. Three of the practice items contained agreement violations. After each practice trail feedback was given to the participants whether the answer was correct and whether they accepted an ungrammatical sentence. During the experiment no feedback was provided. Participants were instructed to read the sentences at a natural rate, but carefully enough to answer the comprehension questions.

3.1.3. Results and discussion

The overall rejection rates for each condition are presented in Table 3. Most participants rated partial agreement in the test items as ungrammatical: 93.8% with preverbal subjects, 81.9% with postverbal subjects and 79.5% with distant postverbal subjects. Full agreement, in contrast, was rarely rejected. The ungrammatical control items, that is singular agreement with non-conjoined plural subjects, were rejected in 98 to 100% of the cases, whereas the grammatical control items with plural agreement were rejected in 1% of the cases. The mean response accuracy to the comprehension questions was 89%.

Repeated measures ANOVAs with factors *word order* (preverbal, postverbal, postverbal + distance) and *agreement* (full, partial) analysing the overall rejection rates of the test items revealed a significant main effect of *agreement* ($F_1(1,47) = 995.58$; $p < 0.01$; $F_2(1,35) = 2175.63$; $p < 0.01$). This

Table 3. Overall rejection rates for each condition

Position of subject	**Full agreement**	**Partial agreement**
Preverbal	1.04%	93.75%
Postverbal	3.82%	81.94%
Postverbal + distance	4.51%	79.51%

shows that full agreement is highly preferred over partial agreement. We further found a significant main effect of *word order* ($F_1(1,47) = 4.48$; $p = 0.016$; $F_2(1,35) = 3.94$; $p < 0.05$), and a significant interaction between *word order* and *agreement* ($F_1(1,47) = 10.23$; $p < 0.01$; $F_2(1,35) = 8.85$; $p < 0.01$) showing that the three word orders are processed differently with respect to agreement.

Paired t-tests revealed that partial agreement is significantly more acceptable with postverbal subjects (4b) than with preverbal ones (4d) ($t_1(47) = 3.02$, $p < 0.01$; $t_2(35) = 3.11$, $p < 0.01$). This provides evidence for Hypothesis 1. The difference between partial agreement with postverbal (4d) and distant postverbal subjects (4f) did not reach significance ($t_{1,2} < 1$). Thus, we were not able to find evidence for Hypothesis 2 in the grammaticality judgement task. This however is not very astonishing, since the grammaticality judgement task is rather an offline data type. Reading time differences might be covered up by the decision processes. Although partial agreement with conjoined singular subjects is significantly more acceptable with postverbal subjects than with preverbal ones, participants nevertheless show a clear preference for full agreement with all three word orders.

The rejection rates for the different segments of the test sentences are presented in Figure 1 for preverbal constructions (4a, b), in Figure 2 for postverbal constructions (4c, d) and in Figure 3 for sentences with distant postverbal subjects (4e, f). As illustrated in Figures 1–3 the sentences are mostly rejected at the verb in preverbal constructions and at the second conjunct (*DP*) in postverbal constructions. These are the critical segments when the language system takes both conjuncts into consideration for the agreement process. Thus, the results also show that the parser operates *globally* in the grammaticality judgement task.

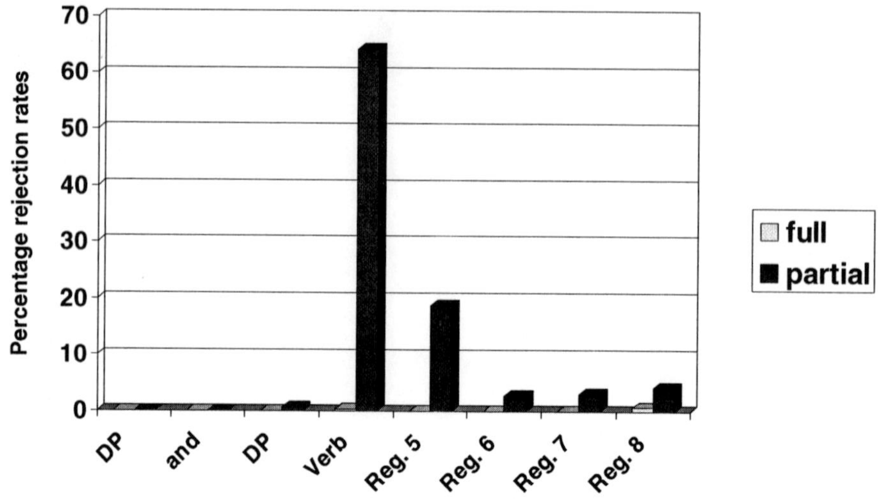

Figure 1. Rejection rates per segment for preverbal constructions

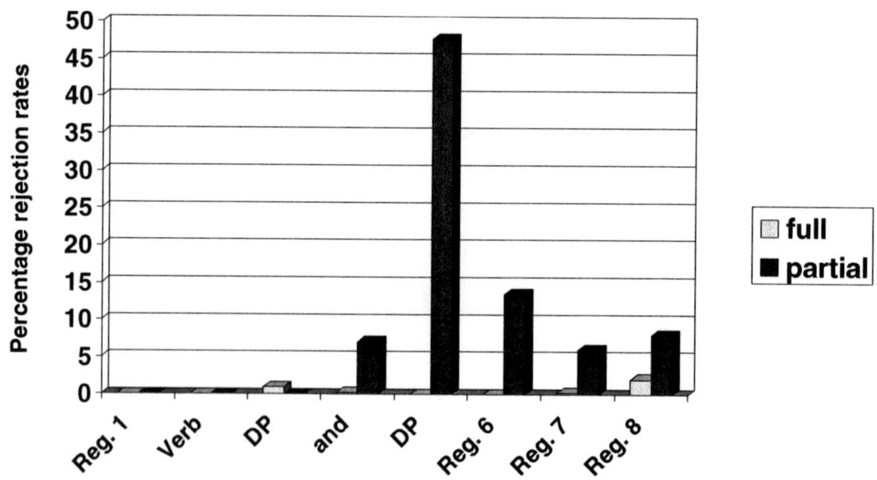

Figure 2. Rejection rates per segment for postverbal constructions

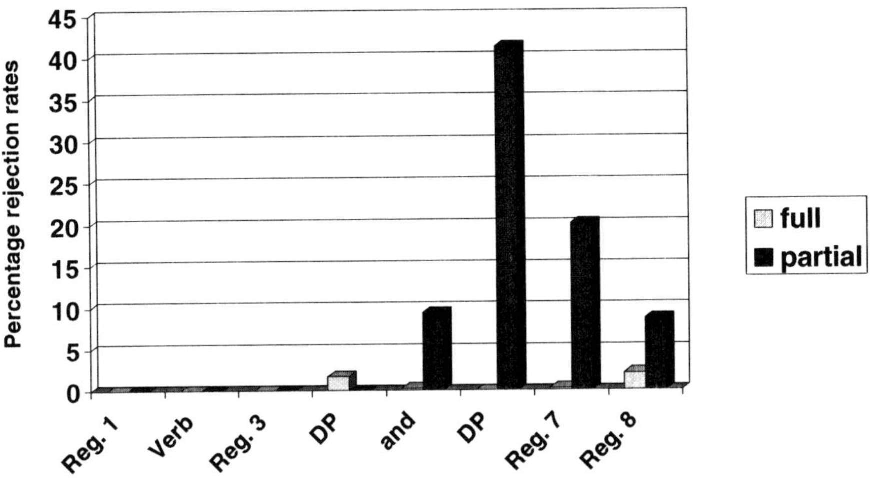

Figure 3. Rejection rates per segment for constructions with distant postverbal subjects

3.2. Experiment 2: Self-paced reading experiment

3.2.1. Subjects

Forty-eight students of the University of Tübingen were tested individually. All were native speakers of German and naive to the purpose of the study. The experiment took about 30 minutes, the subjects were paid for their participation.

3.2.2. Procedure

Participants performed a self-paced reading task using a non-cumulative moving window technique. A trial began with a series of dashes masking the characters in the sentence. To reveal the subsequent segment of the sentence they had to press the middle button of the response box. We measured the time participants spent on a region. Note that except for the decision component, that is the possibility to abort a trial, Experiment 1 and 2 were identical.

3.2.3. Results

The reading times were corrected for outliers. Reading times below 100 ms and above three standard deviations from the mean were replaced by the mean for each condition and for each segment. The mean reading times per segment in ms are presented in Figure 4 for preverbal constructions, in Figure 5 for postverbal

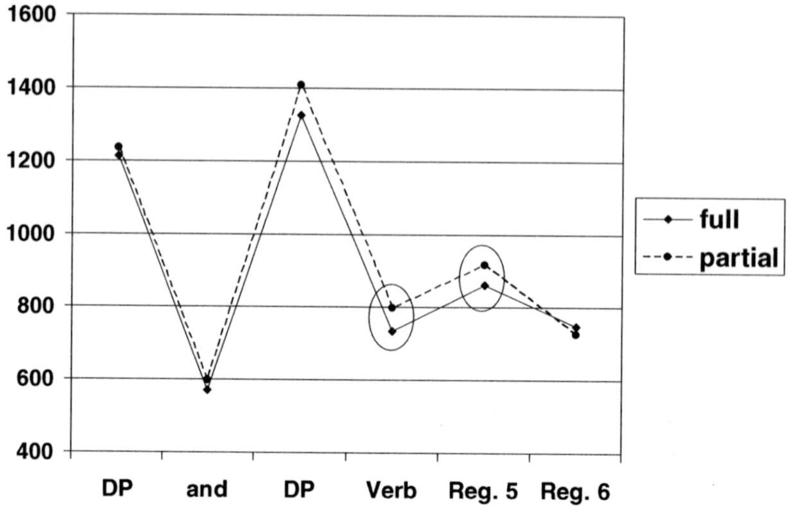

Figure 4. Mean reading times per segment (in ms) for preverbal constructions (Region 1–6). The circles mark significant differences.

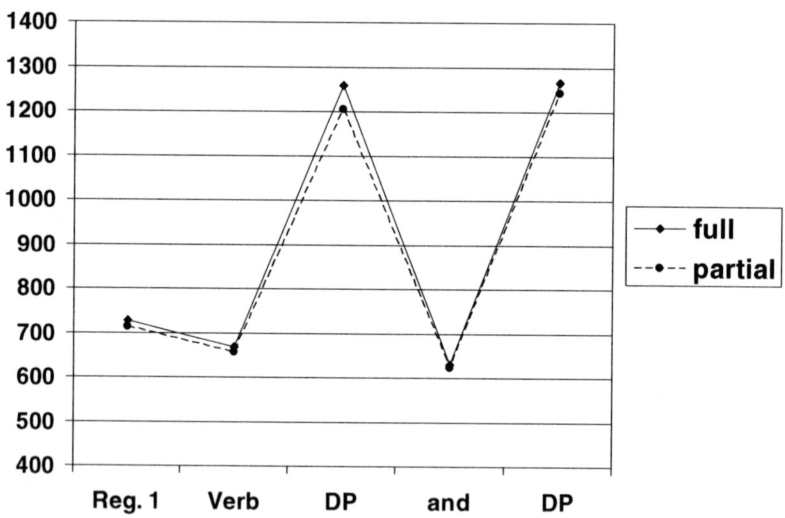

Figure 5. Mean reading times per segment (in ms) for postverbal constructions (Region 1–5)

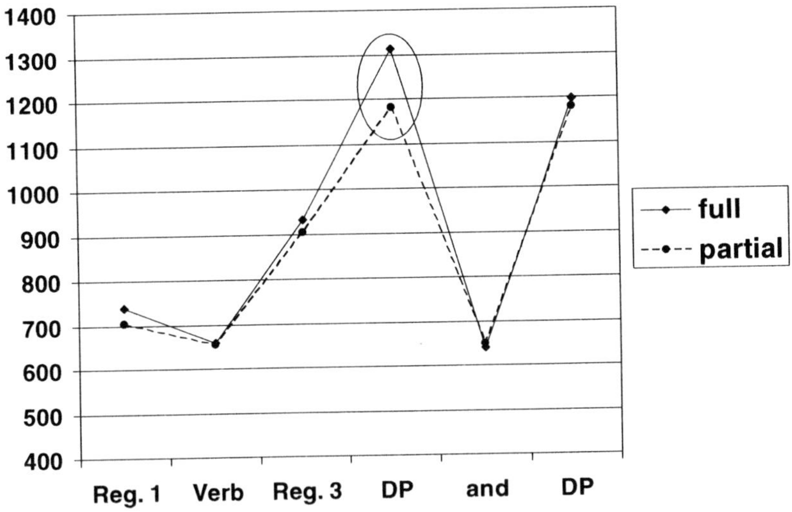

Figure 6. Mean reading times per segment (in ms) for constructions with distant postverbal subjects (Region 1–6). The circle marks a significant difference.

constructions and in Figure 6 for postverbal constructions with increased distance between verb and subject. The comprehension questions were answered 90% correct.

In preverbal constructions (see Figure 4) we found longer reading times for partial agreement compared to full agreement, especially at the verbal segment (Region 4) and at the following spillover segment (Region 5). In postverbal constructions partial agreement was processed roughly as fast as full agreement (see Figure 5). In postverbal constructions with increased distance between verb and subject partial agreement is processed even faster than full agreement (see Figure 6). This concerns especially the first conjunct (Region 4).

In order to compare the three different construction types (preverbal, postverbal, postverbal + distance) it was necessary to look at the relative differences between full and partial agreement instead of taking the absolute reading times into consideration. There are two reasons for this. First, in analysing the *local* critical segments of the different construction types we compared different parts of the sentence. In preverbal constructions the local critical segment was the verb, in the postverbal construction types it was the first conjunct. Second, the critical regions occurred in sentences with a different word order, i.e., they were preceded by different segments and could not be compared directly.

We therefore computed the mean difference scores between partial and full agreement for individual segments within a construction type per subject and per item. Reading times for full agreement were subtracted from the reading times for partial agreement. Positive values indicate that full agreement was processed faster than partial agreement, negative values show that partial agreement was processed faster. A difference score of 0 indicate that there was no difference between full and partial agreement. In order to investigate whether there are differences between the three construction types with respect to agreement, we compared the mean difference scores using repeated measures ANOVAs and paired t-tests. Using one-sample t-tests the mean difference scores were also tested against 0. This allows us to detect significant differences between full and partial agreement within one construction type.

We first compared the three different construction types. ANOVAs with the factor *word order* (preverbal, postverbal, postverbal + distance) analysing the mean difference scores of the *local* critical segments revealed a significant main effect of *word order* ($F_1(1,47) = 7.27; p < 0.01; F_2(1,35) = 9.06; p < 0.01$). This shows that the mean difference scores between partial and full agreement (preverbal: 64.95 ms, postverbal: –54.24 ms, postverbal + distance: –131.71 ms) are different from each other. Paired t-tests showed that the mean difference scores of preverbal (64.95 ms) and postverbal constructions (–54.24 ms) differed significantly from each other ($t_1(47) = 2.70, p = 0.010; t_2(35) = 3.12, p < 0.01$). Partial agreement was processed faster in the postverbal construction type compared to preverbal constructions. The difference between postverbal constructions (–54.24 ms) and constructions with distant postverbal subjects (–131.71 ms) did not reach significance ($t_1(47) = 1.36, p = 0.18; t_2(35) = 1.43, p = 0.16$).

We further looked at the differences between the two agreement types within one construction type. We used one-sample t-tests comparing the mean difference scores between partial and full agreement against 0. Positive t-values indicate that full agreement was read faster, negative t-values show that partial agreement was faster.

In preverbal constructions the reading time differences between partial and full agreement at the verbal segment (Region 4) and at the following spillover segment (Region 5) were significant (Region 4: $t_1(47) = 2.42, p = 0.02; t_2(35) = 2.28, p = 0.03$; Region 5: $t_1(47) = 2.29, p = 0.03; t_2(35) = 2.40, p = 0.02$).[5] This shows that full agreement was read faster. The analysis of the preceding segment (Region 3) revealed no significant difference ($t_1(47) = 1.54, p = 0.13; t_2(35) = 1.62, p = 0.11$). In postverbal constructions the reading time difference at the first conjunct (Region 3) was not significant ($t_1(47) = -1.55, p = 0.13; t_2(35) = -1.31, p = 0.20$) showing that partial agreement is read as fast as full agreement. In postverbal constructions with increased distance between verb and subject the analysis of the first conjunct (Region 4) revealed a significant difference ($t_1(47) = -3.02, p < 0.01$; $t_2(35) = -2.86, p < 0.01$). Here, partial agreement was read faster. We found no significant difference at the preceding segment (Region 3).

Finally, we analysed the *global* critical segments in both postverbal construction types, that is the second conjuncts, using the mean reading times. It is legitimate to use the absolute reading times here and not the difference scores, because we compared identical segments (the second conjuncts) and the two preceding segments are also identical in these two construction types. ANOVAs testing the factors *word order* (preverbal, postverbal, postverbal + distance) and *agreement* (full, partial) revealed a by subjects significant main effect of *word order* ($F_1(1{,}47) = 7.17$; $p = 0.01$; $F_2(1{,}35) = 3.95$; $p = 0.06$). We found no main effect of *agreement* and no interaction between *word order* and *agreement* (all Fs < 1). Hence, there is no difference between partial and full agreement at the second conjunct in both postverbal construction types.

3.2.4. *Discussion*

In the self-paced reading experiment partial agreement was processed more easily with postverbal subjects than with preverbal ones. This provides evidence for Hypothesis 1. In preverbal constructions we found significantly longer reading times for partial agreement than for full agreement. Partial agreement in postverbal constructions was processed as easily as full agreement. If the postverbal subject is more distant from the verb, partial agreement is processed significantly faster than full agreement which indicates that the higher processing load switches the preference to partial agreement. These results provide evidence for Hypothesis 2.

In addition, we found that in the judgement task the decisions in postverbal constructions are made globally at the second conjunct. In the self-paced reading experiment however the difference between full and partial agreement with distant postverbal subjects occurred locally at the first conjunct. Longer reading times for full agreement are probably due to a local mismatch of the plural verb form and a singular first conjunct. No effect was found at the second conjunct. This indicates that with increased distance between verb and subject only the first conjunct is considered for the agreement process.

While partial agreement in postverbal constructions were rated as ungrammatical in the judgement task (offline data), the same sentences caused no processing difficulties or were even preferred in the reading time experiment (online data). This provides evidence for Hypothesis 3.

4. General discussion

In this paper we tested three hypotheses that can be derived from a processing account of partial agreement. According to this approach, the partial agreement pattern results from incremental language processing from left to right. If the subject is in preverbal position, the plurality of the subject is already computed when the finite verb is processed. This should preferably result in full agreement. If the subject is in postverbal position, agreement preferences are influenced by processing load. The higher the processing load the more locally the language system operates, so partial agreement should occur more frequently. In order to test our hypotheses, we compared four different types of linguistic evidence: spoken and written corpus data in German, as well as an incremental grammaticality judgement task and a self-paced reading experiment. In the following we discuss the evidence we found for the three hypotheses in more detail.

In *Hypothesis 1* it is assumed that partial agreement occurs more frequently or is processed more easily when the subject is in postverbal position. We found overwhelming evidence for this hypothesis from all four data types. Partial agreement occurs significantly more frequently with postverbal subjects than with preverbal ones in written and spoken corpus data. The grammaticality judgement experiment revealed that partial agreement is significantly more acceptable with postverbal subjects than with preverbal ones. In the reading time experiment partial agreement was processed significantly more easily in postverbal constructions than in preverbal ones.

It should be noted here that Lorimor (2007) has found similar results in language production experiments with Lebanese Arabic and English speakers. In a picture description task singular verbs were produced much more frequently with postverbal subjects than with preverbal ones. Since word order is not variable in English, Lorimor (2007) compared *Statements* (preverbal structure) and *Questions* (postverbal structure) in her study. We think that her results provide additional evidence for Hypothesis 1 and for the idea that the word order asymmetry is due to general processing mechanisms.

Hypothesis 2 states that partial agreement occurs more frequently or is processed more easily when the distance between the verb and a postverbal subject is increased. We were not able to test this hypothesis with corpus data. We however found evidence from reading times. In postverbal constructions there is no significant difference between full and partial agreement. If the postverbal subject is more distant from the verb, partial agreement is processed significantly faster than full agreement, which indicates that the higher processing load switches the preference to partial agreement. In the grammaticality judgements we did not find a significant difference between the agreement with postverbal and distant postverbal subjects. We assume that this difference is too subtle and can possibly only be detected in an online task.

In *Hypothesis 3* it is assumed that partial agreement occurs more frequently or is processed more easily in online data sources than in offline data. We found evidence for this hypothesis both in corpus data and in experiments. In written corpora (offline data) partial agreement is very rare. In spoken dialogues (online data) partial agreement occurs frequently and is even preferred with postverbal subjects. We were able to show that partial agreement occurs significantly more frequently in spoken dialogues than in written texts. In the grammaticality judgement task (offline data) partial agreement is mostly judged to be ungrammatical with all three word orders. In the reading time experiment (online data) partial agreement is processed as easily as full agreement in postverbal constructions and is even preferred in constructions with increased distance between verb and postverbal subject. This shows that partial agreement is processed more easily during reading than during a grammaticality judgement task.

We did not only find different agreement preferences for online and offline data, we were also able to locate different positions in the sentence that are relevant for the agreement process. During the judgement task both conjuncts were considered for the decision whether a sentence is grammatical or ungrammatical. Partial agreement in postverbal constructions was mostly rejected at the second conjunct. In the self-paced reading experiment, in contrast, the difference between full and partial agreement with distant postverbal subjects occurred locally at the first conjunct. No effect was found at the second conjunct. This shows that with increased distance between verb and subject, that is with higher processing load, the language system operates more locally which results in partial agreement. We suppose that the switch to more local operations is due to limitations of processing or memory resources.

In addition, we were able to reject the proposal that people build up an elliptic structure for postverbal constructions with partial agreement and a phrasal structure for the subject DP in sentences with full agreement. This proposal predicts longer reading times for partial agreement in postverbal constructions than for full agreement, because it is much more time consuming to build up a clausal structure than a phrasal structure. We, however, found the opposite result in the self-paced reading experiment. Furthermore, we constructed the test sentences in a way that it was not possible to incrementally build up a clausal structure for them (see Note 4). When reading the conjunction, participants did not have enough information to build up a complete sentence for the first conjunct, hence they were forced to construct a phrasal structure for the subject DP. It is conceivable although very uneconomical to reanalyse the phrasal structure into a clausal structure at the end of the sentence when the relevant information is available to the parser. In this case, the process of reanalysis however should lead to longer reading times at the last segment of the sentence. We should then find longer reading times for postverbal constructions with partial agreement compared to full agreement, which was not the case.

Overall, our results provide evidence that partial agreement is strongly influenced by processing mechanisms and processing load. Especially the comparison of online versus offline data types allowed us to support this claim. We think that the partial agreement pattern described in the introduction can be explained elegantly by a processing approach and need not be accounted for by syntactic theories. In addition, our results clearly show how important it is to take into account online and offline aspects of the data sources in contrasting data types.

Acknowledgments. The work presented here was done in a project of the SFB 441 "Linguistic Data Structures" at the University of Tübingen funded by the "Deutsche Forschungsgemeinschaft". I would like to thank the project leaders Veronika Ehrich and Ingo Reich, as well as Serge Doitchinov, Sam Featherston, Nele Hartung, Andreas Konietzko, and Janina Radó for valuable discussions and helpful comments. I am especially grateful to Oliver Bott for his kind support in my experimental studies and data analysis.

Notes

1. Marten (2005) presented an independently developed approach of partial agreement within the framework of *Dynamic Syntax* that draws upon the same basic assumption. However, the optionality of partial agreement in V-S word order and the factors that influence the choice of agreement type are not accounted for.
2. The following sentence is a corpus example with negation that was excluded from the study, because only singular agreement is possible.

   (6) … [*die Wirtschaft*] *und* [*nicht die Politik*] ***sei*** *für den Mißbrauch bei sozialversicherungsfreien Beschäftigungsverhältnissen verantwortlich.*
   … [the business] and [not the politics] **is** for the abuse of social… insurance-exempt employment responsible.

3. Lorimor (2007) has shown that the semantic type of conjoined singular subjects influences agreement. In English corpora conjoined mass nouns and deverbals are more likely to take singular agreement (41% with mass nouns, 86% with deverbals) than conjoined pronouns or animate subjects (0% each). However, the corpus data were taken from the World Wide Web. Unfortunately, the proportion of spoken language in these data is thus unclear.

4. Comprehension experiments using the moving window technique in reading allow us to control exactly which parts of the sentence are known to the parser at a given point in time. This is not possible in production experiments. We constructed the experimental sentences in such a way that the parser encountering the conjunction did not have enough information to build up a complete clausal structure at that point. In (7) the experimental items (English glosses) with partial agreement based on a clausal analysis are shown with all three word orders used in our experiments (preverbal subject (7a), postverbal subject (7b), distant postverbal subject (7c)).

(7) a. [A good-natured teacher *goes after the class frustrated out...of the classroom of...an eleventh grade*] and [an inexperienced student...teacher goes after the class frustrated out...of the classroom of...an eleventh grade].

b. [Frustrated goes a good-natured teacher *after the class out...of the classroom of...an eleventh grade*] and [frustrated goes an inexperienced student...teacher after the class out...of the classroom of...an eleventh grade].

c. [Frustrated goes after the class a good-natured teacher *out...of the classroom of...an eleventh grade*] and [frustrated goes after the class an inexperienced student...teacher out...of the classroom of...an eleventh grade].

In order to build up a clausal structure for the test sentences, the parser would have to construct syntactic structure for the sentence parts marked in italics in (7). These parts of the sentence, however, are not available when the parser encounters the conjunction. Since they are not known to the parser until the end of the sentence, it is not possible to build up a clausal structure for our test sentences incrementally. The language system is forced to construct a phrasal structure for the subject DP.

5. The verbal segment is the only segment that is not completely identical in the two agreement types (3rd pers. sg. / 3rd pers. pl.). We however found longer reading times for the shorter segment (singular verb form). Thus, the difference would be even larger if we corrected the data for length.

References

Aoun, Joseph, Elabbas Benmamoun and Dominique Sportiche
1994 Agreement, word order, and conjunction in some varieties of Arabic. *Linguistic Inquiry*, 25(2): 195–220.

Babyonyshev, Maria
1997 Structural connection in syntax and processing: Studies in Russian and Japanese. Ph.D. thesis, MIT.

Citko, Barbara
2004 Agreement asymmetries in coordinate structures. In: *Formal Approaches to Slavic Linguistics: The Ottawa Meeting*. Ann Arbor, MI: Michigan Slavic Publications.

Gibson, Edward
2000 The dependency locality theory: A distance based theory of linguistic complexity. In: Alec Marantz, Yasushi Miyashita and Wayne O'Neil, (eds.), *Image, language, brain*, 95–126. The MIT Press.

Hinrichs, Erhard W., Julia Bartels, Yasuhiro Kawata, Valia Kordoni and Heike Telljohann
2000 The VERBMOBIL treebanks. In: *Proceedings of KONVENS 2000*.

Lezius, Wolfgang
2002 TIGERSearch – Ein Suchwerkzeug für Baumbanken. In: Stephan Busemann, (ed.), *Proceedings der 6. Konferenz zur Verarbeitung natürlicher Sprache (KONVENS 2002)*, Saarbrücken.

Lorimor, Heidi
2007 Conjunctions and grammatical agreement. Ph.D. thesis, University of Illinois at Urbana-Champaign.

Marten, Lutz
2005 The dynamics of agreement and conjunction. *Lingua*, 115: 527–547.

Munn, Alan
2000 Three types of coordination asymmetries. In: Kerstin Schwabe and Ning Zhang, (eds.), *Ellipsis in Conjunction*, 1–22. Tübingen: Niemayer Verlag.

Telljohann, Heike, Erhard W. Hinrichs, Sandra Kübler and Heike Zinsmeister
2006 Stylebook for the Tübingen treebank of written German (TÜBA-D/Z). Technical report, Seminar für Sprachwissenschaft, University of Tübingen.

Zinsmeister, Heike
2006 Treebank data as linguistic evidence – Coordination in TÜBA-D/Z. In: *Pre-Proceedings of the International Conference on Linguistic Evidence 2006*, 210–212.

Index